OBSTACLES TO CHANGE IN
LATIN AMERICA

Obstacles to Change
in Latin America

Edited by
CLAUDIO VELIZ

Issued under the auspices of the
Royal Institute of International Affairs

OXFORD UNIVERSITY PRESS
London   Oxford   New York

OXFORD UNIVERSITY PRESS

Oxford   London   New York
Glasgow   Toronto   Melbourne   Wellington
Cape Town   Salisbury   Ibadan   Nairobi   Lusaka   Addis Ababa
Bombay   Calcutta   Madras   Karachi   Lahore   Dacca
Kuala Lumpur   Hong Kong   Tokyo

65-9707

First published by Oxford University Press, London, 1965
First issued as an Oxford University Press paperback, 1969

This reprint, 1970

Printed in the United States of America

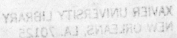

Contents

Foreword

ALL the essays included in this volume were specially prepared for a Conference on Obstacles to Change in Latin America which met in Chatham House in February 1965. It was originally planned to publish these essays together in a volume which should not appear later than the end of the same year. For various technical reasons this imposed a very severe schedule on all those who worked translating, editing and altering the manuscripts in the light of the Conference discussions. Much of the strain fell on the shoulders of my assistant editor, Mr Fred Parkinson, of University College London, who, in spite of being unwell at the time, devoted himself with great selflessness to these demanding tasks.

However, this volume would not have been ready as planned had it not been for the extremely generous, efficient and imaginative co-operation of my friends and colleagues at Chatham House, Miss Hermia Oliver, Miss Katharine Duff, Mr Emanuel De Kadt, and Mr Andrew Shonfield. Working under great and constant pressure and in the shortest time, they helped to edit the manuscripts, advanced most valuable suggestions, and offered scholarly advice which was almost invariably taken. Copying heavily edited manuscripts time and again and at great speed is a most trying job which was faultlessly performed by Mrs Fiona Ramsay, Miss Margaret Youdle, and Miss Carol Robertson.

Both the London Conference on Obstacles to Change in Latin America and the publication of this Volume are part of a larger programme of Latin American studies being carried out by the Royal Institute of International Affairs and St Antony's College, Oxford, thanks to a generous grant from the Ford Foundation.

April 1965   C. V.

Abbreviations

ECLA: (United Nations) Economic Commission for Latin America, *Econ. B.* (*Economic Bulletin*); *Statist. B.* (*Statistical Bulletin*).

IMF: International Monetary Fund.

LAFTA: Latin American Free Trade Association.

OAS: Organization of American States.

UNCTAD: United Nations Conference on Trade and Development (Geneva, 1964).

Introduction

CLAUDIO VELIZ

IN spite of its reputation for frequent and violent political upheaval, perhaps the principal contemporary problem of Latin America is excessive stability. There exists in the region a resilient traditional structure of institutions, hierarchical arrangements, and attitudes which conditions every aspect of political behaviour and which has survived centuries of colonial government, movements for independence, foreign wars and invasions, domestic revolutions, and a confusingly large number of lesser palace revolts. More recently it has not only successfully resisted the impact of technological innovation and industrialization, but appears to have been strengthened by it.

From the essays in this volume it would seem fairly certain that if this traditional institutional structure is not fundamentally transformed, Latin America will not be able to develop at a satisfactory rate. The authors of these essays also agree that the models of development—and therefore of social and economic transformation —based on the historical experience of the more advanced countries of Europe are not applicable to Latin America. Similarly, the nineteenth-century European pattern of political ideologies is not relevant to contemporary Latin American conditions and this partly explains the failure of the traditional groupings—including socialist, communist, radical, liberal, and conservative parties—and the relative success of the grass-roots 'populist movements' with their confusing mixture of nationalism, social-reformism, and authoritarian centralism.

These opinions are particularly significant because those who hold them write with exceptional authority and experience. As well as being academically distinguished, most of them are placed near the sources of political power in their respective countries and have on many occasions advised either their governments or international organizations on specialized problems.

Yet it is above all as witnesses of the rapid rise into political and economic eminence of the so-called middle classes in Latin

America that their experience is valuable and unique. During their lifetime they have seen the beginning of the industrialization of their countries, the coming to power of the middle classes, and their subsequent failure to implement the reforms necessary to ensure further development.

Until recently it was generally expected that the Latin American middle classes, middle groups, middle sectors, or whatever one chooses to call them, were going to behave by and large like their European counterparts and bring about the cultural and institutional changes demanded by the growth of industry. The rising expectations of the mass of the people, the impact of modern technology, the expansion of industrial activity: these factors, in conjunction with the self-interested and determined political activity of a forward-looking, reformist, anti-aristocratic, and generally progressive and modernizing middle class, should have been sufficient to solve the problem of development. But the problem has not been solved. The middle classes have been in power for three or four decades—depending on the country—and have obviously participated in the general process of industrial growth but, also allowing for regional differences, they have been responsible for maintaining or even strengthening the traditional structure and for leading some of the major countries into a situation of institutional stability and economic stagnation. This they have achieved precisely by defending their present interests and future prospects. Far from reforming anything, they have become firm supporters of the Establishment; they have not implemented significant agrarian or fiscal reforms but have displayed remarkable energy trying to become landowners or to marry their offspring into the aristocracy.

Of the many interesting and complex factors which have contributed to this situation of relative stagnation and stability, perhaps two of the most significant are the existence in Latin America of a sophisticated pre-industrial urban civilization and the uniqueness of the region's first decades of import-substitution industrialization.

In Europe it is perfectly possible to establish a direct correlation between the growth of industry and the growth of cities. Although there were great cities with impressive urban cultures for many centuries before the industrial revolution, their size was limited by technological and municipal considerations—the provision of adequate drainage was a sizeable problem—while the absolute predominance of agriculture as the basic economic activity necessarily resulted in the greater portion of the population living in rural areas.

In Latin America the large, dominant city, with highly organized national and municipal bureaucracies, containing vast non-industrial aggregates of service occupations, and with a self-conscious bureaucratic and professional tradition precedes the coming of industry by almost a century. Many years before the First World War, when industrialization was very much a thing of the future, Rio de Janeiro, Buenos Aires, Mexico, and Santiago already occupied a preponderant position in their respective countries and contained an impressively high proportion of the national population. In most Latin American countries 50 per cent or more of the total population lived in three or four major cities, while in Uruguay or Chile almost one-third of the population lived in one city. Even today the degree of urban concentration in centres of 100,000 or more inhabitants is greater in Latin America than in Europe or the Soviet Union.[1]

The cities of Latin America grew as they did on the income arising from the exports of primary products and foodstuffs which characterized the regional economy during the first half of the nineteenth century. Even at that early period, the 'demonstration effect' was felt when the great wealth coming into the hands of the upper groups was used mainly to finance sumptuary imports and to erect mansions, boulevards, and public buildings slavishly patterned after European models. At the same time there was little if any industrial activity, as the wealth from primary exports paid handsomely for all needed imports. But most important was the fact that these vast urban centres harboured a highly literate, perceptive, and self-conscious professional and bureaucratic middle class which also looked towards Europe for inspiration. If the commercial, mining, or agricultural plutocracy imported French wines, English furniture, and architectural and sartorial fashions from the great capitals of Europe, these lawyers, intellectuals, and civil servants eagerly absorbed Positivism, German historicism, and French political radicalism. They formed parties of reform which,

[1] David V. Glass, 'Population Growth and Structure: a Socio-Demographic Study', in UNESCO, *Social Aspects of Economic Development in Latin America* (Paris, 1963), i. 95.

with very few exceptions, were predominantly urban, free-trading liberal, radically anti-clerical, and non-industrial. While in Europe a direct relationship existed between the growth of industry and the quest for reform in the nineteenth century, this was not so in Latin America where 'industrial' reformism, imported from Europe, paradoxically preceded the coming of industry by almost a century. The Latin American parties of reform did not represent a manufacturing interest for the simple reason that there were no manufacturers important enough to constitute national pressure groups.

Between the two world wars, in practically every major Latin American country these reformist groups managed to achieve political power. In so doing without having first become economically powerful through—for instance—industrialization, they reversed the classical sequence of social evolution whereby a group first achieves economic power, then claims political representation, and lastly—most elusive and difficult—aspires to social prestige. In Latin America the rise to power of the middle class and its political leadership had nothing to do with the growth of industry or the individual enrichment of its members. Political power was first obtained on the strength of the popular vote of the newly enfranchised urban masses (not to be confused with an industrial proletariat) who supported them because in fact they represented the only reformist alternative to the traditional ruling groups. Confronted with the social structure of traditional privilege and power, they proposed to demolish it and to replace it by one more egalitarian in which at least all their urban supporters could find a place. Their reformism was mostly social and religious: it included demands for legislation for divorce, state control of education, the extension of social security and the like.

These middle-class groups did not reckon with the almost insurmountable obstacles which a traditional political and administrative structure can place in the path of reform, and although at times they had considerable political power, they were remarkably unsuccessful in the implementation of their programme because they were forced to operate within a system which invariably gave exaggerated weight to the conservative, land-based minority bent on preventing change at all costs. As Sr Celso Furtado indicates in his essay, this is a problem which still has relevance in present-day Brazil. In addition, the Great Depression with its sequel of disruption and the outbreak of the Second World War made for particularly unfavourable conditions for widespread reforms advocated—after all—by a middle-class leadership. This was specially true as the new factor of revolutionary socialism was by then making its first appearances.

On the other hand, these same momentous external circumstances thrust industrialization on the countries of Latin America. Drastic changes in world trading patterns which were eminently favourable for the rapid development of an import-substitution industry at the consumer-goods level affected the whole region with great force. European and United States manufactures ceased to flow to Latin America, and in the artificial and absolute vacuum thus created, a most impressive mushrooming of industry took place. Hence, during the two decades following on the Great Depression, industry came generally to Latin America not as the outcome of a deliberate policy of modernization on the part of a reformist urban middle class, or as the marginal consequence of the distinct way of living of a rising industrial class on the European model, but as the direct result of a historical accident.

Unable to implement their projected reforms, the leading groups of the urban middle classes were drawn to industry not only because of the obvious opportunities for personal gain—especially considering that they had virtual control of the sources of public credit and of the civil service—but because they had a vague hope that industrialization would perform painlessly and automatically the social transformation they had not been able to bring about themselves. Industry became a gigantic *deus ex machina* expected to solve social and political problems, change attitudes, and bring prosperity. To support industry was not only to act on the side of history but was—and still is—patriotic. The leading groups of the urban middle classes, using their influence in the state bureaucracy, became the most enthusiastic promoters of industrial growth: they allocated tenders, granted licences, encouraged doubtful ventures, and channelled scarce foreign exchange and public credit in the direction of friends and supporters. To their evident gratification, industry prospered, and so did their friends. By the end of the decade of 1940, they were not only politically powerful but also extremely wealthy. Yet they were not industrialists, nor were they very clearly aware—as Sr Aníbal Pinto points out—of what was exactly happening under their eyes and what were the implications of this important but fortuitous development.

The extraneous nature of the coming of industry to Latin America must, of course, be set in its proper context. Other areas of the world were affected in the same way but reacted differently. Obviously in Latin America, partly because of the existence of the pre-industrial urban civilization, partly because of a traditional affinity with or closeness to European developments, there were a number of favourable factors to the introduction of modern industry which were not present—say—in Africa or Asia. There was also relatively little difficulty in obtaining capital, while the mass of the urban population—which constituted the majority—was literate and contained a highly skilled minority which proved to be quite capable of adapting to the technical demands of a capital-intensive industrialization. Finally, there was an interesting tradition going back to the colonial eighteenth century which placed great emphasis on the development of manufactures. Latin America had no rural-minded Jefferson but produced at least two dozen major political figures who preached the development of manufactures as early as 1820. This tradition had its modern counterpart in the highly articulate, protectionist, centralist, and nationalist schools of economic thought which flourished in many countries after the First World War.

Nevertheless, two or three decades of this type of 'accidental' industrial growth have not resulted in the creation of an industrial culture which could possibly be regarded as an alternative to the traditional, upper-class cultural complex. Industrialization in Latin America is neither the product of the activities of a rising industrial bourgeoisie nor has it produced one. This situation is fundamentally different from that of the rise of the European industrial bourgeoisie. In Europe in general, but particularly in Great Britain, industry was part of a way of life which also included a new architecture, a different way of writing, a distinct way of educating the young and of appreciating the arts, and a new code of manners and morals. This was a total cultural complex asso-ciated with the rise of industry which in Britain can be perfectly identified with mid-Victorian tastes and ethics. The members of the British industrial bourgeoisie were conscious of their unique way of doing things and were very proud of it. Far from wishing to imitate the manners and morals of the traditional aristocracy, they successfully imposed their own on the nation as a whole. The spiritual and cultural distance which separates the Prince Regent from the Prince Consort, or the Nash terraces from the buildings of the Gothic revival is one which no Latin American middle class has yet been able to bridge. Qualified exceptions to this might be the cases of Brazil, as explained in the essay by Sr Hélio Jaguaribe, and of Mexico and Cuba, where revolutions imposed conditions radically different from those found in the rest of the continent. Elsewhere in the region, the politically influential and now economically powerful urban middle class has moved on to conquer social prestige, the final summit in their ascent.

The aristocracies of different Latin American countries have very little in common save their powers of endurance. They come from different parts of the Iberian peninsula, have decidedly different racial composition, and were formed at different times between the sixteenth and the early nineteenth centuries. Nevertheless, they have all been accepted as aristocracies in their respective social contexts for a very long time. For many generations the same handful of families have always been near the sources of political power, have obviously enjoyed great wealth, and have had a clear monopoly of social prestige. At present, although they have lost a considerable amount of direct political influence and share with other groups the control of private wealth, they continue to have a vital monopoly of social prestige. In fact, in the absence of an alternative set of cultural values and prestige symbols—which the rising middle class proved unable to create—the only possible way of obtaining at least a measure of social prestige is by associating with the traditional aristocracy. This the urban middle classes have done systematically and successfully.

Their children have been entered in the schools patronized by the aristocracy so that they can start making useful contacts at an early age. They have bought land and horses and have painfully learned to practise upper-class sports and games. They have made every effort to join aristocratic clubs and have consciously imitated the dress and speech of their members. They have built and furnished their homes in the styles and districts presumably approved by the aristocracy, and have finally succeeded in becoming very much like them, thinking like them and defending their traditional interests with the zeal of the newly converted.

The upper classes have not viewed this process with distaste. All they need do in exchange for impressive financial and political support is to bestow minimal social favours on their eager imitators, and this they have done effortlessly. The two groups have entered into an extraordinarily successful 'social contract' which, if Latin America were absolutely rather than relatively static, would most certainly last for a very long time. For the present, however, it is fair to conclude that programmes of fundamental institutional change, if left to the reforming zeal of the urban middle classes of Latin America, are unlikely to succeed.

These essays were originally commissioned to form the basis of the discussions at a Chatham House Conference which met in London during February 1965. The purpose of the Conference was to study the factors which prevented positive institutional changes in Latin America.

The discussions among the Latin American scholars, who came from different countries, worked in different disciplines, and started from different premises, showed a most remarkable coincidence of views which is certainly reflected in these essays. These views may very well mark the end of the sincerely held belief that the changes which preceded and followed the industrial revolution in Europe would automatically accompany the industrialization of Latin America. The essays also leave no possible doubt that a sophisticated, pragmatic, and efficient nationalism has penetrated even the most internationally-minded circles, where the consensus of opinion seems to be that the 'classical' Marxist or liberal models of development based on the experience of the more advanced countries of Europe are not applicable to Latin American conditions. The principal task in Latin America at present seems to be the construction of a theoretical model based on the experience of the last decades which can be used effectively to understand, interpret, and direct the processes of social and economic change. Whether the populist experiments are a fitting political answer to these problems is an open question; what is beyond doubt is that any trace of the distressing intellectual habit of always looking elsewhere for ready-made comfortable answers to the problems of the region is completely absent from these essays.

Political Aspects
of Economic Development
in Latin America[1]

ANÍBAL PINTO

WHENEVER attempts are made to isolate the social forces behind economic development it is possible to distinguish two principal alternatives: first, a certain social class may institute such changes as are within its power, and either induce or force the authorities to make the necessary adjustments to implement them. In the countries which are now fully developed, it appears that it was the 'bourgeois entrepreneur' group that was mainly instrumental in performing this function. In the second main alternative the impetus and direction come from above—from the state apparatus—and are channelled through groups or parties which lay down objectives and decide on the means to be used to start the process. The experience of both the Soviet Union and Japan provides the most striking examples of this type, which is also to be found in certain countries which have gained their independence since the Second World War (e.g. India, Cuba, and a number of others).

Neither case entirely corresponds with the transition of the main Latin American countries from economies based on primary exports to a more diversified system, with independent possibilities of development. During the key period of the change-over, between the Great Depression and the end of the Second World War, the industrial bourgeoisie does not appear to have been the prime mover in these changes; nor does the policy of the state—despite

---

[1] All views expressed in this essay without exception reflect the private opinions of the author; they are in no circumstances to be understood as reflecting the views of the institutions with which he happens to be connected. The scope of the essay is confined to the general situation as it appears today, and the observations made apply primarily to the more industrialized countries of the Latin American region; many of them do not apply to the less industrialized areas with the same force. A study of the differences between the less and more highly developed countries in the area may be found in 'Inflation and Growth: Summary of Experience in Latin America', ECLA, *Econ. B.*, vii/1 (1962).

its undoubted importance—reflect the conscious decision of any social or political group or élite to make use of its apparatus to impose them.[2]

In fact, the changes occurred as the result of a vital factor not connected with either of these agents, namely the bankruptcy of the traditional foreign trade arrangements of these countries and the consequent internal reactions. These were the decisive, impersonal influences behind the processes of change in the pattern of development.

This phenomenon took shape and manifested itself through decisions adopted by the state, but if the economic policies pursued during this period, particularly during the 1930s, are examined, it will be found that the protectionist instruments used were not principally directed towards the encouragement of industrialization, but towards the defence of the balance of payments. On the other hand, during the period 1940–5, economic development was the result of the opportunities caused by the war rather than of economic policies promoting industrialization, although some of these were beginning to be adopted in a number of countries.

As far as this phase is concerned, therefore, it may well be claimed that industrialization was a by-product of contingencies originating outside the Latin American economies and their centres of decision. The rationalization of this process came later, slowly, and with difficulty. It was helped by the industrial advances made during those years, and especially by the crisis in exports which weakened the traditional political forces and facilitated the rise— in both private and public sectors—of new groups closely connected with industry.

Nevertheless, this was an immature form of rationalization, as is shown by the weakening of policies of industrialization during the period 1945–50. The revival of foreign trade during this period was not used to reinforce the changes already begun, but was reflected in almost all countries by a slackening of impetus while the representatives of orthodoxy were busy announcing a 'return to normalcy' (i.e. to past patterns of growth), recovering both their reputation and influence in the process.

[2] Although the author has shifted the emphasis slightly, he acknowledges his indebtedness to Hélio Jaguaribe, *Desenvolvimento econômico e desenvolvimento político* (Rio, 1962), who stresses the following main types: national (or 'neo-Bismarckian') capitalism; state capitalism; and 'developmental socialism'.

Another relatively external factor which influenced the problem during this phase was the creation of the United Nations Economic Commission for Latin America (ECLA). The *Economic Survey* published by that body in 1949 has been called a Latin American Manifesto. It was undoubtedly the first systematic statement of the general problems of the region and the policies required for their solution. It explained and justified the process which had been taking place in preceding years, first by criticizing the traditional pattern of growth based on primary commodity exports and its theoretical foundations; and secondly, by demonstrating that the new methods now adopted, above all industrialization, were not merely an emergency solution dictated by exceptional external circumstances but also were essential if the expansion of the Latin American economies was to be encouraged.

During the 1950s both the policies adopted and the actual course of development pursued inclined once more—with the striking exception of Argentina—towards structural diversification in the principal countries of the region, mainly as a result of the two types of expansion produced by the Korean war: in foreign trade, and in import substitution. It was here that ECLA was able to provide the ideological framework that had been lacking hitherto, and which had the additional effect of helping to consolidate the position of those groups which were committed to the encouragement of industrial expansion. This second and most pronounced awareness of the problems of development was most prevalent and important at the highest levels of the state administration, although a few of the more dynamic representatives of private enterprise also came forward as defenders of the new policies. The new trend was seen with greatest clarity in Mexico and Brazil.[8] The development-minded government of President Kubitschek, backed by key interests among the country's entrepreneur class and—this is worth noting—by some foreign investors, represents the most clear-cut case of an autonomous decision to foster domestic industrial development. In recent years the various inter-American agreements

[8] This is not the place to discuss why these countries and not others should be the most conspicuous cases. One obvious fact is that the size of their markets in absolute terms and the stage of development they had already reached gave them more objective or material opportunities to speed up the process, and the time had now come for them to enter more complex areas of industrial development, for instance consumer durables and capital goods.

concluded within the framework of the Alliance for Progress—also an external influence—have helped to generalize these trends by establishing both regional and national goals for development, and by making the allocation of United States credits conditional on the formulation of national development programmes. The Alliance for Progress, ironically, has made respectable a policy which, until recently, had been regarded with hostility by conservative circles. Even though it is alleged that support for the Alliance on the part of certain governments and private interests is often merely nominal, the fact is that the Alliance has made the different countries adopt a definite attitude to development programmes, and this has doubtless had a major influence on their implementation.

Whatever view is taken of the degree of rationalization of this process, no valid grounds exist for rejecting the main contention that in Latin America neither the state nor a rising industrial bourgeoisie has been the principal social force fostering rapid economic development. Although the state has played an important part, this has not been the result of deliberate decisions on the part of a bureaucratic or political élite, but the response to situations imposed by external circumstances. This fact has considerable political importance and it must be borne in mind when other factors are evaluated further on. For the time being it is sufficient to stress that the main changes that have taken place in Latin America have been the consequences neither of gradual, qualitative transformations in the modes of production, coinciding with changes in social relationships and the 'superstructure', nor of a 'peaceful' confrontation (as in Britain) or a revolutionary one (as in France) between social classes associated with either regressive or progressive economic trends.

It is important to emphasize the fact that in the case of a number of advanced countries in the region, the significance of external stimuli or pressures seems to be diminishing. The decline of traditional exports has been accompanied by the exhaustion of easy opportunities for import-substitution. Consequently the way ahead becomes more difficult as countries enter the more complex and demanding fields of consumer durables and capital goods industries. This state of affairs, which is doubtless one of the causes of the deceleration in development noted in recent years, gives added importance to national decisions directed towards increasing autonomy.[4]

Weakness of the Nationalist Factor

As the 'bourgeois entrepreneur' class has not played as prominent a part in the development of the Latin American economies as it did in that of 'central' highly industrialized countries, it is necessary to study more closely the role played by the state.

When examining the various instances in which the impulse and direction from the state are of primary importance in the process of 'take-off', it is possible to distinguish two main types of dynamic forces: one, determined primarily by ideological and foreign policy considerations, is at work in the socialist countries. Today Lenin's formula of 'electricity and Soviets' could well be re-phrased as 'technical progress and changes in the social structure'. A certain type of industrialization founded on the expansion of, and giving priority to, the basic productive activities has assumed great importance in the economic and general policies of these countries, with the 'state' acting as an institutional agent for the ruling political entity, the local communist parties.

The second main force, nationalism, is most characteristic of the experience of the capitalist world. There are appreciable differences between the traditional meaning and the present significance of nationalism in certain parts of the underdeveloped world. The 'chauvinistic' or imperialist interpretation of the past is no longer adequate, since the new nationalism corresponds largely to an aspiration, vague but nevertheless striking, of national affirmation and a desire to narrow the gap separating the underdeveloped from the advanced countries. There are two sides to this nationalism: a negative aspect, derived from the struggle against domination or open tutelage by some foreign power, and a positive aspect based on a desire to define and promote the national personality *vis-à-vis* that of other countries.

The degree of nationalist maturity may be analysed by using an approach similar to that used by Marxists to distinguish class-consciousness: 'in itself' and 'for itself'. Primary nationalism, or nationalism 'in itself', is more or less equivalent to patriotism, that is, an emotional sentiment which does not necessarily lead to

---

[4] This problem has been analysed in two recent works: 'Apogee and Decline of the Substitution Process for Imports in Brazil', ECLA, *Econ. B.*, ix/1; and Pinto, *Chile: una economía difícil* (Mexico City, 1964).

positive action. Secondary nationalism, or nationalism 'for itself', goes farther and deeper, implying the will to affirm and realize more or less defined ideological aspirations. Perhaps a historically significant example of this differentiation is Japan. In that country, the primary nationalistic reaction against the danger of foreign domination has been accompanied by the clear understanding on the part of her political leaders of the need to establish the economic foundations which will allow the country to challenge her more developed rivals.

But the profound internal changes which accompany it constitute an even more significant aspect of modern nationalism in the underdeveloped countries. The bankruptcy of the various forms of subjection or dependence they have undergone has normally been accompanied by the displacement or proscription of the social and political groups identified with the old order. The rise of nationalism has, therefore, had revolutionary implications which have differed importantly from Marxist theory. Although most of these movements draw their inspiration from socialist sources, many of the changes have been brought about not through the social mobilization of the proletariat or peasantry or some Bolshevist minority, but rather under the leadership of various combinations of militarists, technocrats and charismatic leaders, using the apparatus of the state to achieve their objectives. The pattern in such countries as China or North Vietnam may have been different; but here we are only concerned with the experience of the non-communist world.[5]

Bearing this in mind, it can be stated that the nationalist element in the more developed part of Latin America (in contrast to that in certain more backward Latin American regions) has had little or no influence on the action of either the state or the key political groups. This is mainly because in these countries the imperialist presence—a primary motivating factor—has not had the significance or the characteristics it has had in countries which have been exposed to colonial rule or to other forms of open foreign tutelage or intervention. There are well-known exceptions, but apart from the fact that these do not relate to the largest and/or

[5] India, with her large Congress Party, would appear to be a special case. Nevertheless, the differences between India and the communist states may well be more formal than substantial, especially when the cardinal role of Nehru and possible developments after his death are taken into account.

more developed countries, there is a clear difference between the experience of this region and of other backward areas. This does not imply a denial or an underestimation of the existence of an 'imperialist problem' in Latin America, in the general sense that one Great Power exerts visible—and sometimes decisive—influence over the policies of the region, and that powerful foreign business interests are firmly established, both factors giving rise to various frictions with the national interest.

Nevertheless, these problems cannot be compared either in degree or intensity with colonial or semi-colonial experience elsewhere in the world. An empirical demonstration of this fact can be found in the failure of the Communist Party to build up in Latin America movements for 'national liberation' similar to those which have prospered in Asia, the Middle East, and Africa. The simple truth is that there are no progressive masses or national bourgeoisie who feel a vital need to liberate themselves or be liberated. While anti-imperialist or, more concretely, anti-United States sentiments and postures may be found in various countries, they are not as widespread as is often maintained. As a rule, they are restricted to the politically conscious sectors of the intelligentsia and the parties of the extreme Left, without ever resulting in aggressive mass movements. Antipathy or resentment towards the United States may for a number of reasons be discovered in other groups, but these attitudes are counterbalanced by a clear feeling of solidarity with the foreign power in the face of internal Jacobinism and in the Cold War.

Apart from the obvious fact that the countries under discussion here have long enjoyed political independence—although the exact degree of their autonomy may be questionable—the imperialist presence in them has been both more diffuse and more localized than elsewhere. On the other hand, it has made itself felt in the sphere of high politics, in the working of high finance and credit, in control over foreign markets, and in the multiplicity of enterprises brought into the domestic economic system. In the case of the great primary investments like petroleum or copper, this influence has established itself in key centres which are relatively isolated, geographically as well as politically. Finally, imperialist exploitation, as depicted in the Latin American 'social' novel, is, generally speaking, a thing of the past. Today the enterprises with the highest wages and the best working conditions are often precisely those belonging to the great foreign consortiums. In conditions such as these, the impact of imperialism on Latin American nationalism has been considerably softened.

A Few Special Cases

Mexico, Brazil, and Argentina provide interesting examples, as well as contrasts, of circumstances in which nationalism has proved relatively more important. Mexico's relationship with the United States is a case in point.

It would seem that the Great Depression had less importance in Mexico than in other Latin American countries, such as Brazil, Argentina, and Chile, as the prime mover of a new type of economic development. The closing years of the 1930s would appear to have been decisive in the Mexican case, for they coincided with the conflict over the expropriation of the oil companies, and all the nationalist fervours generated by it, the immediate consequences of the Second World War, and the advantages gained from the agrarian reform initiated in 1910 and extended by Lázaro Cárdenas during the late 1930s. Three developments followed: (*a*) the emergence of a dynamic capitalist sector in the countryside; (*b*) the promotion of new entrepreneur elements; and (*c*) the establishment of political power divorced from the old class and their landowning interests.

In Brazil the emergence of a strong sentiment at the same time nationalistic and 'developmental' is a more complex and unusual process. This is a country in which imperialism was less evident and less influential than anywhere else in Latin America. For instance, the export sector was, and for that matter still is, in the hands of Brazilians, even though the mechanisms of foreign marketing may be outside their control. Transactions with other countries are of relatively less significance than in the remaining countries.[6] Finally, the burden of the payments to foreign interest for servicing and funding investments has represented a very small

---

[6] Brazil has one of the lowest coefficients in the capitalist world (and not only in Latin America) as regards the relationship between imports and the national product. The share of imports in the total supply of goods in 1928–9 amounted to 15 per cent, which compares with approximately 28 per cent for Latin America as a whole. In 1948–9 the percentage for Brazil was already as low as 9, while recent estimates fix it at around 6–7. Cf. ECLA, *Statist. B*.

fraction of the total quantity of goods and services available.[7] These economic facts cannot be said to provide a basis for an awakening of nationalism or for the resulting notions about imperialist exploitation; concepts which were used with much effect during the 1950s by some Brazilian intellectuals and radicals, and echoed even in military circles. There are three explanations for this phenomenon.

In the first place the Communist Party, though it is small, has exerted considerable ideological influence, but it must be pointed out that its appeals to nationalism were little more than an expedient for mobilizing anti-imperialist sentiment. The second factor brings to mind the case of Mexico because it was the problem of oil that stood at the centre of political debate, and the slogan 'The oil is ours' was used effectively to bring together widely differing groups. It may finally be said that the nationalist *élan* was a by-product of the speedier economic development registered during the period 1955–9, when Brazil leapt forward to a more advanced phase of industrialization, with a substantial extension of her capital goods, basic raw materials, and durable goods industries such as the motor-car industry. In this instance nationalist sentiment provided the primary impulse, while the anti-imperialist factor was the secondary factor, so much so that it is worth noting that foreign investors were largely responsible for a good part of this spectacular transformation of the industrial structure.

Despite all this, there can be little doubt that the significance attributed to nationalist sentiment in Brazil and Mexico should not be overestimated. It is nowhere near as important as other expansionist factors, such as external pressures, and its effects cannot really be compared with those achieved by nationalist sentiment in the more underdeveloped areas mentioned earlier in this essay.

The case of Argentina is more complicated. Nationalist feeling in that country may be compared with what used to be known as *ufanismo* in Brazil, i.e. a boastful, optimistic, and at times ingenuous evaluation of the national image, either absolutely or in

---

[7] 'Payments to productive factors outside' accounted for less than 1 per cent of the gross internal product between 1945 and 1961, though, in view of the rigidity of income from exports, they constituted an increasing burden on the balance of payments. Cf. ECLA, *Economic Development of Latin America in the Post-War Period* (1963), vol. i, table 113.

relation to other countries. Peronism was in a position to make this attitude its own and to use it for promoting a policy of independent development, but failed to do so. Thus the ultimate objective was gradually obscured and finally lost sight of. An 'infantile imperialism' of scarcely regional scope took its place, and since then nationalism in Argentina has reverted to an identification with the most reactionary groups, so that now it constitutes a further obstacle to the economic development of that country.

Finally, it is remarkable that nationalism should have met with so little response in countries like Chile or Venezuela, where the strongpoints of the internal economy as well as the export sector are in foreign hands. The ideological burden of the campaigns against these interests, i.e. those carried on within the ambit of communist propaganda, has inhibited any disinterested consideration of the subject as a national problem.

State, Politics, and Regional Development

As the significance of nationalism appears to be relatively small, and there does not seem to exist any pattern of 'developmental socialism', it is now necessary to examine the relationships between the state and the political and social forces that have determined its economic policies.

The phase of 'outward growth' has lasted, without interruption but with varying success, from independence [8] to the Great Depression. The latter marks the turning-point towards the second phase of expansion in the main countries of Latin America. Examining this first period of 'outward growth' in the light of some Marxist categories, two important questions call for comment.

Firstly, during this period the state made itself openly the servant of the ruling classes, i.e. both national and foreign property owners in the export sector, their urban supporters, and the landowners, who were frequently connected with the export trade. The political forms of this subservience of the state apparatus to the traditional ruling groups are unimportant, as are the contradictions within the ruling coalition, even though they gave rise to innumerable disputes about the exercise of power, especially in the form of the traditional conflict between the so-called

[8] The exploitation of sugar-cane obviously gave Brazil much earlier access to world markets.

Conservatives and Liberals, with the former being closely connected with the large rural estates, and the latter having their roots in the towns and among financial circles.[9] By and large, all these groups were committed to an economy based on primary exports. Translated into a specific state policy, this meant the promotion of 'free trade' policies with close affinities to the orthodox trade policy pursued by Britain at that time. The 'outward growth' model, therefore, could count on the support of strong and decisive forces and on a dominating ideology. However, these favourable domestic conditions were not the decisive ones for the efficient functioning of the model which—by definition—was subordinated to the ups and downs of the foreign demand for primary exports. The fundamental harmony which existed between the political and economic forces was not reproduced in the relations between the mode of production and the social 'superstructure' of the period of 'outward growth'. This was to have most important political consequences for the later pattern of economic development.

Although during that period productive systems expanded considerably in response to foreign demand, this was basically due to fuller and more intensive exploitation of natural resources and the labour force rather than to the introduction of technological innovations. It was a growth *in extenso* and not in depth. Basic changes in the manner of production, in so far as they took place at all, were confined to the exporting enclaves, particularly those connected with the mining industry rather than with agriculture, though in these there was a wider spread of social relations of the capitalist type.

On the other hand the transformation of the 'superstructure' was far-reaching. A considerable part of the inner structure and the institutional fabric which were the result of a lengthy period of evolution in the developed capitalistic and democratic nations was superimposed arbitrarily on to a basically traditional system

[9] The class struggle, stressed by Marxists as a primary social force in the development of European capitalism, does not seem very important in any of its forms, whether between wage-earners and capitalists, between peasants and landowners, or between the bourgeoisie and the landed aristocracy. Apart from isolated instances, only during the first part of the century, and in certain countries, do real class conflicts play any significant part—for example in Chile with the emergence and struggles of the mining proletariat; and, of course, in Mexico with the agrarian revolution.

of production. This process was greatly facilitated by the free and independent status of the Latin American countries. This is not the place to examine the various questions relating to the incongruence between the façade and the economic structure of these countries. What is important here is to examine the consequences of this phenomenon. In the first place, the incongruence was not incompatible with, nor did it place obstacles in the path of, the traditional process of development because, as has been stated, this was essentially dependent on the external stimuli of foreign demand and foreign investment. The only requirements for these external stimuli to operate efficiently were 'law and order' and a *laissez-faire* economic policy. Nor did the superimposed institutional structure clash with the domestic social reality, because its operation was limited to the property-owning ruling class and excluded all popular participation. This is a fundamentally different picture from the one that emerged after the Great Depression.

There are two principal aspects which call for comment. Firstly, it must be noted that the inherited institutional and juridical system was totally unsuited to tackling the typical problems of 'inward growth', i.e. the internal economic and social adjustments intended to create or promote autonomous growth factors, such as the accumulation of national savings, efficient investment, the extension of the domestic market, modifications and control of external transactions, etc. The old apparatus was completely incapable of functioning under these new circumstances, which demanded efficient state leadership and participation. In the absence of a radical institutional transformation—an unrealistic alternative given the existing political arrangements and the complexity of the problem—the dominating feature of our political experience came once again to the fore and a vast and unsystematic aggregate of administrative mechanisms and partial responsibilities was added to the traditional institutional structure. This is not a specifically Latin American phenomenon, as similar developments have also taken place in Western developed countries during their transition from the traditional to the Welfare State. They seem, however, to have been more pronounced and less effective within the Latin American environment.

The second and most important aspect of this question is its impact on the political system and party organizations. Here again the basic fact is that these countries have inherited a body of political institutions created to satisfy interests, relationships, and objectives which are completely antipathetic to the basic problems of development. Conservatives and liberals defined their respective positions in terms of religious, strictly political, or even regional allegiances. The situation in the 'progressive' parties—for instance in the old Radical parties—was not fundamentally different. For these groups, the main questions were those related to the extension of democratic rights and to their social advancement. They were often devoted to free trade, as were the parties of the Right, and this made any systematic criticism of the traditional pattern very difficult. Yet there were groups and individuals who were not ready to conform. In many parts of Latin America, the nationalist, autarkic ideas of Friedrich List [10] met with strong approval, while the protectionist policies followed by the United States after the end of the Civil War were praised as exemplifying the best possible pattern for national industrialization. But these were isolated voices, of little weight either in practice or for the formation of any relevant policy.

There have been three decades of considerable transformation in the productive systems of the most important countries of Latin America. It is important to discover whether any corresponding changes have taken place in the social and political 'superstructure' of these countries during the same period. If the main criterion is the capacity to adapt to the new objective economic circumstances, then the only general conclusion is that such adaptation as has taken place has been extremely precarious and limited. In fact it can be said that there is not one single political organization in the whole region which—as a body—has defined and adopted a 'developmental ideology'.

It is possible, however, to distinguish two phases in the process of even a limited adaptation to the new conditions. The first covers approximately the decade of 1930 to 1940. During these years the political parties can hardly boast more than a minimal understanding of the economic and social changes which are taking place. The second phase, which begins in the 1950s, is characterized by a slow, embryonic rationalization of those changes, hastened by new development problems which demand complex

---

[10] Nineteenth-century German economist and one of the earliest protagonists of high tariffs to protect nascent industries.

solutions that are difficult or impossible to arrive at on the basis of the crude empiricism which had hitherto proved sufficient. However, even accepting that some limited progress was made during this latter phase, it is still true to say that there is hardly a political party in the whole of Latin America which has accepted a 'developmental ideology' as the framework for both its long and short-term policies. In all fundamental questions, the initiative still lies outside the political apparatus or—occasionally—within small enclaves inside the parties themselves. The ideological focus is still restricted to some small sectors of the progressive intelligentsia, a few technocrats, government advisers, and a handful of entrepreneurs.

It is now important to analyse the inclinations and policies of what can generally be described as parties of the Right and parties of the Left.

The Parties of the Right

Whenever right-wing groups or parties have been in power in Latin America it has been easy to see—through the policies they have chosen to promote industrialization—how unaware they have been of what was really happening around them. Without in the least modifying their traditional ideas or renouncing their affiliation with the vested interests of the primary export economy, they have been compelled by external crises and emergencies to make use of policies and methods which have resulted in completely unintentional changes and to tolerate and even encourage the intervention of the state in economic matters, although this is still anathema to their declared principles.

However, the traditional parties have only to a very limited extent represented the interests of the new industrial entrepreneur group. It would be pointless to look in the whole region for one right-wing grouping explicitly identified with this new social sector. A variety of bonds, ranging from financial support during election campaigns to the defence of the specific claims of the new industrialists, unite both these sectors. Yet with the exception of the most general matters concerning the interests of property-owners as a whole, there has been no complete fusion of their political and economic interests. On the other hand there has been no sharp division either. In spite of the presumed or probable contradictions which ought to divide them, there has been no 'great divide', although some party organizations tend to represent one group rather than the other. The cause of the traditional landowning group, for instance, has been usually adopted by the conservative parties.

There are many reasons for this, and among the most important is the survival of the traditional institutional structure, which has hardly been affected by the developments of the past three decades. At the same time the system of political representation confers a disproportionate political importance on landowners and their electoral clientèle. There also exists a considerable degree of inter-communication between the property-owning groups, which very often unite the different functions of landowner, industrial investor, importer and financier in various combinations within a closely-knit group of people, or even within the same family or social circle.

The obstacles which prevent an adequate solution to the acute problems of agriculture are a principal consequence of this situation. In spite of the weakening of the landowners' political power resulting from the changes of the last decades, no Latin American country has been able to implement a reform of agriculture as profound and extensive as appears essential to remove the disparities and to broaden the domestic base for an efficient development policy.

The property-owning sector, and especially the industrial entrepreneurs, suffer from what can well be described as a 'schizophrenic' outlook, divided between their 'social existence' and their 'social awareness'. On the one hand it is undeniable that during the last few decades the entrepreneur sector has experienced a very remarkable period of prosperity and expansion, especially those groups connected with industry. On the other hand it is equally clear that this has been almost the direct result of the active intervention of the state in the economy. However, in spite of this fact, a nineteenth-century outlook on economics, and particularly on the role of the state in the economy, persists in these circles. This is fed by the attitudes and slogans coming from the 'Great Neighbour' through the various channels of communication it controls. 'Free enterprise', 'free competition', 'private enterprise', 'elimination of state interference'—these are recurrent themes in the entrepreneur's public statements, even though it is obvious that without such 'interference' and state support, neither the past growth nor the present prosperity of the private sector could have taken place, and although many of these entrepreneurs, as individuals or on behalf of specific pressure groups, continually seek favours of the state in the form of more protection, preferential credits, infrastructure investments, subsidized imports, etc.[11]

This flagrant inconsistency has special importance because it has been reflected at the policy-making level of the right-wing parties which have—in this sense—become little more than loud-speakers broadcasting a most unimaginative and mediocre set of conventional slogans. These parties also divorce their day-to-day conduct from their ideology, and this has impeded the rationalization of the events of the last decades in an efficient way which will place the problems and aspirations of the property-owning class within the framework of a development model for a region which differs so profoundly from the fully developed countries, whence they derive their intellectual inspiration.

Finally, it is worth while insisting on the fact that the new industrial sectors have proved unable to form right-wing parties reflecting their interests. In this respect they are at a disadvantage compared with other groups, especially the landowners. It is very difficult to offer a satisfactory explanation of this but, perhaps, the lack of internal differentiation of the property-owning groups

[11] In an inquiry carried out among the industrialists of São Paulo, Brazil, the sociologist Fernando Cardoso collected a number of examples to describe another characteristic expression of this interesting schizophrenia of the Latin American capitalist: -

'Contradictorily and significantly, after listing a series of catastrophes which must happen to the country sooner or later, industrialists, when questioned about the possibilities of expanding the market and maintaining the rhythm of economic growth, express absolute confidence in the future. This false appreciation of the present situation is coupled with an act of faith in regard to the future; motivated by contradictory and far from objective beliefs, they plan greater investments. Once more, these circumstances emphasize the division between their actual behaviour and their individual appreciation of the situation in which they are about to act; they reinvest because, *objectively*, conditions are favourable for new and greater profits; they are *confident* because they *feel* rather than *analyse* market conditions; they see the present situation in cataclysmic terms because, as members of the new bourgeoisie, they still remain faithful to the beliefs and ideologies of the classes from which they have sprung, and are in no condition to understand the changes which have taken place in the Brazilian economy or to find a place in their midst suited to their new interests' (Fernando Henrique Cardoso, *Empresário industrial e desenvolvimento econômico* (1964)).

and the disproportionate representation afforded by the electoral systems to the landowning and local sectors *vis-à-vis* the great urban and industrial centres may have something to do with it.

The Situation in the Left Wing

The parties of the Left seem likewise to have been unable to think out a development policy and use it as the basis of their political strategy. Nevertheless, there are certain striking contrasts with the position of vested interests and parties of the Right. The left wing is relatively immune from, if not in fact hostile to, nineteenth-century *laissez-faire* ideologies. On the contrary, the Left is in principle interventionist, supporting both industrialization and the means of promoting it. It defends the extension of public ownership and is to a large extent nationalist. It favours egalitarian reforms in the social structure and the distribution of income. Though many criticisms and reservations could be levelled against the degree of maturity and coherence of these and other characteristic attitudes, it is plain that in general the tenets of the Left constitute a basis and framework more in keeping with the new pattern of development than the 'free enterprise' source of doctrine and aims of the Right. Nevertheless, this is the by-product of various impulses rather than a reflection of any marked preoccupation with the objectives and means for transforming the social and economic structure.

To clarify this it is necessary to distinguish those forces of the Left which primarily represent middle-class groups, and those which are Marxist in inspiration and are rooted in the proletariat and the agricultural working class. The former were really brought into existence by the activities generated by the 'export model'. During recent decades their social basis has been considerably extended through industrialization and urbanization. For them the state has been a main source of employment and provider of opportunities for social betterment rather than an instrument for promoting development. In some countries, and especially in Chile, these parties have become extraordinarily bureaucratized, not only with regard to the political affiliation of the civil servants, but also because state expenditure and protection have become the principal means of recruiting party supporters. In other countries, such as Brazil, the promotion of interests through the use of state machinery has also been extended to the trade union sector, which was promoted 'from above' under the Vargas régime, creating a very special situation that has some similarity to that of Argentina under Perón and Mexico under the *Partido Revolucionario Institucional* (PRI), where the trade union leadership has been integrated into the political structure of the government party. For these organizations, certain central aspects related to a policy of expansion, such as state intervention, have a particular significance, intelligible in terms of their own vested interests, but scarcely related to the truly economic or 'developmental' objectives of their activity. This has tended to favour middle and working-class groups, whose position in the urban regions and in the capitalist sector of the economy is a relatively favourable one. It has accentuated the tendency to concentrate on technical progress and its rewards, and it has led to a decrease in the importance of traditional activities and their labour force; a large part of the total, if the peasant class and the workers in small-scale industries and artisans are included.[12] Though this tendency has undoubtedly helped to expand the urban domestic market for industrial supplies and complementary services, it is equally true that, apart from relegating the greater part of the wage-earning population to a 'marginal' position, it has meant ignoring almost entirely the equally important problems of accumulation, social priority, and returns on investments—all of them key features of the developmental conception.

A predominant concern with 'redistributive' questions, coupled with an indifference towards what could crudely be termed 'productive' questions, are typical of the 'populist' parties of the non-Marxist Left.[13] At various times during the past years these parties have gained considerable success in a number of countries even though this, as a general rule, has involved redistribution *within* the wage-earning classes rather than any decrease in the living standards of property-owning groups. Hence the striking phenomenon of the gradual trend to conservatism of these groups in almost all countries of Latin America. The aggressive petty-bourgeois reformers of the 1920s and 1930s 'became the sedate,

---

[12] See in this connexion Pínto, *Concentracion del progreso técnico y de sus frutos en el desarrollo latinoamericano* (ECLA/Banco Nacional do Desenvolvimento Econômico, 1964).

[13] Celso Furtado, *Dialética do desenvolvimento* (Mexico City, 1964), gives a penetrating analysis of this problem in relation to experience gathered in Brazil.

technically-minded and moderate statesmen of the 1950s'.[14] Not only have their social anxieties been assuaged, but their interest in policies or decisions connected with development has also declined.

Alongside these 'populist' movements with strong middle-class roots are to be found the parties of Marxist extraction, the communists and various radical socialist organizations, though some, like the (official) Argentine Socialist Party, have little or no connexion with Marxist objectives and tactics. In almost all countries in Latin America, the two fractions of the left wing (the petty bourgeoisie and the working class) have collaborated at various times, or at any rate have never been at loggerheads. It is only very recently that the 'conservatism' of the petty bourgeoisie and external factors (such as the attitude towards the United States and Cuba) have seemed to indicate a growing schism between them.

It might be thought at first that the ideology of the Marxist parties necessarily involves explicit and emphatic views and attitudes with regard to economic development, and more specifically with regard to industrialization and all that this concept implies. But this assumption is only partly justified, particularly if a distinction is made between *verbal* and *written* statements on this subject and actual behaviour. On closer inspection the attitude of the Latin American Marxists turns out to be similar to that of middle-class or 'populist' organizations. In either case, a concern for development has been the by-product of other pursuits, rather than a main objective. In order to justify this statement it is necessary to analyse the principal levels on which the Marxist Left operates.

At the most elementary level, these Marxist groups regard the class struggle in its most 'economistic' sense, i.e. as a struggle to maintain or increase the workers' share in the social product. Because of this similarity with the redistributive policies of the middle-class parties, those of Marxist affiliation have had, and still have, their main bases in the industrial proletariat, the public services, and the urban petty bourgeoisie, these being the groups with the greatest bargaining power and highest relative incomes in the wage-earning sector. Their ties with the peasantry and marginal elements in the towns are limited. Here, clearly, is one of the

[14] See Claudio Veliz, 'Obstacles to Reform in Latin America', *The World Today*, Jan. 1963, pp. 18-29.

causes making for association with the parties of the 'Centre Left' and also of the inability of the Marxist groups to control, or identify themselves with, the neglected masses, who are more inclined to follow charismatic leaders.

Evidently the socialist and communist successes in organizing these privileged classes of workers and employees, and the resulting rise in their income, have had a positive effect on development by enlarging markets for the capitalist sector of the economies. But this has also weakened their solidarity with the neglected workers in the 'underdeveloped' activities and has tended to 'conservatize' the most protected section of the working class and to have blunted its more radical political aspirations. This trend is most marked in what may be described as the new industrial proletariat, that is the workers of the more dynamic, technologically advanced, and productive sectors of the manufacturing industry. As happens in certain developed countries, a breach develops between militant trade unionism, restricted to economic objectives or those affecting the internal affairs of certain firms, and strictly political attitudes. Taken as a whole, the organized workers and the party leaders closest to them tend to take a narrow view of socio-economic problems in general, including development.

The Marxist parties might have compensated for this in other directions, providing better opportunities for pursuing the ideological struggle. Here again, however, their attitude to the problems of development has been oblique or incidental, a by-product of other preoccupations and not the result of directly confronting these questions in their Latin American context. The main reason for this is that in Latin America these organizations have been unable or even unwilling to define their attitude towards the process of economic transformation *within a basically capitalist market*.

Marxist movements in the developed countries have never had to face this problem. Their main objective was the destruction of the existing capitalist order. For the 'reformists', the problem was whether to integrate themselves with an existing system which was not amenable to revolutionary change, and if so how. In the more backward ex-colonial countries, the radical Marxist parties have maintained that only revolutionary change and the pursuit of a socialist policy can open the way to development, and that there is no capitalist alternative. In Latin America the capitalist system was already dominant when an overdue and partial version of the industrial revolution began. Marxist parties were faced with a capitalist development already well under way and this placed them in a dilemma for which their canonical texts provided no satisfactory answer.

They could either, by the use of revolutionary methods, reject and oppose the capitalist alternative of development, or they could accept the *fait accompli* and work out a strategy for living with it without losing sight of their long-term objectives. This problem was passionately discussed in socialist circles during the 1930s and 1940s with the usual virulence of dogmatism that rejects any kind of criticism. Those who inclined to the first alternative were attacked as 'infantile left-wingers' or Trotskyists, while the others were dismissed as reformists, gradualists, and bourgeois agents. The controversy was never settled, since international variables always diluted it and removed it into other contexts, where first 'anti-fascism' and then 'anti-imperialism' (or simply anti-United States phobia) came to be the main watchwords, sometimes even superseding the class struggle at the 'economistic' level.

In any event, an ideological volte-face supervened: the official Communist Party line of broad anti-fascist coalitions and joint action with the 'national bourgeoisie' and other 'progressive' forces to oppose imperialism. This line implied the *de facto* acceptance by the Communist Party—the major component of the Marxist organizations—of the prevailing capitalist pattern of development. The new attitude was in fact a by-product of other considerations, and it has never been clearly and thoroughly enough elucidated to permit the adoption of an explicit policy with regard to economic development.

The reaction of these parties to the role of the state in the process of economic change is typical of their ambiguous attitudes. It might be imagined that they would have championed the extension of public control and governmental direction in the formation of capital and the orientation of investments, but they have paid little attention to such matters except when it has been a question of nationalizing foreign assets in basic activities, such as the public services and the oil industry. This indifference would appear to have originated in traditional conceptions of governmental entrepreneurship in a bourgeois state, and in the possibly deleterious effect of supporting a policy of state control in the common front with the national bourgeoisie.

It can perhaps be argued that these anti-imperialist objectives contributed towards shifting the centres of decision towards the countries directly concerned, and in so doing helped to establish proper conditions for autonomous development. However, even if this were so, it would represent a very small fraction of an overall development policy, which remained undefined even in matters as vital for a socialist party as the extension of state ownership. This is the reason why in these countries most of the measures extending state control over the process of economic development have been adopted without active support by Marxist parties. The net result has been to reinforce domestic capitalism, rather than, as a Marxist would have demanded, to create and strengthen 'socialist cells' in the economy. It is only in recent years that the Marxist parties have become increasingly aware that a capitalist Establishment has grown up alongside them and partly with their assistance; that it is becoming more and more hostile to them; and that it is proving incapable of maintaining its former rhythm of expansion or of solving problems affecting the masses living in rural areas or on the urban periphery.

On the other hand, both the Cuban experience and the effects of the Sino-Soviet controversy have resulted in some Marxist groups adopting an anti-capitalist line opposed to any political collaboration with or placation of the 'national bourgeoisie', who are denied an anti-imperialist function. Though the pro-Soviet groups do not subscribe to the more radical views of their own left wing, it would seem probable that they must to some extent adopt a more hostile and critical attitude towards the capitalist type of expansion that has taken place. There is thus some reason to believe that in the future the Marxist left wing will tend to oppose the prevailing set-up, though it remains to be seen what form their new line will take, how permanent it will prove to be, and what consequences it will have.

The Outlook for the Future

Political considerations have become more significant in determining present and future development in the main countries of the region. For one thing, the pressures originating in the crises or breakdowns of foreign trade tend to play a less important role in the internal dynamism of these economies and thus internal impulses, and therefore the conscious decisions to stimulate and fortify them, are beginning to be a fundamental factor. This trend will be accentuated, since the farther each country has progressed along the path of import-substitution and industrial diversification, the fewer are the stimuli and pressures resulting from its external transactions. Such a state of affairs places the main emphasis on development policies and on those responsible for formulating and implementing them. To an even greater extent than before, this is likely to emphasize state intervention, not for doctrinal reasons but because of the objective difficulties impeding any continued advance.

Despite crises, tensions, and conflicts, wide 'social agreement' has prevailed with regard to economic development during recent decades. Nowhere has any open opposition been registered by groups or forces capable of stopping or reversing current trends. Nevertheless, there are reasons for believing that this state of affairs is changing, and that conflicts may flare up which will lead to more or less profound alterations in the political and institutional patterns which have prevailed hitherto. A new feature of the situation might be the divorce of the extreme left wing from the group which—in theory or *de facto*—has so far supported this development process, and this is likely to be accentuated by international tensions. This breach may tend to be widest wherever it is proving most difficult to maintain past rates of growth, or where any appreciable section of the masses has derived only marginal benefits from it. Alternatively, the same circumstances may unite both groups, or those who have in any way benefited from recent development, in defence of the *status quo*, ironing out any differences between them.

On the other hand, if formidable obstacles in the way of maintaining recent rates of development should threaten to reduce the political influence and standard of living of the middle class, a situation may be imagined in which members of this class will be 'radicalized' and a new opportunity will arise for joint action with an extreme left wing in a more radical mood than before.

In considering the future of political institutions, it is difficult to be optimistic about the stability or soundness of the traditional democratic and parliamentary systems. Paradoxically, the sympathies of the urban and rural masses (which have tended to manifest themselves outside the older political parties, including the Marxists) now favour different political formulae, such as charismatic leaders, movements of the 'neo-populist' type, or even military groups of the 'Young Turk' or—as we should say today—the 'Nasserite' variety. It is generally accepted in Latin America that second-rate imitations of democratic and parliamentary systems are—to put it very mildly—inadequate for dealing with problems requiring immediate solution. The proliferation of parties, parochialism, ideological 'alienation', or the absence of ideologies and lack of basic social or economic homogeneity hardly favour the smooth functioning of democratic and parliamentary institutions. It would be wrong to imagine, as people sometimes do, that a democratic system of the British type is capable of being transplanted, and that the failure of democratic systems in alien surroundings may be attributed to eccentricities allegedly inherent in the Latin American character, or to other equally superficial factors.

One of the features which régimes offering workable alternatives, either overt or covert, to 'democratic/parliamentary' ones have in common is a degree of authoritarianism and/or militarism. This means that the operational scope of parties is more or less restricted, and the power of the executive increased. This last may be exercised through some social organization or through a charismatic personality such as a de Gaulle or Nasser. Mexico provides a classic illustration of these features. Though her government is civilian, its authoritarian nature is nevertheless real, and at least as legitimate, representative, and effective as any of the nominally democratic régimes of Latin America. Various Latin American governments are paying increasing attention to this and are trying, by way of plebiscites and reforms, to by-pass the parliamentary labyrinth, creating direct links between government and people without altering the basic framework of the political system. Both in this and other respects recent French constitutional experience has made a considerable impact on the region. However, past Mexican and present Brazilian constitutional experience are a reminder that both civilian and military authoritarianism may be compatible with the existence of outward democratic forms.

Within the framework of parliamentary democracy, the following patterns may be distinguished:

1. The association, whether explicit or implicit, of 'progressive' groups based on right of centre and left of centre movements, with

the specific tolerance or backing of the radical left wing. This constellation, found at various times in countries such as Chile and Brazil, now seems less common. Venezuela may be moving towards it, though there is a notable antagonism of the extreme left wing to the system.

2. A grouping of the right of centre and the Right appears to be the position in countries such as Colombia and Uruguay, notwithstanding the strictly political conflicts (or simply the struggles for power) between various sections within that combination. It also corresponds to the ruling coalition in Chile during the greater part of the late Alessandri administration (right wing plus Radical Party).

3. Alliances composed of middle-class groups, 'populists', and the extreme left wing, in open conflict with or divided from the right wing. So far this has been a theoretical possibility only. The only country in which there would appear to be any real possibility of something like this happening is Chile, provided the Christian Democrats and the *Frente de Acción Popular* (FRAP), a coalition of Communists and Socialists, succeed in co-operating. Other factors apart, it would seem that international politics make such co-operation difficult.

As regards authoritarian alternatives, these main types call for comment:

1. Governments maintained by force, with the overt presence of, or manifest control by, militarists supporting the traditional property-owning classes, the landowners, and the wealthy. This formula seems to have lost ground, both as a result of the diversification of economic and social structures during recent decades and because it has become discredited internationally. Possibly the last striking example among the advanced countries of Latin America was to be found in post-Perón Argentina.

2. The same formal picture may be obtained through combinations of the military, new property-owning interests, and middle-class groups enjoying the goodwill or support of related political organizations, and at times even some popular or 'populist' backing. This form is undoubtedly more progressive than the first. In some small countries still in the initial phase of the process, industrialization appears to be the primary object of alignments of this sort.

3. 'Authoritarian/popular' régimes—civilian as in Mexico, or military as in the case of Nasser's Egypt—but established on a

more extensive social platform, in which the new bourgeois centre and left factions may unite with the blessing of a large part of the urban and rural wage-earning class. A necessary condition for the success of such an alignment would be the participation of the peasant masses, who, for all practical purposes, have remained outside all popular movements, but whose importance is tending to grow as a result of development taking place. Nevertheless, in countries such as Argentina, Uruguay, and Chile, where the agricultural population is relatively small, a system of this kind must depend mainly on the participation of the urban workers, the Peronist movement being a noteworthy example.[15]

4. A Cuban-type revolutionary and socialist alternative. The general circumstances and specific situation prevailing in other countries have served to point up the difficulties in the way of any duplication of this phenomenon. Even in those countries where the established order seems weakest, and thus revolutionary conditions appear to exist, any crisis may cause a reactionary eruption just as easily as a revolutionary one. For the moment there is every indication that the former is more likely to happen than the latter. However, both the rough Marxist-Leninist mould of the Cuban movement (which it did not show at the beginning and which does not correspond to the outward forms of the régime) and its diplomatic leanings have inhibited its spread to other Latin American countries. Elsewhere, pro-Cuban movements remain restricted to the more radical sectors of the left wing. Naturally there is no intention here to pass judgment on whether the Cuban experience was either necessary or inevitable.

Each of the above patterns, whether actual or hypothetical, has its roots in the economic and social structures peculiar to each country;[16] but each has certain typical features as regards its own objectives and the instruments of its economic and social policy.

[15] 'Nasserism' is extremely topical in Latin America today. Nevertheless, more attention is focused on the external features of the phenomenon than on the very appreciable changes that Nasser has brought about in the social and economic structure of Egypt and, to some extent, Syria also.

[16] The three levels correspond roughly (though not entirely) to the Marxist classification of 'the means of production', 'social relations', and 'super-structure', represented in this instance by the political or party system.

It would be tempting to imagine that there are any clear causal connexions between a rather diversified economic structure, its corresponding social structure, and a rather representative political system.[17] Without denying the relative or general interdependence of these positions, it will be enough to look at one or two countries in order to see that development at these different levels has not been homogenous.

Argentina probably has the most advanced economic and social structure in the region, existing side by side with the weakest political and civil Establishment. Yet she also possesses a most mature working-class movement. All this may be due partly to the Peronist trauma, but also owes a great deal to more distant circumstances like the absence of any political party representing the interests of the landowning class, although this sector is of crucial importance in Argentine society.

Chile has a productive system with some of the features of an underdeveloped economy, such as a strategic single-export sector under foreign ownership and an agriculture relatively impermeable to technical progress. None the less, she possesses a political 'super-structure' similar to that found in most European countries.

Brazil has the most extensive and varied industrial basis in the region, concentrated, moreover, in a restricted area of her territory, where the economic and social features of a developed community predominate. Nevertheless, this situation, which has developed over the last thirty years, still fails to find any clear or organized expression in the political field, for example in a party representing the new industrial interests.

External Political Factors [18]

The external political obstacles to development in Latin America cannot be analysed even perfunctorily within the scope of this

---

[17] In addition to recent efforts by ECLA (e.g. *Social Development in Latin America in the Post-war Period* (1963), and José Medina Echeverría, *Sociological Considerations regarding Economic Development in Latin America*, ECLA, E/CN.12/646), the Centre for Economic Development of the Central University of Venezuela, under the direction of Jorge Ahumada, has also made progress with the integrated analysis of economic, sociological, and political variables.

[18] The external political and economic problems of foreign trade are not discussed here at all. They have been exhaustively dealt with in several studies made by ECLA and other international organizations and they were also the central subject discussed at the UNCTAD Conference in 1964.

paper; nevertheless it can be stated that they have only a secondary importance. The basic dynamic factors at present are domestic— and not foreign—investment and demand. In the new circumstances, external factors continue to be of strategic importance to the dynamic nature of the economies, either as driving forces or as ballast, but their role is essentially complementary, in one way or another, to the domestic forces, for these impose the tempo and control the process. One or two recent revealing experiences may serve as examples. Brazil, at least before 1963, grew at a rate that was exceptional for the region, despite the unfavourable trend prevailing in her external transactions (including the inflow of capital). The recent regression is more related to the political upheavals that have disturbed this country since 1961 (when Jânio Quadros resigned as President) than to any external factors. Chile, at the other extreme, in spite of the acute disequilibrium in her balance of payments, has during the past few years been enjoying a favourable phase of external transactions, measured in real terms of import and export increases. Nevertheless, she has continued to remain practically stationary, at the average levels of the 1950s. The modest revival of the years 1960–2 was basically due to the building programme undertaken by the government. Argentina, at least from 1962 onwards, has experienced an appreciable recovery in her exports sector, but this has not been enough (as it probably would have been in the past) to stop a gradual contraction, evident for some time, which is attributed not without some justification to deficiencies in economic policy and weaknesses in the productive structure. Mexico has been more fortunate, for she has been able to combine a moderate development of her external trade with her own domestic drive. Nevertheless, even in this country there are signs of a decline in the rate of growth, and this may be explained by domestic factors (such as effects on the dimensions of the market of a regressive distribution of income) and not by external events, despite the undeniable importance of the latter.

In short, in so far as these economies have become more autonomous, external obstacles and opportunities have been losing their relative significance in face of the domestic factors affecting expansion.

A second point to consider is the appreciable change in the views of the Great Powers, and in particular the United States, on the industrialization of Latin America. The scope and extent of this change are arguable, but it seems clear that they have become more tolerant of, and at times even in favour of, a diversification of economic structures. A number of factors have contributed to this phenomenon. No doubt one of these has been the fact of industrial growth itself, and another, general considerations advocating more stable dynamic expansion as an antidote to social tensions and political crises. Finally, foreign investment, as a means of avoiding protective barriers and taking advantage of fresh markets, has departed from its traditional preferences (primary exports and public services) in favour of the industrial sector and complementary services.

These, and other factors, have substantially altered the nature of the external impact on Latin American development, but little has been done to analyse the new situation and restate the problem. The left wing, for example, continues to operate mainly with an ideology and attitudes more suited to the earlier situation, partly because it supposes that these are enough to arouse anti-imperialist resistance. The right wing also remains attached to the old order, allotting the same decisive role as in the past to foreign capital (if not to foreign trade), partly for political reasons but also as a means of avoiding its own responsibility in the savings/investment process at the present time.

The perennial problem of the solidarity of foreign interests and the conservative groups of each country, both more or less hostile to the manifold implications of industrialization, is now reasserting itself. When in the past references were made to the existence of these foreign interests, they contained an implicit suggestion of an identity of interests between private investors and the United States government. But as the political preoccupations of the White House for its 'back-yard' were limited, in fact relations between Latin America and the United States were shaped above all by business circles rather than by Washington. The famous dictum 'what is good for General Motors is good for the United States' exactly fits the inter-American situation. One only needs to substitute 'United Fruit', 'Standard Oil', or 'Anaconda' for 'General Motors' to see the point.

In certain respects, as compared with other regions, this situation has not changed appreciably. In no region (except perhaps in the oil countries of the Middle East) does private business have greater influence on the formulation of the policies of the State Department.

Nevertheless, it is certainly true that from the Roosevelt administration onwards, changes have been dictated above all by the increasing diplomatic importance of Latin America as the rearguard of the Big Neighbour, engaged as the latter has been in international conflicts and struggles. In general, Washington's attitude has tended to take an independent line from private interests whenever a more liberal policy has been called for to maintain this Latin American rearguard. Official toleration of oil expropriation in Mexico (which ten or twenty years earlier would have given rise to intervention or some demonstration of force) probably constituted the first and most dramatic sign of this new divergence between the 'micro-vision' of the investors and the 'macro-perspective' of United States policy.

Because of the Cuban Revolution, and during the brief Kennedy interregnum, this process continued with increasing clarity and on a larger scale. As the Cold War assumed a new importance in inter-American politics, the more perspicacious groups in the United States became convinced that the old 'holy alliance' (between foreign investors and the local reactionary groups) could not meet the new contingencies. The Alliance for Progress is the formal expression of this change. It is neither, as some have stated, a panacea for Latin American development, nor, as others suppose, merely old imperialism writ new. It is obviously not a panacea because its available resources cannot even begin to counteract the unfavourable trends in the region's export trade in primary products.

As regards the old problem of imperialism, the insistence on the 'new look' would suggest that nothing of substance has changed in inter-American relations. This is evidently incorrect, if changes in the international field and various other factors are taken into account. Even if imperialism has not disappeared altogether, the truth is that it nowadays presents itself in a very different form and substance. To insist on its essentially unchanging nature, while ignoring the concrete elements which characterize it at present, can only be described as 'metaphysical deviationism'.

To the extent to which it expresses a decision of the United States to escape from outmoded traditional groupings in Latin America and to look for a broader and more progressive social and economic platform, the real significance of the Alliance for Progress is to be found at the political level. The new orientation has placed the traditionalist groupings on the defensive or has weakened their resistance by holding out prospects of external credits. The Alliance has also made respectable a number of ideas and objectives which until recently have only been supported by the Latin American Left.

These implications have not been fully appreciated by the Latin American Left, but they have been fully grasped by the more retrograde interests in both Latin America and the United States. The Right has complained that the reforms proposed by the Alliance are impelling them to undertake a leap into the dark, while US conservatives complain that Washington is promoting a 'socializing' type of policy, ignoring, if not antagonizing, private foreign investors.

Nevertheless, the attitude and programmes adopted at Punta del Este in August 1961 have encountered certain obstacles that cannot be ignored. In the first place, the reduction in the feeling of urgency aroused by the initial phase of the Cuban Revolution has at the same time cooled the reforming zeal of the United States government. Though this change will probably not modify the long-term attitude of the United States towards Latin America, it may well considerably slow down policies in the intervening period. And in the second place attempts to alter the old causal nexus of ideas, 'domestic reaction-foreign interests-United States', are encountering difficulties.

One of the serious drawbacks in the scheme of an Alliance for Progress is the weakness of 'moderate democratic' organizations in Latin America. These can hardly be thought to constitute a clear alternative to the right wing, while at the same time they are unable to ally themselves with the radical left wing, since this does not fit in with the international image of the Alliance for Progress. Faced with the danger of losing the bird in the hand, there is a growing tendency to rely on the traditional 'holy alliance'. One alternative is to search for a military/progressive combination, but the authoritarianism implicit in this concept is undermining the campaign in favour of the much heralded 'democratic progress'.

The other obstacles relate to United States private interests. Though the situation differs noticeably in each country, it is possible to distinguish two variations. In the first the key points in the economic structure are under foreign control, especially in the export sector and basic services, while the second comprises economies in which the main investments have been made in the industrial sector and in the service industries. Both types, and principally the former, involve actual or latent inconsistencies in relation to the diversified development policies which the Latin American countries are or may be pursuing. There is the possibility of clashes and conflict with foreign interests, and also with the government of the United States or others representing it.

In the former case, it would seem difficult to put into practice any autonomous and stable policy of development while vital nuclei of the economic system are under outside control and operated according to a set of criteria that may differ from, and at times conflict with, such a policy. Large-scale undertakings (such as copper in Chile or oil in Venezuela) form part of international complexes which allot resources and take decisions with an eye to the position of the industry and the market, and not to the specific situation or convenience of any given undertaking in any particular country. The problem becomes still more complicated when these activities are linked with provisioning the metropolis and are retained as such for emergency purposes, or when they can be classed as strategic, thus restricting openings in other markets, e.g. those of the communist countries.

On the other hand it may well be argued that this type of investment, frequently of high 'technological density', represents a vital source of funds for development, that such funds cause a permanent drain on the scarcest and most vital factor in the internal effort —foreign exchange—and that, in the above conditions, these transactions imply a high degree of instability as regards their provision.

Foreign investors in the secondary and tertiary sectors, integrated with and dependent on the domestic market, not only contribute to the diversification of the productive structure, but are also eventually committed to national development in the sense that profitability and expansion are subordinated in greater or lesser degree to the dynamism of the system, which certainly does not occur with the traditional type of investment in primary production for export. Nevertheless these types of foreign interest may also come into conflict with the national interest.

An admittedly subsidiary but not altogether unimportant factor concerns the quality of these investments from the point of view of their importance to development. A foreign enterprise which is to fill an impojtant gap in the industrial framework cannot be considered in the same way as an undertaking which manufactures non-alcoholic beverages or consumer goods typical of an 'affluent society'.

Since all these investments presuppose claims on available foreign exchange, the most important aspect is that the servicing of this accumulated and permanent capital (unlike other types of funds brought in from outside) may be more or less divorced from the countries' ability to pay, which depends on the export of primary materials. In so far, then, as they are unable to devote an adequate proportion of their ordinary income to these obligations, another source of conflict arises, which cannot be attributed to nationalist animosity. Because of the significance of investments for her domestic market, the position of Brazil in this respect is extremely revealing.

Whenever there are problems which, although directly affecting private foreign interests, also involve their governments, any controversy between a Latin American country and a foreign enterprise will tend to develop into a cause of conflict or rupture with Washington or some other capital, and will thus impede decisions which, rightly or wrongly, it is proposed to take in response to the needs of accelerated economic development. A purely hypothetical situation may serve to illustrate the point: Country A, for some good reason, adopts a resolution which seriously injures a foreign undertaking (for example, it nationalizes a basic export industry). This will lead to protests from those who have suffered damage, and intense action on the part of lobbyists and other agents to mobilize the government, let us say, of the United States, in their defence. Naturally, the reaction will depend in part on the influence of the source of the protest, and the extent to which the particular case is of importance to the northern country. But another factor which will be equally, if not even more, influential is whether the action in question has been taken by a friendly or a hostile government, or one which inclines towards the 'other side' in terms of the Cold War. It seems beyond question that in the former instance the action is more likely to be condoned than in the latter, unless there is a disposition to challenge the power involved directly.

The present problem raises a variety of questions. For example, will a government which is diplomatically friendly to the United States be able to muster sufficient determination to stand up to a powerful foreign concern, even if it believes this to be necessary? If it possesses this determination and proceeds, will it cease to be considered 'friendly', or may it be impelled to move in some other international direction, even though this may not have been initially considered desirable? Or, rather than being interested in surmounting difficulties for development, will the government concerned be precisely interested in forcing an international political break? These and other contingencies are by no means unrealistic, given the probable political and economic evolution of Latin America.

Although external attitudes and decisions liable to clash directly with changes in the main Latin American economies are less influential today than they used to be, it is evident that other factors have acquired an importance which inadvertently may render the process of development more difficult. An especially clear case is the influence of the IMF on the politics and economics of Latin America. Apart from its influence on questions relating to external trade and foreign exchange, this international financial institution has in practice turned into a kind of surety for good behaviour, whose opinion is decisive in obtaining credit from other international organizations and even lending governments themselves. A sharp controversy has taken place in Latin America between 'structuralists' and 'monetarists' in connexion with the diagnosis of inflation and the policies to be adopted towards it.[19] Relevant to this study is the relationship or contradiction between the so-called 'IMF orthodoxy' and the process of development. At the risk of oversimplifying this question, it can be said that this contradiction takes place at two different levels. There is the explicit orthodox belief that stability is essential in matters of political economy, to which is sometimes added the rider that this is a necessary condition for healthy development. But, for reasons for which there is a good theoretical explanation, in Latin American experience development has gone hand in hand with an appreciable degree of monetary

[19] A large number of articles on this subject have appeared in the journal *Trimestre Económico* published by the Fondo de Cultura Económica of Mexico. *Latin American Issues*, ed. by Albert O. Hirschman (1961), has a bibliography on the subject.

imbalance in internal and external relations which has been reflected in the balance of payments. More important still in existing conditions, it is quite probable that a dynamic process will continue to generate, and coexist with, pressures militating against stability. Thus, though the terms 'development' and 'stability' are not antagonistic or mutually exclusive, in practice a choice between the two is or will frequently be offered in the sense that priority for the objective of development may imply a certain degree of imbalance, or that the attainment of stability will presuppose reduction in the rate of development.

It would be incorrect to maintain that its preoccupation with stability means that IMF policy implies or proposes to sacrifice the ultimate objective of development. In actual practice, this emphasis on stability, in conjunction with the actual methods recommended or imposed, has meant more stability and less development, and the former has frequently failed to be achieved, while the latter has been jeopardized. But it is not merely that the IMF views the Latin American situation through a glass which may be—and this is also questionable—appropriate for developed economies, in which dynamism is self-generating and only requires care to ensure a general equilibrium. This dissociation is also reproduced at the level of instruments of economic policy. International orthodoxy considers certain instruments to be 'healthy' (generally because they have been hallowed by the practice of the industrialized countries), and others by their very nature—so to speak—to be 'reprehensible'. In Latin American experience, some of these 'reprehensible' factors have been of key importance (especially exchange controls and certain discriminatory action, and monetary expansion in favour of the public sector). The making of far-reaching changes within a historically brief period, and a subsequent failure or difficulty in adjusting obsolete institutional and administrative machinery in order to keep abreast of them may account for this.

The IMF's offensive against various heterodox trends of thought has been accompanied by an insistent clamour for their replacement by others, thought to be theoretically more 'healthy'. However, the dismantling of the 'reprehensible' instruments has not been compensated by the prompt substitution of adequate alternatives which —generally speaking—demand a higher level of institutional development. Consequently the capacity for action on the part of the political economies has been weakened, or in more than one case there has been a combination of opposing factors in which the 'reprehensible' instruments continue to be used sparingly or in disguise, while the 'healthy' ones are being formally superimposed, with extremely precarious results.

An additional classification is necessary to prevent mistaken interpretations, given the highly schematic form of this analysis. It is not intended here to offer an apologia for the crude and pragmatic methods that have characterized the working of the Latin American economy and which, not infrequently, have created as many problems as they were intended to solve. But the problem evidently cannot be tackled on the basis of simplifications frequently suggested by foreign organizations and observers. It would be better if, from the outset, attempts were made to understand the assumptions underlying this heterodoxy without presuming that it is merely a manifestation of frivolity or irresponsibility on the part of the authorities of underdeveloped countries, and without calling on foreign experts to 'reveal' (as any book on the subject currently in circulation could easily do) the 'proper' and 'healthy' forms within which Latin American economic policies should be conducted.

There would appear to be clear evidence of a contradiction between the objectives and priorities advocated by the Alliance for Progress, and the general and particular outlines of the policy of the IMF, backed as it is by foreign financial centres and private interests. If, as some expect or hope, the Alliance for Progress becomes just another declaration of good intentions, this conflict will not become explicit. If, on the other hand, it should succeed in acquiring substance, its accent on progress (and not on alliance, as A. O. Hirschman aptly remarked) would clash with the alternative emphasis of the IMF on the stability and 'soundness' of the economy.

To conclude this sketch of the external factors affecting regional development, it is necessary to recall a general feature that exerts an extensive and profound influence on the political framework of development. This is the much described and analysed 'demonstration effect', i.e. the process of absorption of customs, ideas, institutions, etc. originating in, or transmitted by, the developed countries. Certain aspects of this phenomenon are of interest.

In the first place, the region is vulnerable to the most formidable propagator of consumer goods and aspirations of the 'affluent society'—the United States. Secondly, by virtue of their higher absolute levels of average income (in comparison with Africa or Asia), the degree of its concentration, and the absence of an autonomous industrial culture which might offer an alternative way of life, the more developed countries of Latin America are much more vulnerable to this 'demonstration effect.' Thirdly, at present—in contrast with the past—the 'demonstration effect' not only involves the oligarchies—as is sometimes thought—but also middle-class groups and the better-paid sections of the working classes. The reproduction of aristocratic consumer habits, typical of the old Latin American society, has given way to the mass consumption copy of the 'democratic' market, except that now the goods are, on the whole, produced domestically rather than imported. There is, of course, no question of objecting to the absolute increase of the consumption of new goods and services but rather to their social and economic cost.

The mass consumption of durables is a comparatively recent phenomenon in industrialized countries, and occurs wherever a sufficient level of income has been attained to provide the majority of the population with a reasonable standard of living. It reflects the degree of productive diversification. In Latin America, on the other hand, such consumption takes place in circumstances in which the average income is extremely low,[20] while a large part of the population lives precariously at a mere subsistence level, and development has transformed or modernized only a limited sector of the productive economy.

Thus consumption of durable goods can only expand if it is protected by a considerable concentration of income; but while this is taking place and a market is being established, a displacement of resources will necessarily occur which will prevent their being used for the development of basic activities and the improvement of the standard of living of the mass of people, who are excluded from this restricted area of 'capitalistic' development in the economy.

It is easy to appreciate the differences between this type of evolution and that which characterizes the developed Western

[20] Average real income per inhabitant in Latin America has been estimated at some $420 a year, as compared with $1,470 for Western Europe and $2,791 for the United States. See references and methodology in ECLA, *Economic Development . . . in the Post-War Period*, table 49.

countries and those of the communist world.[21] What is important here is to examine the political consequences of the 'demonstration effect', of which the principal is the 'compromise' between the better organized and more influential groups and what might be termed, somewhat harshly, our second-rate caricature of the affluent society. Any decision aimed at increasing resources for investment and/or diverting them towards those activities and groups which were neglected or overlooked in the earlier advance will meet with much greater resistance than is imagined. A typical case revealed in the process of planning for fiscal reform is the difficulty of working out a tax system which discriminates between goods and services according to their degree of priority, which is essential in view of the inherent difficulty of reproducing the tax patterns of industrialized countries based on personal income tax. Every effort in that direction arouses strong opposition among entrepreneurs, workers, and consumers connected with the envisaged activities, and these usually enjoy powerful political backing.

On the other hand, whatever the opinion regarding this type of development, it is certain that the progress of the economy has come to depend largely on the behaviour of the 'dynamic' consumer durable industries, the private investment they attract, and the activities complementary to them. In these circumstances, any policy affecting them may prejudice the rate of expansion in the short term, though some re-allocation of resources might well establish more favourable conditions for the future.

The reconciliation of these trends is undoubtedly one of the major tasks facing the strategy of economic development at the present time, and one which most clearly emphasizes the importance of political factors for its solution.

[*Aníbal Pinto, Professor of Public Finance, University of Chile, Director of the ECLA/BNDE Centre in Rio de Janeiro. His principal publications include* Chile; un caso de desarrollo frustrado (*1959*) *and* Chile, una economía difícil (*1964*).]

[21] See further, Pinto, *Concentración del progreso técnico.*

Populism and Reform in Latin America

TORCUATO S. DI TELLA

THE dynamic forces of reform in Latin America are not the same as those which successfully operated in Europe during the past century and a half. In Europe—as exemplified by the case of Britain—modernizing reform was brought about first by a Liberal Party based on the rising middle class and then by a Labour Party centred on the trade unions. This pattern is not viable in Latin America or in the rest of the underdeveloped world. In the place of Liberalism or Labour, there is an assortment of political movements which, for lack of a better word, have been often grouped under the omnibus concept of 'populism'. The term is slightly derogatory, implying something distasteful, disorderly, and brutish: something of a kind that is not to be found in socialism or communism, however one may dislike these ideologies. Populism also smacks of improvisation and irresponsibility, and by its nature, is not regarded as functional or efficient. The term, it should be added, has been coined by ideology-mongers from both the Right and the Left. It may be defined as a political movement which enjoys the support of the mass of the urban working class and/or peasantry but which does not result from the autonomous organizational power of either of these two sectors. It is also supported by non-working-class sectors upholding an anti-*status quo* ideology.

The differences between the various political situations covered by this term are permanent and important enough to merit a detailed analysis, which is essential for an understanding of the character of social change in the developing world. The reasons why the 'European model' does not apply ought to be investigated, and the various sub-types of populism described in detail. In this way the various strategies open to political-reform parties will be made more apparent.

A Shrinking World

Populism cannot be explained away as characteristic of under-developed or 'uneducated' areas. European countries were also once eminently rural, backward, and low in their standard of education, without exhibiting such a prevalence of populist forms. There were exceptions, notably in France under Louis Napoleon, but the phenomenon never produced the epidemic traits it shows in the *tiers monde*. The reasons for this are related to the fact that the developing countries of today are not only poor in absolute terms, but they are on the periphery of richer, central areas. They suffer from what economists call the 'demonstration effect'. Whether or not this 'demonstration effect' works in the sphere of consumption exactly as some economists seem to think, the fact remains that it has powerful cultural repercussions. The intellectual élites of underdeveloped countries cannot avoid suffering from an extreme form of 'demonstration effect', which should properly be called a 'fascination effect'. The existence of foci of the intensity of the United States, Britain, France, or the Soviet Union distorts their perspectives to such an extent that it is almost impossible for them to find adequate answers to the problems of their own countries. This was not the case with the intellectuals of eighteenth- or nineteenth-century Europe or the United States, who did not have the opportunity to imitate more advanced nations. It is an effect of the peripheral situation of these countries, made acute from the moment they entered into the world market.

The existence of a variety of competing foci only aggravates the problem. The intellectuals of these countries have become so accustomed to get their spiritual sustenance from abroad that the pattern is maintained even when there is a reaction against the standard cultural centres, which are then accused of 'imperialism'. There is either a shift to another focus of fascination in the charmed developed part of the world—Moscow replacing Paris—or at times an underdeveloped country takes on the role: it may be Cuba, Egypt, or China. The interesting fact is that, as little is known about these countries, opinions about them are formed once again by the news agencies of the 'imperialist' powers. These agencies shape not only the opinions of that part of the population which absorbs the contents put forward by the mass media, but also of the rebellious intellectuals, who simply take the logically extreme opposite view. This logical opposite is usually as little suited to guide action intelligently as the platitudes coming from the international news agencies.

In the other strata of the population the cultural 'demonstration effect' works just as intensely, if in a less sophisticated way. The mass media raise the levels of aspiration of their audience, particularly in the towns and among the educated. This is what has been aptly called the 'revolution of rising expectations'. Social psychologists are discovering here what tyrants have known since antiquity: give them an inch, and they will take an ell. The moment the lid is unscrewed from a traditional society, no one can predict the amount of pressure which will force its way out. This process is relatively sudden, because the modernizing trends have great force behind them. Radio, the cinema, the ideals of the Rights of Man, and written constitutions—they all tend to produce effects greater than those produced in the European experience. Yet economic expansion lags behind, burdened by the population explosion, by lack of organizational capacity, by dependence on foreign markets and capital, or by premature efforts at redistribution. A bottleneck necessarily develops, with expectations soaring high above the possibilities of satisfying them.

Representation without Taxation

In these conditions, it is difficult for democracy to function properly. In Western experience democracy was traditionally based on the principle of no taxation without representation. In the developing countries, the revolution of expectations generates a desire to have representation without ever having been taxed. Groups lacking sufficient economic or organizational power demand a share in both the goods and the decision-making processes of society. They no longer 'know their place', as European workers knew theirs until recently.[1] They form a disposable mass [2] of supporters, larger and more demanding than any Louis Napoleon would have dreamed of.

[1] European workers probably still do, according to some of their critics, notably Professor S. M. Lipset. See his well-known analyses in *Political Man* (1962). In a sense, one might expect a generalized lack of status-respect to be generated in a developing nation similar in some of its effects to the one originating in the American frontier situation, but with different causes.

[2] Gino Germani uses this concept in his works on the subject. See also his *Política y sociedad en una época de transición* (Buenos Aires, 1962).

Here another aspect of a developing society should be taken into account. In many a place and time there have been any number of reasons for being disgruntled, but in Latin America the number is at its highest. The chasm between aspiration and job satisfaction, particularly for the educated, is probably one of the main sources for what sociologists call 'status incongruence'. Impoverished aristocrats, newly rich businessmen not yet acceptable in high society, and ethnic minorities, they all add to the possibilities for creating this type of individual and group. When social rigidities make it difficult for them to regain a balanced status situation, the incongruents develop resentments, brooding over new ideas and ways of changing things. They are a great danger to any stable and sanctified social order, because they can use their resources—which on some counts are high—in order to get even with society. It has been contended that it was people of this sort who found enough motivation for pushing through the industrialization of some of the major powers of today.[3] The incongruents create social or political tension wherever they may be found but mainly in countries in the process of development, and more so in present-day developing ones than in those of the period of 'classical' European development.

The incongruent groups (generally of above-average status) and the mobilized, disposable masses complement each other. Their social situations are different, but what they have in common is a passionate hatred of the *status quo*. This feeling is different in quality from the one intellectuals may develop as a result of their professional activities—except if they happen also to be strongly incongruent, a state of affairs not uncommon in underdeveloped areas. The opposition of the incongruents to the Establishment is also different in kind from that expressed by the organization-minded, distribution-orientated trade unionists. As for those who belong to the mobilized, disposable mass, they have no patience with the complicated ways, principles, and ideas of the trade unionists who have built an organization by their own efforts. They will be more attracted by the antics of the incongruents than by the penny-mindedness of the aristocracy of labour. In such a situation, the prospects for a pluralistic

[3] See Marion Levy, 'Contrasting Factors in the Modernization of China and Japan', in S. Kuznets and others, eds., *Economic Growth: Brazil, India, Japan* (1955); and Everett C. Hagen, *On the Theory of Social Change* (1962).

democracy based on the strength of voluntary associations after the European model are poor indeed.

The Strength of the Populist Coalitions

Instead of a Labour movement, or a Liberal coalition, as happened in Britain, a populist coalition of some kind is likely to be formed. The Liberal or Labour alternatives are unattractive for the following reasons:

1. At present, Liberalism is no longer basically an anti-*status quo* ideology. In the major Western countries it has become tinged with the ideology of the dominant classes, and thereby tainted with 'imperialism'. It may also be identified with local groups with substantial foreign interests. To that extent, it is useless as an ideological weapon to the reformist groups of developing countries. It is, moreover, used as a justification for the politics of the upper classes, who are generally linked with foreign capital and commercial groups of importers and exporters.

2. Similarly, the example of the Labour movements in the developed countries is not followed with any great enthusiasm by local trade unionists or left-wing politicians. The acquiescence of those Labour movements in the official foreign policies of their own countries appears to be one of the main factors determining their lack of prestige in Latin America.

3. In addition, the formation of a Labour movement demands intensive participation of the ranks and a gradual acquisition of organizational experience. Where there is a sudden increase in the numbers of the urban working class, this process can hardly take place. In an underdeveloped country small groups of the working class that have some experience of participation and bargaining usually become too 'reasonable' too soon, losing contact with the newly mobilized masses pouring in from the countryside, or just awakening from a slumber of centuries in the cities.

4. The intellectuals, to the extent that they are not to be found in the incongruent groups, tend to develop an ideology both rationalist and humanitarian, like Marx's own version of Marxism, but unlike Lenin's. The newly mobilized masses, and the incongruent élites—including many 'youth' movements—demand much headier stuff than this. Besides, the ideology of most intellectuals is distorted by the 'fascination effect' referred to above.

5. The proliferation of incongruent groups at the various social levels of the community produces a large number of potential élites, who are capable of providing politically relevant answers to the problems of their countries and are prepared to lead the masses or the middle class. In this case—in contrast to that of the intellectuals—the capacity to provide political solutions is based principally on emotions, no matter how much these may have been rationalized.

There were fewer incongruent groups in nineteenth-century Europe and there were also fewer uprooted masses at their disposal. The 'demonstration effect' had not intervened to raise the aspirations of the masses and of the educated and semi-educated groups of the middle class. The slowly organizing sectors of the working classes, on the other hand, provided an interested audience for the theories of the rationalist-minded intellectuals.

As a consequence of the impossibility of forming a strong political movement of a Liberal or Labour type, other combinations have taken the lead on the side of reform (or revolution). They have as a rule been formed by elements drawn from various social classes, and with an ideology more radical than their class composition would have led one to expect. Given the present international situation, and the prevailing cultural and political atmosphere, reform parties in underdeveloped countries tend to adopt numerous elements from among the radical ideologies available in the world market. These ideologies (mostly varieties of socialism or Marxism) are based on the experience of the European working classes. But in the underdeveloped world, they are adopted by reform parties that comprise many social elements in addition to the urban or rural workers. This does not create a great problem, because the ideologies are used instrumentally, as a means of social control and mobilization of the masses, to an extent unparalleled in the older countries. The corpus of the doctrine is reinterpreted and blended with nationalist elements, and, above all, ritualized out of recognition. In India the Congress Party became socialist (or rather *socialistic*). Nasser also is converted to socialism. The Malagasi Republic has a government vowed to democratic socialism. *Aprismo*—derived from the initials of the Peruvian *Alianza Popular Revolucionaria Americana* party—claims to apply Marxism and dialectical materialism to Latin American conditions. The governing parties of Venezuela and Costa Rica are accepted as special members of the Socialist International. All this is meaningless. The word 'socialism' is now as malleable as the word 'Christian' and it is well on its way to becoming as useful for ruling the masses as it once was for arousing opposition against them.

In the *tiers monde* countries the masses are clamouring for goods and benefits that are farther out of their reach than ever was the case in the European experience at a given level of economic development, i.e. in relation to a given size of the cake of the national income. This is what makes it necessary for the upper or middle classes (even where they are on the side of reform) to use ideologies of appeal, in case they are unable to channel the political energies of the masses in the required direction. The need for ideology is rendered even more urgent by the fact that it is necessary to integrate not only the masses, but also the intellectuals and some of the incongruent groups. The lower strata of the masses could be adequately served by a personalized, charismatic leadership, provided it were felt to be strongly anti-imperialist or anti-oligarchic. But the other groups, particularly the marginal or under-occupied intellectuals, demand greater ideological sophistication. The juggling with concepts to be found in the writings of Lenin, Mao Tse-tung, or Fidel Castro should be judged with this fact in mind. It is their capacity to become sacred words, objects of a belief to which one is committed, that matters, not their vulnerability to the criticisms of an Oxford philosophy don.

Types of Populism

The sources of populist strength are:

(i) an élite placed at the middle or upper-middle levels of strati-fication, impregnated with an anti-*status quo* motivation;

(ii) a mobilized mass formed as a result of the 'revolution of expectations'; and

(iii) an ideology or a widespread emotional state to help communication between leaders and followers and to create collective enthusiasm.[4]

4 See Di Tella, 'Monolithic Ideologies in Competitive Party Systems: the Latin American Case', *Trans. 5th World Congress of Sociology* (1964).

In order to appreciate the perspectives of populism in a given country, the conditions facilitating the creation of the élite as defined in point (i) must be analysed.

Typically underdeveloped countries—as opposed to relatively more developed countries which will be discussed later—lacking middle sectors and which are dominated by a small upper class, provide the most fertile ground for various types of populism. The usually stagnant economic and social conditions, added to political repression by a conservative government, tend to drive many sectors of the middle class or the bourgeoisie into opposition. Even sectors of the army or clergy are affected in this way. Conditions are ripe for what Marxist theory would call a 'bourgeois' revolution; but there are several kinds of what in fact may turn out to be more broadly based revolutions of the 'socialist' or 'Nasserite' variety.

What is likely to happen depends on the exact identity of the groups driven into the reformist camp. These may either (1) include numerous elements from the upper middle class, the military, and the clergy, or else (2) they may only attract lower middle-class individuals, including intellectuals. For the purpose of this division, incongruent groups should be classified according to their main, or average, class composition. Another criterion which should be applied is whether groups attracted to the camp of reform are (1) fairly widely accepted, or (2) socially rejected, by the dominant social circles of the class from which they come.

These two criteria are important, because they permit an assessment of the degree of radicalism of the anti-*status quo* populist movement: it is suggested that a situation in which the second alternative of either criterion prevails is likely to show a populism more radical than in the case of the former alternatives occurring. Where the movement includes elements from the lower middle class only, or the intelligentsia—apart from the working classes—it will be less involved with the dominant classes than if it also includes groups from the upper middle class. But this should be read *ceteris paribus*; because the second criterion indicates that in cases in which the components of the populist movement are rejected within their class, they will be turned much more radically against the *status quo* than in the opposite case. It could be that a populist movement with components from the upper middle class, clergy, or military, rejected within their classes of origin, would turn out to be more radical than one including groups from the middle class only, who are accepted within their social *milieux* and therefore lack sufficient drive to challenge the dominant social order.

If the two criteria are crossed, the following fourfold table is obtained:

TABLE 1

Characteristics of Populist Movements in Typically Underdeveloped Countries classified according to Non-Working-Class Participation

	Accepted within their class	*Rejected within their class*
Including elements from upper middle class, military, or clergy (apart from lower strata).	Most moderate alternative. It may easily lose its populist character and become conservative.	Intermediate alternative with strong tendency to use violent means, but accepting most basic values of the existing social order.
Including only elements from the lower middle class or intellectuals (apart from working classes).	Intermediate alternative, with tendency to use legal means, but fairly radical criticism of basic values of the existing social order.	Most radical alternative. Oriented towards a social revolution with alteration of basic property pattern.

The two extreme diagonal cells are easily identified as the most conservative and the most radical. The other two are intermediate, one of them tending to be a 'loyal opposition' having important long-term interests and values at variance with those of the dominant Establishment, while the other exhibits a violent, usually authoritarian, reaction against the dominant social order, but without too wide a long-term differential of interests or values in relation to it. But the political context may be such that it forces the latter type to become progressively more radical, placing it in the extreme bottom right cell. Each of the four cases will be dealt with in detail later; in the meantime some clarification will be useful.

First, in a situation in which a populist movement arises within a basically traditional society the *status quo* is assumed to be conservative. The same is true where a populist government is in office but the basic social pattern is maintained, leaving intact a social *status quo* to which the government itself may be opposed. Where social changes have been more radical, *status quo* will be used for the structure existing before the upheavals and those surviving elements which still present problems afterwards.

Secondly, it will be noticed that incongruent groups as such were not used to produce the divisions which are illustrated in the fourfold table. This is because the essential factor, as far as the nature of the populist movement is concerned, is whether its components are accepted or rejected within their original *milieux*. Probably it is the incongruent groups that are rejected, thereby providing the main source of non-working-class components in the two right-hand cells of the table. This is a tentative hypothesis, not further explored in this paper.

Thirdly, the social conditions in a given country leading to the emergence of a certain type of non-working-class populist group are not analysed systematically here, because this would require a more intensive treatment.[5] But many references are made to this problem in dealing with each of the types of populism listed. One may put forward a basic proposition here: the typically underdeveloped condition of countries in this first group makes it possible in many cases to have important groups of the middle class, as well as military and clergy, aligned against the oligarchic Establishment. If this were not so, the two upper cells would probably present a void, or contain only a few examples. As we shall see later, this condition applies in the case of the second group of countries under study, namely those in a relatively more developed condition.

The typical populist movement represented in each cell is shown in table 2 on p. 57.

It must be borne in mind that only typically underdeveloped countries are included in the present scheme. This applies to practically the whole of Africa, Asia (except Japan and Israel), and Latin America, with the exception of Argentina, Uruguay, and Chile. Countries like Brazil and Mexico—particularly the former—which contain a rather developed region within a generally underdeveloped country, also belong to this category, but many of

---

[5] An attempt to lay down some bases for this study will be found in Di Tella, *El sistema político argentina y la clase obrera* (1964).

these must be treated as hybrids, i.e. in terms of a juxtaposition of two nations in one country. The situation in the relatively more developed countries of the *tiers monde* will be dealt with separately (see table 3, p. 73).

TABLE 2

Types of Populist Movement in Typically Underdeveloped Countries classified according to Non-Working-Class Participation

	Accepted within their class	*Rejected within their class*
Including elements from bourgeoisie, military, clergy (apart from lower strata).	Multi-class integrative parties (Mexican PRI) (Indian Congress Party)	Militaristic reform parties * (Rojas Pinilla's régime) (Nasserism)
Including only elements from lower middle class or intellectuals (apart from working class).	*Aprista* parties	Social - revolutionary parties (Castroism) (Chinese communism)

* This table refers only to the more underdeveloped parts of Latin America, thereby excluding Argentina, Chile, and Uruguay. Otherwise Peronism would fall into this category, including, as it does, some illegitimized elements from the bourgeoisie, military, and clergy. But the fact that it exists in a much more developed country sets Peronism distinctly apart from Nasserism. See table 3, p. 73.

Each of the four types of populist party of the typically underdeveloped areas will now be described. The Argentinian and Chilean cases (particularly Peronism and the Ibañez movement, and the Popular Front of Communists and Socialists), are dealt with later on, in considering the relatively more developed countries.

Multi-Class, Integrative Parties

In addition to working-class membership, these populist parties comprise numerous groups drawn from the middle class and which are accepted by it. These parties are broadly integrative, covering a wide range of interests which may find expression through factions and other special groups within the parties where there is ample scope for bargaining. Even when formally autocratic, in practice these parties allow their constituents much freedom of manoeuvre. The Congress Party of India is the best-known example. The typical Latin American case is the *Partido Revolucionario Institucional* (PRI) of Mexico as it is now constituted, although in the earlier stages of the Mexican Revolution the governing party may have been nearer to the *Aprista* type, enjoying little support among the higher reaches of society.

Possessing a strong organizational structure, with their own fairly well-developed bureaucracy, and controlling the associated groups (such as local committees and other voluntary groups), populist parties usually enjoy trade union support. In the Mexican case this is manifestly so; it is less markedly so in the case of the Indian Congress Party.[6] While personal charisma of the leader or President may be important, this is less so than in other types. Enjoying the support of the bulk of the middle class these populist parties have no need to establish a *direct link* with the masses, as is the case when a rather isolated and socially rejected leadership faces a majority consisting of sectors favouring the maintenance of the social *status quo*. Supported and accepted by the middle class, parties of this type do not risk going too far in the direction of demagogy or of arousing class animosities. In cases such as these, ultimately some form of pluralism based on Western democratic forms tends to prevail, but given the social structure of the country, these opposition parties represent a small minority only. In the Mexican political spectrum there is on the Right a small party enjoying support from some groups of the upper classes, and on the Left another small party identified with both working-class and intellectual elements. In India the situation is similar: there is the Swatantra Party on the Right, and a number of small groups on the Left (Communists and Socialists), none of which can threaten the solid majority of the governing party for the time being.

Of all the possible populist varieties, this is the most moderate, the one in which the link between the masses and the leaders is least marked by strong emotional involvements or personal charisma,[7] and one which lacks an elaborate and sanctified ideology. The bonds of organization in this case are rather weak,

[6] Although this typology has been developed especially for Latin America, it may be applied to other similarly underdeveloped regions.

[7] So much so that it is even doubtful whether the term 'populism' can be adequately applied to this type of movement. The term will be retained, however, with the proviso that this is a special type of populism.

being mainly financial and bureaucratic. This lack of structural rigidity may be due to the absence of an external challenge. A great majority of the population is still rural, largely unmobilized, and relatively unaffected by the influence of mass media. As the process of industrialization gains momentum, there may well be a tendency for this type of party to lose its popular support and to become a modern conservative party, finding itself in opposition to a newly formed populist group. Among other examples are the Republican Party in Turkey and the Kuomintang of China during its early period of existence. The *Partido Revolucionario Auténtico* of Grau San Martín and Prío Socarrás in Cuba also came close to this type.

In Brazil, the Vargas government, from its inception in 1930 until its demise in 1945, approximated to this model. Though not acceptable to the upper classes, it was certainly widely accepted among the middle class. However, the special conditions prevailing in the case of Brazil—'two nations in one'—complicate the situation. The more developed part of the country demands a more modern political structure, approximating to the European model: a large conservative party (*União Democrática Nacional*) finds itself facing a Labour Party (*Partido Trabalhista*). But the fact that the country as a whole is at a lower stage of growth serves to maintain the strength of many traditional patterns. Thus the almost permanent governing coalition of Vargas's heirs, composed of the *Partido Social Democrático* and *Partido Trabalhista*, in power from 1946 to 1964, has its equivalent in the PRI in Mexico (its two components separated, though permanently allied). The right-wing opposition parties (*União Democrática Nacional* and the *Partido Social Progressista* of Adhemar de Barros) are each much stronger than the equivalent Mexican section. On the Left also, the Communist Party is potentially stronger than its Mexican equivalent. It is tempting to extrapolate these tendencies and forecast a polarization of the political spectrum in Brazil on the following lines: on the Right, the solid mass of the *União Democrática Nacional* plus its *Social Progressista* ally; on the Left, the *Trabalhistas* supported by the Communists; with the multi-class integrative populist party (*Social Democráticos* plus *Trabalhistas*) torn asunder in the process. But this science-fiction model would be possible only under very 'developed' conditions—it would be rather similar to the British variety. The fact that the whole of Brazil is still far from being as developed as the São Paulo region makes this extrapolation unrealistic. Whether in opposition or in the government, the multi-class integrative party, or the coalition that takes its place (*Social Democráticos* plus *Trabalhistas*) is likely to remain an important element of the Brazilian political scene for a long time to come.

This type of populist party tends to be powerful irrespective of whether it forms part of the government or opposition, and to concentrate on economic growth rather than social reform. Some reforms conducive to economic development—like agrarian reform—will be accorded priority, but not much will be done to antagonize the capitalist sector of the economy. An important state sector may develop for the purpose of launching new enterprises in fields in which private capital has found it difficult to enter on an adequate scale. Enjoying strong support among the various social classes, governments of this type are in a position to embark on foreign policies relatively independent of the main world powers. In this sense it is interesting to note that Brazil— before the 1964 coup—and Mexico have been the two principal countries in Latin America to follow an independent foreign policy, most noticeably in respect of Cuba but not entirely confined to that issue. Anti-American feeling is no stronger than that prevailing in other countries of Latin America: it is their governments that are stronger. The size and importance of Brazil and Mexico merely add one more relevant factor in this instance. That size by itself would not be enough is shown by default in the Argentine case. It is the combination of national importance and a strongly backed *populist* government that makes such an independent foreign policy possible. This is not to say that other political combinations would not make the pursuit of such policies equally possible: Argentina under Perón, Chile under Frei, and Cuba under Castro are cases in point.

The Aprista Parties

The *Aprista* type of party is based on the support of the working class and important segments of the lower middle class, but not the upper middle class, military, or clergy. The middle-class segments joining the *Aprista* coalition tend to be accepted within their class, though not necessarily by the upper classes, the bourgeoisie, or the military. The party is at once more monolithic and strongly organized than the type just analysed. It does not contain so many divergent class interests, or provide such an opportunity for pressure groups to operate within its ranks. The Peruvian *Alianza Popular Revolucionaria Americana* (APRA) party is the most representative example of this type. This is perhaps truer of its flourishing period before 1950 than since then, when it has shown signs of decay. Highly integrated with an important basis of voluntary workers, the party's organizational structure is in some ways similar to that of the communist-cell variety. The tradition of anarchism and other small-scale working-class organizations is to be found in this type of party also, but strong authority and charisma have been vested in the leadership. Education, social work, co-operatives, and other cultural activities reminiscent of the European Social-Democratic tradition are accorded importance in the everyday activity of the party. Ideology, to an extent unknown in the multi-class integrative type, plays an important part in maintaining solidarity. APRA's ideology was consciously elaborated from Marxist elements, ostensibly being an application of dialectical materialism to Latin American conditions, and at variance, therefore, with Lenin's application of the same basic dogma to Russian conditions.[8] This ideology—the object of a special cult by its followers—has been made more esoteric by the addition of Einstein's theory of relativity to Marxism in an attempt to justify the adaptation of political values and strategies to conditions differing from country to country.

The political outlook of the party has undergone an evolution not altogether different from that of German Social Democracy: from a tough adherence to revolutionary principles to an acceptance of moderate democratic forms; and from an insistence on outright nationalization of foreign enterprises and large local concentrations of industrial or rural capital to a gradualist reformist programme. The transition from the more radical to the more moderate form of ideology has had its parallel in the amount of participation of the party in government in the immediate post-war period—from 1945 to 1948—and in an agreement to accept the role of loyal opposition to a conservative government they helped to elect: President Prado's régime from 1956 to 1962. In the

[8] See V. R. Haya de la Torre, *Treinta años de Aprismo* (Mexico City, 1956), and H. Kantor, *The Ideology and Program of the Peruvian Aprista Movement* (1953).

process, accusations of betrayal have been common, especially from intellectual groups, but the party does not seem to have lost too much of its popular support.

In parties of this kind there is, in moments of crisis, a tendency towards a three-way split. This was clearly seen in the case of *Acción Democrática*, APRA's sister-party in Venezuela. During President Betancourt's period in office, a thorough reassessment of the party's ideals had to be made in order to ensure survival in the conditions of the post-Pérez Jiménez period, in the face of continuous threats from the army and unrelenting pressure from oil interests. To this was added the complicating factor of the Cuban Revolution, which at the beginning had the support of the Venezuelan government. But as the extremist followers of Fidel Castro tried to extend their revolution to Venezuela, clashes became inevitable. The left wing of *Acción Democrática* split away to become the rebellious *Movimiento de Izquierda Revolucionaria* (MIR), which led an unsuccessful revolutionary movement and was outlawed. Its support among the masses does not seem to be substantial. The remaining body of *Acción Democrática* also divided into two parts, but this division was later healed. The party continues to be a party of reform, enjoying popular support—as evidenced in the last elections—but finds itself hampered by compromises both in the domestic and the international field.

In Peru APRA also lost its left wing—APRA *Rebelde*—as well as many supporters, but its political capital was so high that it still manages to command the support of an important third of the electorate.

Parties of the APRA type are usually supported by the trade unions, which are not as a rule either too strong or too bureaucratic. Trade unions linked to this type of party were not created by the state, as were those associated with the multi-class integrative parties of Mexico and Brazil. Indeed, trade union support appears to be an essential aspect of this type of populist party, and when it dwindles or disappears the *Aprista* movement may be said to disappear as such, or change towards a centrist party, of the type of the *radicales* in the Latin tradition. Recent trends in Venezuela and Peru may serve as pointers to the future strength of *Aprista* coalitions. Trade union support rather than ideological considerations would appear to be the decisive factor.

Aprista movements often have rival parties on their Right or Centre-Right, leaning on the upper classes and some groups from the middle class with little or no support from the trade unions, though with some popular following. In Peru, for instance, there is *Acción Popular*, President Belaúnde Terry's party, as well as a small party that used to be headed by ex-President Prado. It also has a left-wing rival, at present in the form of *Castrista* groups recruited from among intellectuals and some sectors of the urban working class. On the other hand, when weakened by the internal crises referred to above, new populist movements may arise to compete for its popular following. This is the case of ex-President Odría's party (*Unión Nacional Odriísta*). Though during his presidency Odría was supported by conservative forces, he also made some efforts in a Peronista direction. This was more evident once he was out of office. Now he is attempting to form a populist party of a 'Nasserite' variety which would have support—if successful— among some groups high up in the social scale, among former military colleagues, and among sections of the urban working class but not from organized trade union sources.

In Venezuela the *Unión Republicana Democrática* (URD) occupies a position similar to that of *Acción Popular* in Peru, but it probably cuts somewhat into the popular support of the Odría type, because there is no equivalent of the latter. Some attempts have been made to form an unequivocally conservative party, and there is also the Christian Democratic *Comité Organizador por Elecciónes Independientes* (COPEI), which started as a fairly small, right-wing group, but is now trying to develop a more reformist programme and to eat into the support of the *Acción Democrática* and the URD.

A party of the *Aprista* type cannot exercise power with any degree of confidence equal to that of the multi-class integrative parties. Although its members and political clientèle may have economic interests and attitudes at variance with those of the upper classes, because of its fear of antagonizing the armed forces and other potentially hostile groups, the policy of the party tends to remain moderate. This weakness is particularly evident at the international level, and in recent years has led the party into adopting an extreme anti-communist and anti-Castro position. Heavy emphasis is laid on an alliance with organized labour and similar forces in the United States and Europe, involving to some degree the acceptance of the foreign policy of those countries. Organizations like the ICFTU work closely with *Aprista* parties at the trade union level providing them with funds, but they are a dubious political asset. Cultural relationships are established with the Congress for Cultural Freedom and other similar organizations with even more damaging effects among the local intelligentsia. Policies such as these could spell the continuous weakening of *Aprista* parties as engines of social reform, while maintaining organizational strength among the middle class. If this happened they would resemble the centre parties of more developed countries, as do the *Radicales* of Argentina and Chile. On the Left, their place might be taken by parties of other populist varieties, or by a social-revolutionary *Castrista* or a Labour party, depending on the exact level of development.

Other cases of *Aprista* parties in Latin America are Juan Bosch's *Partido Revolucionario Democrático* of the Dominican Republic, Figueres's *Partido de Liberación Nacional* in Costa Rica, Arévalo's *Partido Revolucionario* of Guatemala, and the *Movimiento Nacionalista Revolucionario* (MNR) of Bolivia. The latter is probably not very typical, because its roots are less of the Marxist-cum-Liberal variety, leaning as it did at its inception during the war on militarist groups with pro-Axis sympathies. Since then, however, the party has developed a structure and ideology of the APRA type interspersed with some elements of the multi-class integrative parties, particularly as regards its semi-monopoly of power, but with less participation of the upper middle class in its ranks.

'Nasserite' or Militarist Reform Parties

The two types of populism analysed hitherto—multi-class integrative and *Aprista*—tend to emerge where social conditions set the bulk of either the upper or the lower middle class against the dominant order. The reform parties, under these conditions, have to represent the feelings and sentiments prevalent among the mass of the respective class, i.e. upper middle class for the integrative, and lower middle class for the *Aprista* parties. It is for this reason that these parties cannot afford to be 'tough-minded'.[9]

---

[9] This word is used in the sense given to it in H. J. Eysenck, *The Psychology of Politics* (1954), meaning a tendency towards authoritarianism and aggressiveness.

When, however, anti-*status quo* elements constitute but a small section of their class, they find themselves in an insecure position and may well develop authoritarian and emotional attitudes. It is these characteristics which make them bellicose and distinguish militarist-reform 'Nasserite' and social-revolutionary parties from the two previously discussed.

Militarist-reform parties in underdeveloped countries are based on a part of the armed forces that rebels against the *status quo*, the military adopting the role traditionally played by the bourgeoisie in promoting economic growth and social reform. Often the only major social group with any degree of organization and discipline, the military provide a combination of modernization and authoritarianism essential for or at least highly propitious for the development of a backward country. Parties thus formed usually *after* the seizure of power do not, as a rule, show a high degree of ideological consciousness, being centred on the figure of a charismatic leader. A one-party state tends to be formed, as in Egypt, or a close approximation to it, as in Iraq under Kassem and his followers. The aristocracy and most of the upper middle class withhold support from the régime, and are at most half-heartedly tolerated: it is not the rule to eliminate them outright. What appears to happen is that a *new* upper or upper middle class is formed under these régimes, mostly made up of high-ranking bureaucrats, military and political leaders, and sometimes a newly-formed capitalist class, partly private and partly state capitalist. If this latter group is allowed to develop to any significant extent, the party moves into the first type, i.e. that of the multi-class integrative party. This is probably what happened in Turkey, where during the first stages of the Kemalist revolution the situation was similar to that of Egypt under Nasser.

A 'Nasserite' party includes in its ranks a large part of the population and of the professional and trade union organizations. Unions are formed as state-controlled mechanisms, and the element of voluntary association in them, as well as in the party, is feeble. The link between the masses and the leader is direct, and reinforced by a good deal of xenophobia. Intellectual support for the régime would to some extent depend on whether Marxist or Liberal ways have been predominant before, though there are exceptions to this. The lower middle classes tend to follow the lead of the military more readily, lacking as they do a tradition of forming political parties of their own.

Foreign policy is usually self-assertive and aggressive, reflecting a strong government and a large number of historical grievances. The internal opposition, springing from the remains of the upper classes and bourgeoisie, is usually not legalized and is rather small and often powerless. There may be left-wing groups in opposition —both legal and illegal—which, if allowed to develop, could spell the end of the régime. This seems to have been the case during the last stage of Kassem's rule.

The examples hitherto cited have been taken from outside Latin America, since 'Nasserism' is not to be found in this area in a pure form. The traditional militaristic dictatorships of the nineteenth century do not conform to this type, as they were more often than not of the conservative kind. In cases in which they were to some extent developmental, as during Porfírio Díaz's rule in Mexico, they enjoyed wide support among the aristocracy and upper middle classes but they were not *populist*. As for Peronism, which some people considered a form of 'Nasserism', it tends to make its appearance in relatively more developed countries, and therefore differs markedly from the 'Nasserite' variety. Arbenz's régime in Guatemala does not belong to this type although he was a military officer. The bulk of the military failed to support him, and his party must be classed as having been essentially *Aprista*, showing some tendency to evolve into the social-revolutionary type as a result of the alliance with the Communists. Rojas Pinilla's régime in Colombia comes closer to the 'Nasserite' model, though it was short-lived and unsuccessful. Colombia's two main parties, Conservatives and Liberals, have long been traditionalist, operating under strictly oligarchic control, with little participation on the part of the middle class. An unstable coexistence evolved in the 1930s under outwardly liberal-democratic institutions, but with limited participation on the part of the population. This was broken during the late 1940s. Rojas Pinilla was eventually put in power by an army coup, ostensibly to restore the original situation. Soon, however, he tried to pursue a new political line, which may be described as both developmental and 'Nasserite'. An attempt to form a populist party—of the *Aprista* type—had been made before 1949 by Eliecer Gaitán, without much success. Rojas Pinilla tried to inherit this tradition, alongside some of the cadres of *Gaitanismo*, as well as some socialist intellectuals. His attempt failed as opposition from traditional quarters proved too strong. Colombia has now reverted, with minor changes, to the traditional two-party system. Neither of the two parties is populist, but there is a small leftist fraction of the Liberals, which shows some social-revolutionary tendencies. The followers of Rojas Pinilla have a party of their own, with scant electoral following. It would be interesting to try to determine which will be the variety of populism to develop in Colombia. That country presents a historical anomaly, as, in spite of several attempts at getting it started, populism has not been widely accepted.

Another approximation to the type is the *Unión Nacional Odriísta* in Peru where the liberal-democratic régime was much less developed at the time of Odría's army coup in 1948 than in the Colombian case. Unlike Colombia, Peru had an earlier populist movement: the APRA. Odría came to power as a conservative, and governed the country as such. An attempt was made to pursue a Peronista policy, and even today the memory of his government is cherished by some sectors of the urban workers because of his public works programmes. Odría, however, has little or no organized union support. His is probably an embryonic 'Nasserite' movement, with few prospects of achieving power.

Conditions in Latin America are on the whole not appropriate—economically, socially, and politically—to permit 'Nasserism', or military reform parties, to be successful. An additional reason for this is that it is not easy for military and religious elements in Latin America to play an anti-imperialist role which their counterparts often perform in the Middle East. In the Middle East crude xenophobia and ethnocentricity tend to lead both religious leaders and army into the anti-Western camp, without passing through any other sophisticated ideological stages. In Latin America there is no important religious or racial difference between the dominant local strata—from which the religious and army leaders are drawn—and the Western powers. The difference between Protestantism and Catholicism, or between Anglo-Saxons and Latins, or *mestizos*, pales when compared to the centuries of animosity against European Christianity to be found in the Muslim and Arab world. Ethnocentric attitudes capable of being harnessed to anti-imperialism do exist at the lower echelons of the social pyramid in Latin

America, but this is a place where the Latin American military are not to be found.

Social-Revolutionary Parties

Castroism presents a typical example of a Latin American social-revolutionary movement. The Venezuelan MIR may be regarded as an attempt to reproduce the same phenomenon, which has not, so far, met with any success. The Bolivian MNR and the Guatemalan Revolutionary Party under Arbenz have a few traits in common with *Fidelismo*, but in neither case was the process of conversion from the *Aprista* to the social-revolutionary model completed. Processes of this kind may be regarded as typical of the formation of social-revolutionary movements in Latin America. Castro's revolution was backed at the beginning by a coalition of the *Aprista* type, and during the first months of Castro's rule claimed as such.

Social-revolutionary movements in underdeveloped countries are based on:

1. Some elements drawn from the urban working class, which is neither numerous nor well organized in such countries.

2. Support from the peasantry, particularly from the poor peasants and agricultural labourers.

3. An élite of professional revolutionaries, mainly drawn from the lower middle class and intelligentsia, strongly at odds with their own class of origin, which tends to develop 'tough-minded' attitudes as a result. Whether this is because of their own status incongruence, or the chasm between aspirations—produced by middle and higher education—and job opportunities, or whether it is strictly a result of ideology, is irrelevant to the present purpose. What matters is that this group is essential to the strength and fighting power of the movement. If social conditions in the country do not produce such a group in significant numbers, no amount of training in leadership can replace it.

On the basis of the last of these three characteristics the social-revolutionary movements of underdeveloped countries find themselves in a different category from Marx's traditional model of a revolutionary working-class party. It is not only that in place of the urban workers there are now peasants or rural workers. Far more important is the prominent role played by the professional revolutionaries alienated in varying degrees from their class of origin. Important consequences derive from this fact, enabling the movement to be included under the general type of populism. Social-revolutionary movements introduce far more important changes in the property relations of a society than do other populist parties. But this still does not make them fundamentally similar to the model of a working-class revolutionary party, which is largely hypothetical, since most important parties of our kind in practice show clear tendencies towards reformism.[10] By contrast, the problems of social control facing a social-revolutionary movement after its advent to power in a society of marked social discrepancies are rather different from those facing a party whose main source of strength is the organized working class. This has led some observers to point to the similarities, under capitalism and socialism, in the process of forcing predominantly peasant societies into the strait-jacket of industrialism.[11]

The internal structure of social-revolutionary parties is, as a rule, monolithic, with an ideology at the core of its loyalties, and with occupational, trade union, and cultural groups under the firm control of the party. The backbone of the process of development, the party is in this sense the equivalent of the army in the case of 'Nasserite' régimes. Opposition, usually from the Right and Centre Right or liberal sources, is not tolerated, and its bases tend to disappear as the revolutionary process gains momentum, dispossessing the erstwhile privileged classes in the process. Social-revolutionary parties in the present world situation quite naturally tend to favour the fostering of close relations with the countries of the Soviet bloc. Economic assistance is likely to come from there, as well as trade union support via the WFTU, and cultural assistance through a variety of Soviet-sponsored organizations. This reliance on foreign sources of power should be contrasted with the relations of the *Aprista* parties with the Western bloc. By controlling the whole state apparatus, the social-revolutionary movements are in a strong bargaining position, but the partner and ally with which they have to deal is strong and powerful also. The relationship is of the

[10] The French and Italian Communist Parties are typical cases in point in the recent political experience of developed countries.

[11] R. Bendix, *Work and Authority in Industry* (1956) develops this point of view, taking his evidence from Great Britain, the United States, the Soviet Union, and Eastern Germany.

government-to-government type, except where the social-revolutionary party, out of power, is trying to organize subversive activities. In that case, dependence on foreign aid may be greater, but this is counterbalanced by the capacity of the revolutionaries to organize successful guerrilla activities. As for the *Aprista* parties, they have much less power in their own territory, but have to deal with less powerful allies and protectors (trade unions and left-of-centre political groups from Western countries) which are to some, however slight, extent at odds with the main power structure of their own countries. Given their bases of strength in the local society, the multi-class integrative parties, are, by contrast, freer from foreign interference.

A social-revolutionary government failing to develop a strong party structure may be forced to rely more heavily on the army, changing itself thereby into a movement of the 'Nasserite' type. The Algerian revolution may be facing this problem within the next few years. On the other hand, if the revolutionary tasks are not tackled energetically, a kind of coexistence may be arrived at, and an evolution started towards the *Aprista* type. Until the recent coup d'état it appeared as if Bolivia were moving in this direction.

The Situation in More Developed Countries: Peronista Parties

In the relatively more developed countries within the *tiers monde* it is more difficult for populism to emerge because higher rates of literacy, urbanization, and industrialization have given the working and middle classes greater organizational experience of their own. They do not enter as easily into vaguely defined populist coalitions, and are more immune from emotional appeal. Expecting a more contractual approach to politics, they want to know exactly what is going to be offered to them in return for their loyalties.

Actual conditions may not always correspond to those stated above, and may hardly begin to approximate to the conditions in the world's major industrialized countries. But it is nevertheless useful to bear in mind these general differences from the earlier group of countries in order to understand political behaviour in the relatively more developed countries like Argentina, Uruguay, and Chile.

Another important characteristic of such more developed countries is that the bulk of the middle class both sense favourable possibilities for social climbing and are the main beneficiaries of the

existing prosperity. This leads them frequently to rally to the conservative side. The situation in the typically underdeveloped countries, however, may be such that the middle class, and even large
segments of the upper middle class, are being driven into the anti-
status quo camp, and adopt radical ideologies. Once development
and/or industrialization is achieved, the middle class have fewer
complaints against the existing social order. Thus the two types of
populist movements rooted in the existence of socially rejected
political élites within the middle class are less likely to occur
under these conditions. Such élite groups as may appear are often
of the right-wing variety. As for the working class, their increased
organization and weight often lead them to seek expression through
instruments of their own making. They are not so easily contented
as before with the crumbs of power gathered by a populist coalition, particularly one of either the multi-class integrative or the
A prista type.

This generalization may appear to be contradicted by the spread
and continued strength of *Peronismo* in Argentina. This movement
was clearly populist; it had a strong popular following, was supported by army circles, a sizeable sector of the clergy, and some
important groups of newly risen industrialists. These latter groups
constituted a social reject from the upper middle class and were a
principal source of leadership, finance, and ideology. Before the
advent of *Peronismo* Argentina had a semi-liberal régime, which
offered the middle class wide political participation through the
Unión Cívica Radical, and to the upper strata of the working class
in the Socialist and Communist Parties as well as the trade unions.
The 1943 military coup, which was markedly fascist, suppressed all
opposition, alienated the intellectuals, but slowly, under the leadership of Perón, succeeded in assembling the components of a populist coalition. The élite trade unions were coerced into becoming
larger, mass unions, and were given much stronger organization
and finances. Some important social reforms were enacted.

To the extent that *Peronismo* was a populist coalition, the hypothesis, stated above, as to the relative difficulty of organizing such
movements in relatively developed countries stands invalidated.
On the other hand it would seem that the main cleavage line, as
shown in elections and political participation, sets the working
class apart from the bulk of all other classes (with the exception of
those small minorities that had been instrumental in the formation

of *Peronismo*). Most of the active sectors of the middle class, including an exceptionally large assortment of voluntary organizations, turned against *Peronismo*. To this extent, then, the hypothesis is validated, establishing *Peronismo* as a class-based movement.

In order to have a populist movement in a relatively developed country, it would seem to be necessary to have a very strongly motivated anti-*status quo* minority among the middle or upper reaches of the social pyramid. When, for reasons of status incongruence or other factors,[12] such a group springs into existence, a populist coalition will very likely emerge. But it will be a populist coalition of a different type from those existing in the underdeveloped areas. For one thing it will have comparatively little support among the lower middle class and intellectuals, and for another its trade union sector is likely to loom much larger. Control, however, will remain in the hands of élites drawn from the upper strata.

This type of coalition is likely to be less permanent than the others witnessed before, because the social structure tends to absorb the anti-*status quo* group into its upper sectors. A relatively prosperous society offers numerous opportunities of satisfaction to any frustrated group drawn from the middle, and especially upper middle, class. The moment this happens, the populist coalition loses one of its legs and tumbles down. This seems to have been the case in Argentina. After the downfall of Perón it became evident that there were few industrialists, military, or clergy left in the camp of populism. They had either turned safely conservative, or into *Radicales*, or had lost interest. The populist movement stands for a while uncomfortably on one foot—that of the trade union movement. As this foot is stronger than it would be in the case of a really underdeveloped country, the party lingers on, developing a tendency to assume the shape of a labour movement. Rightist ideological traits are shed, intellectuals are attracted, trade unions become accustomed to survive without state support, elements from the lower middle class enter the movement. Part of the rural and typically populist following is lost, which makes it more difficult for the party to win elections—*Peronismo* now commands approximately 35 per cent of the votes cast—but brings it closer into line with European working-class tradition.

[12] A detailed interpretation of that phenomenon is given in Di Tella, *El sistema político argentino*, pp. 54–65.

Other combinations leading to a populist party in this type of country are much less likely to materialize. Table 3 reviews the range of possible situations.

TABLE 3

Populist Movements in Relatively Developed Countries classified according to Non-Working-Class Participation

	Accepted within their class	*Rejected within their class*
Including elements from bourgeoisie, military, or clergy (apart from lower strata).	This case could not arise, as the bourgeoisie, owing to the prosperity of the country, would not have any desire to get involved in a populist coalition. It could not, therefore, permit some of its members to take such a step.	This case can arise when some reasons (mostly temporary, like war - induced booms) create a strongly motivated anti-*status quo* minority group in the bourgeoisie, clergy, or military. *Peronismo*, in its heyday, is the typical example.
Including elements from the lower middle class or intellectuals (apart from the working class).	This case is possible because the lower middle class have reasons to be against the *status quo*, particularly in a country not yet fully developed. The *Radicales* could be included in this category, though they often lack enough popular support, especially from trade unions and other organized sectors. Under Yrigoyen in Argentina, or the first Popular Front in Chile, they came close to the pattern. Frei's Christian Democrats in Chile may also be included.	This case would be again the social-revolutionary one. In developed countries it is unlikely to occur. If it did, its working-class component would be stronger, *vis-à-vis* the professional revolutionary élite, than in the case of a really underdeveloped country. The present Socialist-Communist coalition in Chile has elements of this type.

The only clear case of populism among those included in this table is *Peronismo*. The others merely approximate, to varying degrees. They present *incipient forms* of the European model parties—Labour or Liberal—rather than clearly populist ones in the sense in which the term has been used in this paper. It is instructive to compare tables 1 and 2 with table 3. The place occupied in the earlier tables by the multi-class integrative parties is now empty. Even in the case of underdeveloped countries these parties would be classed as moderate. The *Apristas* have been replaced by the *Radicales*, the main difference being the reduced certainty of securing working-class support. The workers now have their own ideas as to what kind of political organization they want (usually urban socialist parties, like the Chilean *Partido Socialista Obrero* of Luis Recabarren or the Argentinian *Partido Socialista* of Juan B. Justo). As for 'Nasserism', it has been, not surprisingly, replaced by *Peronismo*. There is, then, some similarity between those two movements after all; but the differences are even greater and they are principally due to the previous existence of an important liberal régime and the strength of the trade unions, both conditions to be found in the case of *Peronismo*. The social-revolutionaries should have been replaced by Marx's ideal working-class revolutionary party, absorbing the remains of a savagely proletarianized middle class, but as this latter condition does not obtain in the more developed countries, the type gives way to a Labour version as found in fully industrialized societies.

Probably by this time it has become clear that the present author considers populism the only force on the side of reform in Latin America. The problem, then, is how to adjust to the harsh realities of populism. This is no easy matter. Rejection in the name of liberal ideals is as futile as uncritical acceptance. For Latin American intellectuals a possible way out of this dilemma may be the adoption of independent attitudes allowing for the maintenance of working relationships with populist movements. This is something which has hardly been attempted as yet.

[*Torcuato Di Tella is Associate Professor at the Institute of Sociology of the University of Buenos Aires. His principal publications include* El sistema político argentino y la clase obrera (*1964*) *and* La teoria del primer impacto del desarrollo económico (*1965*).]

Land Tenure and Development in Latin America

JACQUES CHONCHOL

THERE appears to be a close relationship between the changes needed in the present systems of land tenure and the possibilities of accelerating the process of development. Unless far-reaching agrarian reforms are implemented, most Latin American countries will be unable during the next few years to speed up economic progress and satisfy adequately the profound longing for greater prosperity and freedom.

The Need to Change and Develop

This need is determined at present by three principal factors, found to a greater or lesser degree in all the countries of the region: the increasing rate of demographic growth, the aspirations arising from awareness of the living standards of more highly developed countries, and the growing political consciousness of the masses.

Latin America today has the world's highest rate of population increase. Between 1925 and 1945 the annual rate of increase was of the order of 2 per cent. During the 1950s the rate was generally over 2 per cent and forecasts for the next fifteen years indicate that it will go up to about 3 per cent. This means that the total population of the twenty Latin American republics, which amounted to 206 million inhabitants in 1960, will grow to 360 million by 1980. At the end of this period, Latin America will have to feed, clothe, house, and, to a large extent, provide work for 150 million more people. This is an increase of 70 per cent over the figures for 1960.

The population is not only increasing unusually fast, but it is also striving to improve its standards of living. There is a growing demand for better food and clothing, better education, and more consumer goods. Real and profound ambitions are becoming increasingly felt; this does not merely affect restricted circles or minor groups among the urban middle classes, but permeates the greater part of the population. The development of these aspirations has been encouraged to a significant extent by what economists call 'the demonstration effect', that is, the realization by the low-income groups that there are others who live better than they do, and their desire also to achieve this improved standard. In open societies this realization and its political consequences are inevitable. In consequence, besides the requirements arising from the increasing population, there are also the demands stemming from these developing ambitions: in a social climate of growing political awareness these tend to gather force rapidly.

The peoples of Latin America are participating more effectively than ever before in the political processes of their respective countries. At the same time politics appear to be increasingly focused on the opportunities for improving the living conditions of the masses. In this connexion, certain factors are worth bearing in mind. One is the extraordinary speed with which the political participation of the population in the electoral system has increased during recent years. In some countries of the region the number of electors has increased tenfold within a few years, and in practically all of them the growth of the electorate has been impressive in absolute as well as in relative terms. All this has doubtless been assisted by granting votes to women, and, in some countries, to the illiterate.

The centre of political contention has tended to shift rapidly away from what used to be the great dividing issues a few decades ago, such as the antithesis between secular and religious society, lay education, the responsibility of the state in education, and so forth. In the forefront are matters connected with economic development, social welfare, and the equitable distribution of income.

Recently, moreover, new models of economic development have made their appearance in Latin America, models which find political expression in a number of populist movements—the Cuban Revolutionary movement, the various groups of Marxist inspiration, and the Christian Democrat groupings—whose importance is increasing in several countries. All these new groupings and forces, which are engaged in a political struggle both with the traditional sectors and among themselves, have brought to the attention of the people new formulas claiming to provide more justice and welfare. This is not only shaking the foundations of the traditional political structures but it is also tending to strengthen the conviction of the people that a rapid improvement in their living conditions is not only just and necessary, but feasible.

In this connexion the countries of Latin America have accepted the necessity for implementing fundamental reforms in the existing social and economic structures. This was expressed, for example, in the Punta del Este Charter and in the programme of the Alliance for Progress. Despite all the obstacles, delays, and progressive shifts of emphasis which the latter programme has experienced, it has brought about a change of attitude—at times perhaps more apparent than real—in two respects. There is now a certain estrangement between the United States government and the more conservative Latin American groups which were its natural allies in the past. The second feature is the formal admission by all governments within the region that it is not possible to achieve economic development without changes in the present social structure. The publicity given to the need for these changes has no doubt contributed to convince the people of their necessity and practicability.

The combination of the demographic problem, the upsurge of new aspirations, and the growing political consciousness of the masses presents a considerable challenge. Without economic growth and social transformation capable of satisfying the needs which these factors engender, the inevitable result will be a situation of progressive political instability, the frustration of the aspirations of large sectors of the population, and the lack of any firm foundation for erecting the conditions essential to a dynamic, progressive, and democratic society.

Consequently the next few years present the region with two basic alternatives. Either reforms will be implemented which will create conditions for accelerated development, or else such problems as underemployment and unemployment, monetary instability, balance of payments difficulties, and a lack of opportunities for improvement for the large majority of the people will continue to grow more acute as they aggravate each other. In a situation of stagnation, which increasing sections of the population are now no longer willing to accept, conditions will become ripe for social upheaval. This, in turn, will increase the likelihood of

strong régimes, whether of the Right or of the Left, able either
to effect or prevent change by force.

Agrarian Reform, Industrialization, and Integration as
Dynamic Factors of Development

Before the crisis of 1929, economic development in the Latin
American countries largely followed the traditional pattern of
colonial countries producing mineral, agricultural, and raw
materials for export to the more industrialized countries, whence
they imported the manufactured goods they required. This was the
traditional pattern referred to by ECLA as 'the pattern of externally induced development'. The crisis of 1929 and the following
years brought a fundamental change.

The patterns of international demand and supply were suddenly
disrupted, and Latin America was faced with a dramatic change
in its terms of trade. Since then, moreover, a number of factors
have tended to slow down the rate of growth of exports of
agricultural products which, as has been stated, have made up a
considerable proportion of total exports. Areas which traditionally
served as export markets for Latin America, like the United States
and Western Europe, have populations which are increasing
relatively slowly, and thus there is no substantial rise in their
demand for Latin American agricultural exports. At the same
time, because these are countries with a high level of income, their
income-elasticity of demand for farm products is low. Moreover,
it should be noted that it is precisely these countries that have had
the greatest success in expanding agricultural productivity, and have
therefore been able to replace by home production a number of
foodstuffs they would otherwise have had to import. The only
exceptions are tropical agricultural products, but in that sphere
Latin America has been faced with increasing competition from
other areas, such as the African countries. All these factors have
resulted in a declining rise in the demand for agricultural and
livestock products from Latin America in those industrialized
countries which have been the traditional Latin American markets,
and there is no doubt that this tendency will be aggravated in the
future.

The countries of Latin America have since the 1930s attempted
to deal with this situation, which had been imposed upon them by
external circumstances, through a policy of industrialization geared

to the substitution of previously imported consumer goods. This policy has for thirty years been the driving force behind economic development in the region. However, there are now clear signs that it is encountering a number of difficulties which suggest that, unless fundamental changes are made in the economic structure of Latin America, industrialization will be unable to continue to play the same dynamic role as hitherto.

One of these difficulties lies in the fact that the substitution of those types of manufactured consumer goods and capital goods which were relatively easy to produce has now been largely completed, and that the markets for these types of products are relatively restricted given the present economic and social structure. Approximately one-half of the population of the region, those depending for a living on agricultural activities, together with appreciable sectors of the urban *Lumpenproletariat*, hardly constitute a good market for manufactured consumer goods: their income is too low and there is no hope of improving it under present conditions. It is not possible to accelerate the expansion of these industries in future unless there is a fundamental change in the prospects of this considerable sector of the population.

There is another difficulty in the way of industrial development. Manufacture is at present passing through a stage of transition, from a preponderantly light industry to an industry at the threshold of producing capital goods, semi-finished goods, and products with a much higher degree of processing complexity. Apart from considerably increased investments and much more complicated techniques, this also calls for much larger markets than the existing national markets of the Latin American countries. With the exception of Brazil, which today has a population in excess of 70 million, Mexico with some 40 million, Argentina with rather more than 20 million, and Colombia with some 16 million, all the other countries in Latin America have populations of the order of 10 million or fewer inhabitants, and although all are experiencing rapid demographic growth, there is no doubt that the sectors which are at present economically capable of constituting a market are a very small proportion of the total population.

In view of these very small national markets, it is difficult to make heavy industry pay unless a policy of integrated industrial development is pursued for the whole of Latin America. But this process of economic integration is still well beyond what the various countries and the economic power groups in each appear to be prepared to consider.

Finally, it should be mentioned in this connexion that, contrary to the optimistic view advanced by many theorists, industrialization alone has not been capable of creating sufficient employment to absorb the growing labour force resulting from the natural population growth in the towns and the rapid process of urbanization now taking place in Latin America, which is intensified by the backwardness and lack of prospects in the agricultural sector. One indication of this is the existence in almost all the large cities in the region, where industrial expansion has tended to concentrate, of considerable shanty towns, referred to by such names as *callampas*, *favelas*, or *barriadas*. These shanty towns mostly consisting of *Lumpenproletariat* elements, either unemployed or very irregularly employed in marginal services and in building activities (as unskilled labourers), present not only the housing problem which is most frequently associated with them, but demonstrate the incapacity of industry and its related activities to absorb productively this labour force, drawn to a large extent from the rural areas.

The economies of Latin America have not evolved according to the theoretical sequence of development whereby industry, as it expands, should, as a result of the better wages offered, attract workers away from the land thus making it necessary to improve agricultural technology in order to maintain farm production at the required levels. In Latin America the flow of rural labour to the urban areas has been much greater than the number required for industrial expansion. Apart from the causes mentioned earlier in connexion with the economic limitations of the domestic market, there have been other factors contributing to the relative inability of industry to offer an adequate solution to the problem of the productive employment of an increasing labour force. These have included a rate of demographic growth, which is today more than twice as high as that of the European countries during the corresponding period of their industrial development; the fact that the present industrial technology created in the economically advanced countries, and introduced from them, shows a labour-capital ratio which is lower than that which prevails in the technologies of the initial stages of industrialization; the increasing flow of workers from the countryside to the cities owing to lack of prospects for social and economic advancement in the rural areas; and, finally, an evolution of agricultural mechanization and technology, which is frequently inappropriate to the stage of development reached by many Latin American countries. These four factors have likewise contributed to accentuate the lack of balance between the growth of the labour force and the opportunities for industrial employment.

Latin America, then, has begun its industrial revolution without having undergone an agricultural revolution. Its agriculture today is largely based either on traditional structures, methods, and systems, or else on modern systems which are not related to the present stage of development. Bearing in mind that viable prospects for future industrial expansion are to a large extent dependent on the incorporation of the rural sectors into the national communities, the improvement of the standard of living of these sectors and that of the urban *Lumpenproletariat*, and the economic integration of the region, it is easy to see that industry alone, during the next few years, will not be capable of constituting the great energizing factor for development in the countries of Latin America. This can only be achieved by the combination of agrarian reform, industrialization, and regional economic integration. It is on these three factors simultaneously—which basically imply the political conception of a new continental nationalism—that emphasis will have to be laid during the years to come.

The Structure of Land Tenure

The basic features of Latin American agriculture are the great concentration of land in the hands of a few people and the landlessness of great masses of the rural population.

The table on p. 82 shows that in Latin America there are 105,000 agricultural and stock-breeding holdings of more than 1,000 hectares each, representing 1.4 per cent of all holdings and covering 470 million hectares, or 65 per cent of the total included in the agricultural and stock-breeding land-rolls. This gives an average of 4,500 hectares for each of these holdings.

At the other extreme, there are 5,445,000 holdings, constituting 72.6 per cent of the total, with less than 20 hectares each and occupying 27 million hectares, that is 3.7 per cent of the total included in the rolls. This gives an average of less than 5 hectares for each of these holdings.

Distribution of Land in Latin America

Size-groups	Holdings			Areas		
	No. (000s)	% of total	Cumula- tive %	Hectares (million)	% of total	Cumula- tive %
Below 20 hectares	5,445	72.6	72.6	27.0	3.7	3.7
20–100 „	1,350	18.0	90.6	60.6	8.4	12.1
100–1,000 „	600	8.0	98.6	166.0	22.9	35.0
Above 1,000 „	105	1.4	100.0	470.0	65.0	100.0
TOTALS	7,500	100.0	—	723.6	100.0	—

Source: Compiled on the basis of data quoted in 'Economic Growth and Social Policy in Latin America', *International Labour Review*, July–Aug. 1961, p. 62.

In reality, there is an even greater concentration of landowner-ship than would appear from the above figures, which relate to unit holdings. It is frequently the case that a number of these large holdings belong to one person or family, who manage them either directly or through indirect arrangements with administrators, tenants, or partners.

These figures also show that of the 111 million rural inhabitants in 1960 and the 30-odd million making up the economically active agricultural population, only some 100,000—and these are probably largely urban and not rural residents—own 65 per cent of the total agricultural land in the region. Disregarding the less than 2 million landowners who may be considered to belong to the intermediate category since their holdings cover from 20 to 1,000 hectares, the balance—representing some 28 million active men and, if we include their families, a total rural population of some 80 million—is made up of smallholders with insufficient land to earn a minimum subsistence on their properties, and more especially of agricultural labourers who do not own any land at all.

The form taken by land concentration and the sizes of the large properties vary from country to country. These differences depend on the amount of land, the types of agriculture, and the historical evolution of the systems of tenancy, but in almost all countries the relative concentration of land in the hands of a few people is extraordinarily high. Among the most notable forms of land con-centration in Latin America is, first, what has been termed the complex of estates and smallholdings which may be the subject of either direct or indirect forms of farming. Other characteristic forms of this concentration are the large cattle ranches, the big agricultural undertakings organized along capitalist lines, producing either for the external or for the domestic market, and the large properties which are either not farmed at all or hardly so and are situated in remote areas.[1]

The concentration of land in these different units is associated with other characteristics. These relate to extensiveness or semi-extensiveness of land use, single crop or diversification of production, the degree of capitalization, its integration with the market, and the mobility of the various factors of production. As it is not possible within the limitations of this work to analyse the specific peculiarities of each of these types of large agricultural enterprises, we shall merely examine in general terms the main effects of this great concentration of land and the characteristics which are found most commonly associated with it on the potential for agricultural progress and for the general development of the countries of the region.

Effects of Land Concentration

One of the most important negative consequences of the concentration of landownership in a few hands is the inefficient use of the most abundant productive resources of agriculture in Latin America: the land and the labour force. In the large traditional estates which are the most typical, and also quite often on the large modern plantations which rely mainly on the cultivation of a single crop, we find an extraordinary degree of underemployment of agricultural land and labour.

In the case of the traditional complexes of estates and smallholdings and the large stock-breeding ranches, extensive agriculture and cattle-breeding are practised on a large scale, which results in the underemployment of labour and in a low physical and economic return per unit of surface area. For those who have available large land areas as well as an abundant supply of labour, extensive methods of farming are very advantageous. With the use of only small amounts of effort and capital—apart from the land—and

[1] According to Solon Barraclough and Edmundo Flores, 'Estructura agraria de América Latina', in *Curso de capacitación de profesionales en reforma agraria* (Santiago de Chile, 1964), vol. i. pp. 211–84 (mimeo.).

very little risk, it is possible to obtain a personal income which is more than satisfactory from the point of view of the owner's economic and social requirements, and for his exercise of political influence. Profits therefore result from the availability of a large quantity of land in the hands of a single owner, accompanied by a plentiful supply of labour which is usually not organized in any way, and which possesses neither land nor any immediately available alternative type of employment. These people are therefore obliged to sell their services at the price imposed by the few leading landowners. Frequently the total value of the wages paid on these large traditional-type estates represents less than 10 per cent of their gross product. Moreover, an important proportion of these wages is not paid in cash but in concessions such as the temporary assignment of a marginal plot of land for the worker's own crops or the right to graze a few animals on the estate's pastures. This enables the landowner to carry on the productive process without the necessity of relying on any appreciable amount of working capital, while exerting social and political power over the peasant attached to his estate as a result of the concessions granted to him.

In such a situation there can be no incentive towards improving technology or increasing capital investment, the two basic conditions for a change-over from traditional-type agriculture to modern methods. Nor is the landowner, under these conditions, much influenced by possible economic stimuli from the market. Everything, indeed, tends to accentuate the desire and urge to accumulate land which, by virtue of the political influence of the owners, pays only a minimum in the way of taxation, and tends to maintain a high real value in the midst of the continuous monetary devaluation process of many of the Latin American countries. In addition, this system results in the land remaining as natural pasture or being subjected to a minimum of agricultural use: its value is greater as a source of personal income, social prestige, and political power than as a factor of agricultural production.

Even among the large modern undertakings of the plantation type, it is not difficult to find many instances of large reserves of useful land being kept unproductive, as the owners are not interested in using them for crops or activities distinct from their main enterprises for the external market. On the other hand the single-crop system, which is typical of these modern properties, normally gives rise to acute seasonal underemployment among the labour force.

In the more remote areas the usually absentee owners of vast unused tracts are only interested in securing public works and improvements such as roads. The value which these add to their lands will enable them after a few years to reap a rich financial reward without any need for the slightest effort in operating them or incorporating them in the nation's productive processes.

The effects of land concentration on the potential for general social, political, and economic development are, however, even more serious than those relating to the supply of agricultural products.

Land concentration gives rise to a very unequal distribution of agricultural income which is also—on average—well below the income obtainable in other sectors of the economy. This, in concrete terms, implies a state of sub-human living conditions for the majority of the population of the countryside. About one-third of the population of Latin America lives in abject poverty: this constitutes one of the main difficulties in the way of attempts to extend the domestic market, an essential condition for the process of industrial growth.

Despite variations in average income per capita, there is considerable similarity in the uneven distribution of agricultural income. Peru, Chile, and Costa Rica are three very dissimilar countries with widely different agricultures and economic systems, yet the three share more or less the same degree of inequality in the distribution of agricultural incomes. Although the categories used in the tables on p. 86 are not precisely comparable, the tables do, none the less, provide a fairly clear idea of the relationship between social stratification and the distribution of agricultural income in these three countries.

In Peru, real income per capita is approximately $140.[2] In Chile, according to the same United Nations source, annual per capita income is almost two and a half times higher than in Peru—approximately $320 in 1960—and only a little over 30 per cent of the population is directly engaged in agriculture as compared with well over 60 per cent in Peru. Nevertheless, the income distribution pattern in both countries is strikingly similar in its gross

[2] ECLA, *Gross Internal Product at Market Prices in 1950 Dollars* (mimeo, 1962).

Income Distribution in Peru

Social groups	Percentage of active population	Percentage of income obtained
Large landowners and capitalists	0.1	19.9
Technicians, top executives, and small capitalists	0.4	6.3
Middle class (employees and skilled workers)	20.0	46.7
Proletariat	22.8	14.2
Mountain-dwelling peasant class	56.7	12.9
	100.0	100.0

Source: Edgardo Seoane, *Surcos de paz* (Lima, 1963), p. 33.

Agricultural Income Distribution in Chile

Social groups	Percentage of active population	Percentage of income obtained
Working classes	87.2	34.0
Middle classes	0.4	0.4
Upper classes	12.4	65.6
	100.0	100.0

Source: Marvin J. Sternberg, *Chilean Land Tenure and Land Reform*, Univ. of California thesis, Sept. 1962, p. 56.

Distribution of Net Income derived from Agriculture in 1961 in the Central Tableland and the Province of Guanacaste in Costa Rica

Groups of Holdings	Percentage represented by each group	Percentage of income obtained by each group
Permanent labourers and smallholders ..	81.0	38.0
Family holdings	10.2	10.5
Large estates	7.9	29.8
Very large estates	0.9	21.7
	100.0	100.0

Source: Walter E. Chryst, *Land Tenure, Income Distribution and Selected Aspects of Economic Development* (mimeo, 1962), p. 42. This document forms part of a study of the position of land tenure in Central America under the auspices of ECLA, FAO, and ILO.

inequality. Costa Rica, one of the most progressive countries of Central America, provides the third case. There, in 1960, over 60 per cent of the population was classified as rural. And although the per capita income is one of the highest in the region—almost $250 per annum—the pattern of distribution again shows the same inequality evident in Chile and Peru.

The following picture, then, though schematic and somewhat simplified, is not far removed from actual reality. In Latin America there is a very small group of 'top people', consisting of the owners of large and medium-sized properties with their traditional outlook, and of the capitalist operators in agriculture, who produce for export and occasionally for the domestic market. This small group, which represents only a tiny percentage of the total agricultural population and which is in some cases largely made up of absentee landlords or persons who are primarily engaged in non-agricultural pursuits, concentrates in its hands the greater part of the landed resources and a substantial share in the income from the agricultural and stock-rearing sector. Moreover this is the group which benefits from all the social and political advantages of the existing system, which at best is typified by a social régime of benevolent paternalism, and at worst by a slave-like oppression of the lower groups.

In certain countries, or in certain regions of some countries, between this tiny but dominant group and the lower groupings, there is a small rural middle class. It consists of independent family enterprises with adequate holdings of land, certain types of agricultural partnerships, or tenant farmers with a certain amount of capital, and some categories of employees responsible for supervision and accounts on the large estates. The numerical and social importance of this group is very small, except in certain special areas or places such as the northern part of the Argentine pampas region and the wine and fruit-growing areas of that country, the horticultural areas and farms near cities such as Montevideo, São Paulo or Havana, and certain new settlement areas or irrigation lands, such as those found in Mexico.

Finally, there are those 'down below' who constitute the broad masses of the rural population, forming distinct groups with more or less specific characteristics. One of these groups is formed by the rural proletariat of the plantation areas (sugar-cane, cotton, bananas, rice); another by the horsemen of the great cattle ranches;

a third by the under-endowed smallholders who are found as owners, tenants, or squatters in practically all Latin American countries; and, finally, the great mass of wage-earners without land on the traditional properties, who are paid only by concessions or a combination of cash and concessions (the *huasipungueros* in Ecuador, the *inquilinos* in Chile, the *conuqueros* in Venezuela, the *colonos* in Brazil, the *peones* in the Argentine, or the Indians in Peru). This enormous mass, despite differences in income between the various groups of which it is comprised—which are determined by the demand for labour in each region, the degree of organization into trade unions in the small number of cases where this applies, and the greater or lesser social and political power of the small, landowning, dominant group—constitute the 'pariahs' of the Latin American agricultural sector. This is the group with the fewest possibilities, expectations, or opportunities of improvement. Their only real chance of breaking through the social and economic barriers which surround them is by moving to an urban area. For those who remain in agriculture, there is no other prospect under the existing order than to continue to lead the sub-human existence already led by the majority of them at the present time. The situation is aggravated in those places where the majority of the peasants consist of Indians still living for the most part according to traditional values quite different from those of the dominant community, with which they are not integrated. The reactions and way of life of these Indians are totally at variance with those necessary to people pursuing economic development as a rational aim. Attempts must be made to integrate them with the national community and to modernize their mentality. But if this is not accompanied by real prospects of improved conditions, the only result will be to create masses of uprooted and frustrated people, which is bound to have disastrous human and social consequences.

The existing situation, then, constitutes a basic obstacle to the evolution or perpetuation of a democratic society. There is a profound contradiction between the existence of the present structure and the rural system in Latin America on the one hand, and the possible development of a democratic régime on the other. As has been rightly pointed out by Erich Fromm,[3] the democratic character of a system can only be judged by the degree to which it

[3] *May Man Prevail?* (London, 1961).

allows of political liberty, personal liberty, an economic system operating in the interests of the great majority of the people, and a social system allowing the individual free and responsible participation in the life of the community. There is not the slightest doubt that the concentration of land in the hands of the few, together with its various economic and social consequences, represents the main obstacle to these four basic and complementary factors which are necessary to enable any truly democratic society to exist in the Latin American countryside.

Finally, it remains to say a few words regarding certain specifically economic effects of the concentration of land. There are two distinct sectors of agricultural production in Latin America: production for export and production for the domestic market. The former has always tended to enjoy priority in the eyes of governments and landowners, and to attract the major share of investment funds; its growth has been restricted only by market conditions essentially outside the control of the Latin American countries. Despite the increasing needs of a fast-growing population, production for the domestic market has expanded much more slowly than for export. This is mainly because the uneven distribution of income restricts demand, because the traditional agriculturists do not respond to the existing stimuli of the domestic market, and because there is little incentive to employ new and more efficient techniques. All these reasons are closely connected with the concentration of land in the hands of the few. The lack of dynamism in agriculture is an obstacle to the general development of the economy through its negative effects on the balance of payments and its inflationary pressures, and because it leads to a reduced state of physical well-being of the labour force.

With regard to the balance of payments position, exports from Latin America, among which agricultural and stock-rearing products are of basic importance, have been tending to grow slowly.[4] Per capita, their real value increased only by 6 per cent between the pre-war (1934–8) period and 1958–60.[5] On the other hand, because the expansion of production for the domestic market has been so

---

[4] In 1950 they represented 53 per cent of the value of total exports from the region, and in 1959, owing to a fall in agricultural and stock-rearing prices, they represented only 40 per cent of the total value of exports (see *Problemas y perspectivas de la agricultura Latino-Americana*, a document submitted to the Joint ECLA/FAO Division at the ECLA Conference at Mar del Plata, May 1963).   [5] Ibid.

slow, the volume of physical imports of agricultural and stock-rearing products doubled between the two periods. Among these, imports of milk products increased fivefold, whereas those of meat products and cereals doubled.[6] All this has adversely affected the availability of foreign exchange for importing capital goods, transport equipment, and other items indispensable for general economic and specifically agricultural development.

As regards the inflationary process, it is clear that, despite the efforts of the Latin American governments to protect the consumer, the rise in the cost of foodstuffs is one of the factors which has most contributed towards pushing up the cost-of-living index. Between 1950 and 1960, for example, in Argentina, Brazil, Chile, Peru, and Uruguay this increase in the cost of food has been anything from 12 to 75 per cent greater than that in the general cost-of-living index.[7]

Finally, as regards the physical capacity of the labour force, a close relationship obviously exists between the quantity and quality of the diet of the working class and its capacity for physical effort and resistance to illness. As has been shown in the classic studies of Josué de Castro and in other more recent inquiries, large sections of the Latin American population do not get nearly enough calories and proteins, and the situation is becoming worse rather than better in a number of countries; quite apart from the consequences in human terms, this constitutes a main obstacle to progress.

These are, in brief, the main reasons for the view that without substantial agrarian reform, implying drastic changes in the present systems of land tenure, in the orientation of agricultural production and stock-breeding, in farming methods and in the distribution of agricultural produce, it will not be possible in the near future to speed up the economic, social, and political advancement of the countries of Latin America.

[*Jacques Chonchol was Director of Agricultural Economics at the Ministry of Agriculture, Chile, and Regional Adviser of FAO in Programmes of Agricultural Reform in Latin America. At present he is the Executive Vice-President of the Instituto de Desarrollo Agropecuario in Chile. His publications include* El desarrollo de América Latina y la reforma agraria *(1964) and* El desarrollo de la nueva sociedad en América Latina *(1965), with Julio Silva S.*]

6 Ibid.   7 Ibid.

Some Implications of Foreign Investment for Latin America

VICTOR L. URQUIDI

For better or for worse, Latin American development is likely to involve a net use of foreign capital for the next two decades at least, and possibly beyond. There are three main sets of reasons for this: (1) a prospective 'trade gap' of considerable magnitude, largely related to import demand resulting from development itself; (2) a probable lag in raising the rate of domestic savings, due in part to the mounting pressure of population growth on current consumption needs; and (3) the presently increasing technological lead of the highly developed industrial countries. These are interrelated and interacting factors, and they should not perhaps raise much question were it not for the hope or expectation, frequently expressed outside Latin America, that at some point in the not too distant future this region will be able to get along, at higher levels of income and at new stages of social maturity, and even begin to help other, less fortunate and more overpopulated, underdeveloped areas of the world, without foreign capital assistance; and were it not also for the fact that Latin American opinion seems to be growing increasingly hostile to foreign capital in general.

The Extent and Influence of Foreign Investment

The expression 'foreign capital' is all-encompassing and means different things to different people. In an underdeveloped area such as Latin America, from a financial point of view it signifies a liability to non-residents, i.e. to persons, business enterprises, banks, governments, etc., in other countries, and to international agencies. The total liability is represented by fixed-interest obligations (loans and bond issues) and equity (so-called direct investment), usually on a long-term basis, but short-term obligations, other than purely monetary ones, should probably also be included under certain circumstances. A rough estimate of Latin America's foreign liabilities as of 1964 indicates the following: direct foreign investment of some $14,500 million and loans and portfolio debt of some $10,500 million,[1] including in the latter balance of payments arrears which are in process of being consolidated as medium and long-term debt.[2] Since Latin Americans also own assets abroad in the form of direct and portfolio investments, the net liability may be somewhat less. There is also the question of short-term and liquid assets held abroad by Latin Americans, often for long periods, of which much has been said in recent years but of which no reliable estimate is possible. In any event, Latin América's privately-held foreign assets are beyond the reach of the authorities and are only of minor potential significance to the region as a whole.

The above are to be taken as orders of magnitude only, since any degree of accuracy in the data is difficult to achieve. The first question to be asked concerns the size and relative importance of the overall liability. At about $115 per capita, foreign-financed capital formation accounts for less than one-tenth of presently available tangible capital in Latin America, less than 6 per cent of it directly foreign-owned, the rest being indirect claims. Foreign liabilities amount to about two and a half years' exports of goods and services. Current annual service on all foreign capital is less than 2 per cent of gross product, and some 13 per cent of exports of goods and services. On the other hand the contribution of net foreign financing to domestic saving (15 per cent of GNP) is the equivalent of less than 2 per cent of GNP.[3] On the face of it, foreign capital does not seem, on the whole, to constitute an undue burden on Latin America, particularly since there would be no question of having to repay or buy out all liabilities at short notice. However, the annual service ratio of one-seventh of current income

[1] The estimate of direct foreign investment is based on the following sources: ECLA, *Foreign Private Investment in the Latin American Free-Trade Area; report of a Consultant Group jointly appointed by ECLA and the OAS* (Apr. 1961); ECLA, *Survey 1963* (1964); US Dept of Commerce, *US Business Investment in Foreign Countries* (1960). That of loan and portfolio liabilities is derived from ECLA, *External Financing in the Economic Development of Latin America*, Doc. E/CN.12/649 (7 Apr. 1963), table IV–16, supplemented by the ECLA *Survey 1963*. An approximate guess has been made to bring the totals up to 1964.

[2] The above estimates, and all figures cited below, exclude Cuba, for which information on a comparable basis is not available. US private investment in Cuba in 1959 was valued at close on $1,000 m.

[3] ECLA, *Economic Development of Latin America in the Post-War Period* (Santiago, 1963), table 33, and ECLA, *Survey 1963*, tables 222 and 231.

from exports of goods and services is perhaps a little high, as it is the equivalent of some $1,400 million that otherwise would be available for essential imports.

General statements about most topics in Latin America must be qualified by their greater or less applicability to certain countries. In the case of foreign direct investments, somewhat over 35 per cent is located in Venezuela, largely in the oil industry, and perhaps a similar proportion in only three more countries: Brazil, Mexico, and Chile; and another 10 per cent or so in Peru and Colombia. In the last five, foreign private capital is mostly in manufacturing industry and mining. Between 1950 and 1959, Venezuela absorbed close on 50 per cent of new foreign investment in the region. Thus it follows that some of the percentages indicated in the previous paragraph are widely different as between Venezuela and other countries: for instance, if Venezuela is omitted, the annual service on all foreign liabilities is reduced from 13 to about 10 per cent of current exchange earnings; and taking earnings on direct investment only, the ratio to exports of goods and services declines from 10–11 per cent to about 6 per cent. The ratio of per capita foreign liabilities to gross product per capita in Venezuela is probably of the order of 0.6 per cent, whereas in Mexico it is about 0.16 per cent. In Venezuela foreign debt is only a small fraction of direct investment, but in Mexico, and more so in Brazil, Chile, and Argentina, it is in excess of direct liabilities to private investors. In the last three countries the ratio of external indebtedness to current exchange earnings is inordinately high, whereas in Mexico it is moderate. The contribution made by foreign capital to gross capital formation is generally higher in Venezuela and Peru than in Mexico or Brazil; it is also higher in some of the smaller countries. Thus the significance of foreign capital to each Latin American country varies considerably from the financial and balance of payments point of view, and as a supplement to domestic savings, but given certain other conditions, most countries would be able to absorb appreciably higher amounts without undue strain.

This raises the question of the role that different types of foreign capital have played in Latin America's economic development, and what types are likely to be required in the future. Historically, direct foreign investment, and a sizeable amount of portfolio investment, accounted for much of the growth of railways and power, mining and oil, and some commercial agriculture. On the other hand governments usually floated foreign loans to meet budget deficits, often occasioned by military expenditure, and to refund previous debts. Private foreign capital was attracted by the profitability of exports in an expanding world market and contributed to general development only to the extent that the export sector became interrelated, directly or through budget revenues, to other sectors of the economy. The well-known pattern of pre-First World War foreign investment, partially extended through 1929, and in the case of Venezuelan petroleum and Peruvian mining up to recent times, does not require elaboration. The advent of the automobile and the Great Depression, combined with the Mexican Revolution, marked the end of the old pattern : public road construction led to different kinds and sources of foreign financing and opened up the domestic market to agriculture and industry; the world trade crisis in the 1930s and, later, wartime restrictions in the early 1940s, spurred industrialization; and Mexican nationalism showed that foreign capital could be subjected to control and, if necessary, repudiated.

The emerging pattern is one in which Latin American governments, and public sector agencies, have increasingly borrowed abroad from other governments, mainly the United States, and from international organizations to finance modern social overhead requirements, including roads, ports, dams, and power installations, while private foreign investment has had to meet frequently stringent conditions for natural resource development (in some countries virtual exclusion) and turn its attention to manufacturing industry for the protected domestic market. In particular, as world markets for Latin America's traditional exports have become more competitive or relatively oversupplied, and as industrialization has advanced in the region, foreign equity investment has tended to become integrated into the modern development model, within the limitations of the national and regional markets. It seems likely that this new pattern will prevail for some time, and the opportunities for increasing foreign investment in manufacturing —subject to some qualifications referred to below—appear to be considerable. At the same time, long-term foreign borrowing by the public sector, as further infrastructure needs are met, is bound to be related increasingly to overall development programmes which in turn raise the prospects of both domestic and foreign private investment in industry. This does not exclude some foreign equity investment in mining, or even petroleum, but for both economic and political reasons it may be presumed to be of limited scope.

At the present stage of development, and especially in the new approach to external financial co-operation and domestic effort under the Alliance for Progress, it would appear also that the next decade or so will see a transfer of capital to Latin America, mostly through public bilateral and multilateral programmes, in order to help expand basic overhead facilities, improve agriculture, and reduce the lag in housing, education, and public health. Policy is wisely concentrated for the time being on these aspects, in recognition of the fact that a broad strategy of development and social improvement requires definite breaks-through in productivity and resource utilization. Direct foreign investment is in a sense secondary and complementary, and not the primary object of policy under the Alliance. This is borne out by recent data. Latin American net long-term loan disbursements and similar transactions were $892 million in 1961, $760 million in 1962, and possibly higher in 1963 and 1964, as against an annual average of $332 million in 1956–60 and only $93 million in 1951–5. Foreign direct investment, which had averaged $325 million in 1951–5 and as much as $581 million in 1956–60, has declined to less than $300 million annually since 1961. If Venezuela is left out of these estimates, the net disbursements on loans become slightly higher in the recent years, but the change in the rate of private direct investments is less marked, since much of such investment had been made in the 1950s precisely in Venezuelan petroleum, and the overall decline in 1961–4 is influenced by actual disinvestment in that country. Private direct investment in the rest of Latin America is running at the rate of about $400 million a year, as against loan disbursements of $800–900 million. It should be noted also that in addition to long-term loans Latin America has received an annual average of $105 million in official grants during 1956–60, and of over $130 million since 1960.[4] Under the programme of the Alliance for Progress, as stated on various occasions, it is expected that not more than some 15 per cent of gross capital transfers to Latin America will be private direct investment, the bulk of foreign aid being provided by international agencies and United States official agencies, and an undefined amount by European and other sources of capital.

[4] Data in this paragraph from ECLA, *Survey 1963*, tables 25 and 26.

Foreign Capital and the Trade Gap

It is important to remember that the need for foreign capital in
its various forms in Latin America does not arise, in the context
of the Alliance for Progress, merely from a consideration of basic
capital requirements involved in development programmes. External capital is more than a supplement to domestic savings, more
than 'aid', more than the means of helping to finance certain
programmes or projects; it must also be regarded as the principal
means of covering the 'trade gap' and ensuring currency stability
once long-term influences on the latter are taken into account.
The 'trade gap' is a calculation made on certain assumptions about
export demand prospects and probable import demand plus services
on both sides of the account; its magnitude is interdependent with
all the other variables, including the capital movements meant to
offset it and the income on such new investments. For Latin
America, a number of estimates were made recently by a group
of ECLA consultants for the 1964 UNCTAD Conference.[5]   From
an annual average of $627 million in 1951–5, $1,133 million in
1956–60, and $1,058 million in 1961–2, the current account deficit
by 1970 may be expected to reach not less than $1,520 million at
1960 prices, under rather optimistic assumptions, and as much as
$4,320 million in case import-replacement programmes should not
get fully under way. An intermediate hypothesis about imports
yields a figure of $2,570 millions. In all three cases, per capita
gross product is expected to rise at 3 per cent per annum, and
exports at 3.1 per cent;[6] both of these projected rates are above
post-war experience.

Assuming the trade and services gap at somewhere in the neigh-
bourhood of $2,500 million by 1970, it would be one and a half
times larger than that of recent years. But even on the lower (less
likely) estimate, the 50 per cent increase in the trade gap is a

[5] ECLA, *Latin America and the UN Conference on Trade and Development,* Doc. E/CN.12/693, 20 Feb., 1964, Ch. 1, sec. D and Annex 3.
[6] The text of the report (ibid.) repeatedly mentions a rate of 2.7 per cent
for the export projection, but the tables contain an implicit 3.1 per cent.
The difference involves as much as $480 m. in 1970 and would place the
minimum current account deficit at $2,000 m. and the maximum at
$4,800 m. On the other hand the 3 per cent growth projected for per
capita product is probably overstated, for which reason the actual level
of imports may be lower in each of the projections. Additional income
and interest on new foreign investment was not reckoned, but would
not appreciably alter the orders of magnitude involved.

formidable amount to finance, for Latin America cannot draw on its depleted monetary reserves (or secondary IMF compensatory financing) for long, nor could it, obviously, rely on eternally renewable short-term financing. Moreover, a net transfer of long- and medium-term capital of over $1,500 million would probably require something close on $3,000 million of gross disbursements, in order to make possible the scheduled repayments on existing loans and other debt obligations plus their increment through 1970. It is clear that $3,000 million exceeds the amounts now envisaged under the Alliance programmes, which have aimed at an average annual $2,000 million of gross inflow, probably rising slightly towards 1970.

The implications of the above seem fairly obvious, although generalizations should not be carried too far. One way of putting it would be to say that unless the developed countries of the world are able to shape their policies towards lending, from all the various sources, upward of $2,000 million gross a year to Latin America by 1970, allowing for some private direct investment of the order of, say, $400–500 million, the region will be unable to carry out its development programmes to achieve an increase of income per head of at least 2.5 per cent annually, as expected under the Alliance. An alternative for the developed countries would be to modify their trade policies in order to facilitate a further increase in Latin America's exports and raise their value through price support or compensation. If exports of goods and services went up by 4 per cent annually instead of 3.1, it would mean an additional $1,000 million annually to Latin America by 1970. Or if the commodity terms of trade recovered the average 1950–4 level, it would mean virtually wiping out the current account deficit (other things being equal). A combination of trade policy and long-term financing policy might be a happy medium!

For Latin America, one alternative, which is desirable in itself regardless of the projected trade gap, but all the more necessary in view of it, would seem to lie in the direction of maximum efforts to contain non-essential imports and to expand the import-replacement process;[7] in other words, to aim deliberately, through national and regional efforts, at a narrower trade gap. This in turn brings up a host of other problems bound up mainly with the

---

[7] In the sense of increasing the ratio of domestic supply to aggregate demand, which in many lines need not involve an actual reduction in imports.

feasibility of a more rapid structural change, in agriculture as well as in industry, as part of a speedier pace of development. In order not to beg the question, it may be assumed that efforts in this direction, unless everyone is underestimating the potentialities of the changes taking place since 1961, will achieve only limited success by 1970, although better results may be obtained thereafter. In this light, the persistence of the trade gap beyond 1970 can be taken almost for granted, and perhaps as far as 1975, with a possibility that it may remain moderate in the following decade. However limited, it will imply a net capital inflow into Latin America, unless Latin America meanwhile has been able to syphon off a large share of world liquidity that it could gradually draw upon.

A variant on the above approach, and perhaps a partial condition for it, would be a very determined effort to achieve a good measure of regional integration by 1970, or at the latest by 1975. Regional integration, in the sense of not merely lowering intra-regional trade barriers but of attempting co-ordinated expansion of industrial capacity in major sectors and fuller utilization of complementary opportunities in agriculture and livestock, might imply, for any given rate of investment, a higher rate of growth in output and more intensive import-replacement in critical industries where economies of scale are specially important. To the extent that this may be achieved, a more optimistic projection of the trade gap would be reasonable, for Latin America would be able more efficiently to supply its own capital and intermediate goods requirements, thus releasing resources for other purposes, and to produce manufactures for export at prices approaching competitive world prices.

The role of direct foreign investment in industrial integration within Latin America could be of great significance. There is hardly any sign, however, that anything is being done so far in this direction. On the contrary, foreign investors are mostly duplicating in all major countries, at least for the time being, the kind of industrial installation where some complementarity might have been hoped for, and Latin American public and private opinion is reacting defensively against the possible encroachment of foreign capital on regional industrial integration possibilities. It must be recognized, furthermore, that LAFTA, in which nine countries participate so far, has not, after considerable progress in its first three years, found a practical approach to industrial integration, much less to anything remotely resembling complementarity in future agricultural development. A qualified exception may be made in connexion with the five-country Central American Common Market and Economic Integration Programme, but co-ordinated expansion of industry to avoid needless duplication and ensure the benefits of economies of scale is still bogged down, after eight years of discussion, in a monopoly-versus-free-competition controversy and in the larger consequences of the uniform smallness that afflicts the Central American republics.

Population Growth and the Savings Gap

If the net use of foreign capital is now regarded from a different point of view, namely as a supplement to domestic savings, the question may be put this way: to what extent would Latin America be able to raise its marginal rate of savings by means that will also discourage imports and replace the import-component of domestic output, particularly in durable consumer goods and capital goods? The ratio of gross fixed investment to gross product has been approximately 17 per cent during the last fifteen years, with net external financing accounting for less than 2 per cent. The investment ratio varies as between different countries: it has tended to be higher in Argentina, Venezuela, and Colombia, slightly lower in Mexico, and considerably below the regional average in Chile and Central America. The external component of gross savings has been proportionately greater in Chile, Bolivia, Ecuador, Central America, and Argentina than in Brazil, Mexico, or Peru.[8] It is difficult to draw any general conclusion from all this, for many other factors have to be taken into account. In the case of Bolivia and part of Central America, ability to raise the domestic savings ratio is limited by low levels of income and general backwardness; in the case of Argentina and Chile, it is a question bound up with structural imbalance and social and political factors; in another part of Central America, in Brazil, and in Mexico, there is no doubt that fiscal policy, especially adequately progressive taxation, could be instrumental in making available a higher share of internal savings to finance development. The essential point is that a policy to achieve a higher ratio of domestic savings does not necessarily enable a country to dispense with foreign financing unless it is part and parcel of a fully worked out development policy

[8] Cf. ECLA sources cited in n. 3, various tables.

implying structural change and, especially, a rational import-replacement process. Since Latin America's development also requires increasing the rate of net investment, the implications for a savings policy are abundantly clear, particularly if marginal capital-output ratios, as may be expected, should become less favourable.

On the other hand, in view of the many difficulties likely to be encountered in enlarging and deepening the capital market in most Latin American countries, a good case can be made for specific types of foreign financing to meet part of local costs of certain programmes or projects as well as the import-component. This is being recognized in the practices of some international and other lenders, and may contribute to the use of foreign capital where a purely aggregative analysis would appear to indicate it as unnecessary. In the case of private direct investment, there is an association of capital and technology that also has an important bearing on the problem, and will be referred to later.

An increase in the domestic savings ratio is also related to a problem hitherto given little attention in Latin America: rapid population growth. Population estimates for Latin America are in themselves dynamic, as new census results are analysed and various corrections are introduced. The Latin American Demographic Centre, sponsored by the United Nations and the Chilean government, has been instrumental in bringing to light the gloomy prospect, so far as development efforts are concerned, of an increase in the population at a geometric rate of 2.9 per cent annually up to 1980. In five countries in which the decline in death rates can no longer continue at a rapid pace or in which birth rates are on the low side—Argentina, Bolivia, Chile, Cuba, and Uruguay, accounting in 1960 for only one-fifth of Latin America's population—the expected demographic increase is estimated at 1.9 per cent per year, which is high enough. In the remaining fifteen, the overall rate is estimated to be 3.1 per cent for the next fifteen years,[9] with rates exceeding this average in a nation already as large as Mexico. Since these unprecedented rates of growth are the result of decreasing mortality combined with sustained fertility, the proportion of non-working population tends to rise, and the dependency ratio to increase even more. At the same time the rate

[9] Derived from data in ECLA, *Statist. B.*, Mar. 1964, table 3.

of urbanization has been high, and rural-urban migration will continue unabated.

All the implications of this prospect need not be explored here.[10] It suffices to draw attention to the strain it will impose on the investment effort on the one hand, and to the requirements in terms of basic consumption in the broad sense of public expenditures for education, health, welfare, housing and food subsidies, in addition to the foreseeable consumption bias of any increase in the real income of the bulk of the population. While business savings can be expected to gain in importance as development proceeds and as modern forms of organization of production expand, the possibility of high marginal rates of personal savings seems to be limited both by the consumption needs of the lower income groups and by an eventually higher marginal taxation of middle and upper incomes. Even if the tax burden is successfully increased, the growth of the strategically important public sector savings will probably lag. This will be the result of the political pressure to provide public services at low rates or at a loss, the inherent difficulty in reducing long-standing deficits in public transportation, the expansion of educational and other social functions, and the need to increase greatly the provision of what, for want of a better term, may be called the 'technical and administrative infrastructure' of development (extension and marketing services, research grants, assistance to small business, foreign trade promotion, etc.). Development in Latin America can be expected to require public sector consumption to an extent perhaps not envisaged in the case of other underdeveloped areas where the pattern of population growth is more modest. In so far as this trend combines with other, structural, factors affecting the overall savings ratio, efforts to raise the latter may be less successful, and development as a whole may have to rely more heavily on the use of external financing than would otherwise be the case.

The Demand for Technology and Foreign Investment

Looked at from yet another angle, the function of foreign capital in an underdeveloped area—its basic historic function—is to

---

[10] For a general analysis and its application to India and, secondarily, to Mexico, cf. A. J. Coale and E. M. Hoover, *Population Growth and Economic Development in Low Income Countries: a Case Study of India's Prospects* (Princeton UP, 1958).

enable skill and technology to be transferred in the guise of capital goods in order to help raise productivity and income. Latin America has been importing skill and technology for over 450 years, but the oases of technological modernity even today stand out in a vast desert of backwardness and ignorance. Some excuse can be made for Latin America throughout the period of colonial rule, and perhaps during the early independence turmoil; certain civil war and revolutionary years were also unattractive for technological progress. If the matter were pursued fully, educational advance and incorporation of new techniques of production might turn out to be confined to a few countries and limited to short periods of relative political stability. The recent discovery that Latin America is spending barely 2 per cent of its GNP on education provides as good an index as any of the damaging effects of the social and political structure that emerged in the nineteenth century and has somehow survived, with the three notable exceptions of Mexico, Bolivia, and Cuba, into the middle of the twentieth. Today, after some thirty years of active industrialization, it is doubtful whether the region devotes more than one-twentieth of 1 per cent of its GNP to industrial research. This means that the lessons of modern Western industrialization and of the Soviet rise to power have been largely lost upon the Latin Americans. It signifies also that the region is in a state of technological subservience from which it will not easily become liberated even partially. And this is compounded by the lag in agricultural knowledge and research that afflicts most Latin American countries, improvement of which is basic to any development programme and any attempt to raise the income of the 60 per cent of the population still dependent for its living on primary production.

Whether this state of affairs, particularly on the educational side, is solely the fault of Latin American society or is the partial result as well, paradoxically, of the influx of foreign capital and technology—more precisely, of the particular form taken by this transfer—may perhaps best be left to the historian and the sociologist. The important question at this stage is what can be done about it, how it may affect development in the coming years and, in the context of this paper, what particular relevance it may have to foreign investment.

Education is a national affair, although international agencies have done much in recent years to stimulate a re-evaluation of educational methods and to induce long-range planning. Basically a matter of allocation of resources, the raising of educational levels involves special efforts to increase the availability of suitable teaching personnel. Latin America is beginning now to benefit from foreign and international grants and low-interest loans as well as guidance for teacher training, school, and university installations and equipment, and scholarships abroad. Although some private funds play a role in this process, it is through public agencies and international organizations that most of the external co-operation is likely to be given. Given good communication and a proper understanding of the issues involved, as well as of the national sensitivities on the subject, the 'foreign investment' in education may contribute considerably to bridging the technological gap, or at least preparing the ground for its reduction. Thus the real returns of such investment, in terms of development, may in the long run prove to be quite high. Latin Americans value this contribution of the industrially developed countries, especially if channelled through international organizations. This is a means also of ensuring that progress in educational techniques, from whatever source, may be assimilated by Latin America without undue delays.

There is no comparable experience or outlook in technology as such. Latin America, unlike, for instance, Japan, has been slow to adopt foreign technology, and even slower to undertake its further development in the light of its own conditions. This is in no way to disparage the various national efforts in scientific research and in applied agricultural and other research, and the many international programmes for co-operation in training, research, and experimentation, as well as specific technical assistance. Unfortunately these initiatives have been limited. With regard to industrial technology, both the Latin American effort and the international concern with the problem have been of a much smaller order of magnitude. The United Nations has only quite recently turned its attention to studying the means of transferring industrial technology to the underdeveloped areas. Unlike much modern agricultural research, industrial research in the Western countries is essentially the province of private enterprise—and remains private property—although a not inconsiderable part is being sponsored by governments. But there is no system, and little thought has been given to creating one, whereby the extraordinary progress in industrial technology of the last twenty years may readily be made available to the newly industrializing nations.

The crux of the matter—for Latin America at least—seems to be that the transfer of industrial technology, whether embodied in capital goods, in technical and advisory services or in research activities, is not regarded as a public, international responsibility, but as private business. It thus becomes chiefly associated with private foreign investment. There are many sides to this question, and only a few points can be raised here.

It is frequently argued that there is, on the one hand, a good deal of 'free' technology, in the sense that it is not restricted to use by or through particular business enterprises, but may be purchased by any potential entrepreneur, public or private. To this extent, a Latin American independent private company or an official development bank with the proper ability may apply the results of foreign research, say in electronics, food processing, or chemicals, at little basic cost, to the manufacture of a new product. But it is doubtful that this has happened to any significant extent, for there are other considerations, concerning the type and spirit of Latin American entrepreneurship, organizational, financial, and marketing aspects, and competitive influence, plus the ubiquitous and intangible know-how, that need to be taken into account as risk factors.

Through licensing arrangements an independent Latin American industrial firm is enabled to engage in new lines of production, to improve its processes, and to gain access to the well-proven results of private industrial research in foreign countries. In many cases the Latin American enterprise may be publicly owned. There are many advantages in licensing, chief among them the assurance of ready access to further technological developments in the same field, thus avoiding obsolescence, and the accompanying advisory services that help the enterprise to gain the proper know-how. However, it may be presumed that licensing arrangements entail a number of conditions that tend to establish a pattern of dependency between a Latin American firm and the foreign manufacturer, frequently involving a financial interest by the latter or at least certain restrictions imposed on the licensee. Conflicts of interest have arisen in many cases, and a relatively free and unobstructed system of licensing is difficult to imagine under present conditions.[11]

[11] The use of foreign patents, although it may also involve some restrictions, need not be regarded as of primary importance in the modern

As in the use of 'free technology', many inadequacies and weaknesses handicap the Latin American entrepreneur. It is no accident that one coffee-producing country, with an ample domestic market, was unable to manufacture soluble coffee successfully until it finally turned the business over to a foreign-owned subsidiary of a well-known giant enterprise.

Probably the bulk of foreign industrial technology in the last two decades has been transferred to Latin America through fully or partially-owned subsidiaries of important North American and European companies. This is a broader transfer than mere licensing, for behind it are all the motivations that lead foreign private capital to carry out investment abroad, either to gain a position in the domestic market, to forestall competition from other industrial countries, to maintain its position as a leader in the field, to lighten its tax burden at home, or for other reasons. The full technical, administrative, and financial resources of the parent company are put to work as part of the process. Even where local capital participates in the enterprise, with as much as 50 per cent or more of the capital, the business is essentially a foreign business, governed by policies and controls laid down by its home office. Thus, subject to various qualifications, technology is imported at the price of financial and business domination by foreign companies; the basic decisions are made abroad.

The main qualification to the above is the degree to which different Latin American countries have succeeded, by means of appropriate legislation and skilful policy, in wresting from the foreign interests some of their power, at least in the more obvious matters of submission to national courts of law, disclosure of accounts, employment practices, participation of nationals in management, fair commercial practices, compliance with exchange regulations or import controls, and the like. In most countries, major foreign companies are scrupulous in meeting these requirements, and contribute to the country's development not only by producing manufactures and thus creating income and employment and raising productivity, but by upholding high standards of wages and social welfare. Another obvious qualification is the extent to which in many countries local capital and initiative have

technological scene. On the difficulty in general of transferring technology to independent producers in underdeveloped countries, see W. P. Strassman, *The Network for Diffusing Manufacturing Technology among Nations* (unpublished MS, Michigan State Univ., 1963).

increasingly participated with the foreign stockholders in joint ventures and tended to maximize national interest in the policies and practices of the enterprise.

But none of this alters the basic issue, which is that, in the absence of large-scale industrial research in Latin America, or of internationally-sponsored arrangements to facilitate access to new technology and its transfer under appropriate conditions, the outlook for some time ahead is that foreign private investment, in varying degrees of ultimate control, will tend to be associated with technological progress in manufacturing. This prospect is reinforced by the lag in education on the one hand, and by the evident capacity of the industrially-developed countries to forge ahead to ever higher levels of technology on the other, thus not only maintaining their lead, but perhaps increasing it as well.

In the long view, many implications suggest themselves. First and foremost, the need to strengthen higher education and allocate increasing resources to scientific and industrial research, if only to be able to copy and adapt foreign technology, and where appropriate, innovate. Secondly, if industrial expansion is to become generalized, at some stage the loan policy of international lenders will have to achieve sufficient flexibility to shift away from the basic infrastructure into the development of manufacturing industry on a large scale and into the financing of the technological transfer. Thirdly, Latin American countries will have to work out a policy whereby domestic capital may gradually buy into, or buy out, those foreign subsidiaries in which 'simpler' or more widespread technology is employed, in order to accept new foreign private investment, preferably in the ' dynamic ' technological fields where the lead is more likely to be kept by reason of the cost of research or other factors. Fourthly, a certain amount of pooling of knowledge and resources will become necessary among the countries of the area, possibly in connexion with further advances towards regional integration, but even independently of the latter.

Latin American Attitudes and the Need for a New Approach

It is worth-while considering, at this stage, whether Latin America is prepared to accept a net inflow of foreign capital of the magnitude and type necessary to meet the three major objectives relating to economic development that have been discussed; namely, covering the trade gap, enabling a sufficiently high rate of investment to be carried out, and ensuring a steady stream of modern industrial technology.

It is only necessary to go back to 1957–9 to realize to what extent the policy of the lending countries, and, through them, the international financial agencies, has changed in regard to what is now the major component of foreign capital inflow into Latin America. The trend is in the direction of programme-financing, and away from the project-by-project approach. Accordingly, the logic of financing part of the local costs—including the purchase of domestically manufactured materials—is gaining ground as against the strict import-component scheme; long-term, low-interest loans, with extended grace periods, are now current; external financing of housing, education, and health programmes, as well as agrarian reform and long-term farm credit, is an essential feature of the social objectives of development. There are new sources of lending, such as the Inter-American Development Bank, through which Canadian and European capital is added to the United States and Latin American capital funds specifically allocated to Latin America. Various European countries have now instituted or sponsored bilateral lending programmes.

Before 1960 a conservative orthodoxy dominated foreign lending to Latin America, with minor exceptions such as the Development Loan Fund of the United States and transactions under the latter's Public Law 480. There will undoubtedly continue to be complaints about the lending practices of different agencies and the particular conditions they require of certain countries. There has been, however, vast progress, and the way is open, through multilateral channels such as the Inter-American Committee for the Alliance for Progress, to increase mutual understanding. As the formulation of development programmes in Latin America improves, and as it is supported by better project preparation and evaluation, a larger and smoother flow of long-term funds is likely, from public and from private sources. A sizeable part of the private medium and long-term loans is still essentially a device by the lending country to finance its exports of capital goods, and perhaps, to some extent, a means to gain influence, but a beginning has recently been made in the granting of untied loans by foreign banks and in the floating of government bonds through underwriters who have succeeded in placing them in both North America and Western Europe.

The sharp increase in foreign indebtedness that has taken place in Latin America in the last few years has, nevertheless, given rise to some misgivings. One, that is shared both by lenders and borrowers, is the burden that it may place on the payments position of the borrowing countries over the coming years. Although short-term 'bankability' judgements of a country's capacity to pay have gradually been replaced by sophisticated economic and financial evaluations that take into account the expected success of the development programmes and the intangible advances in education, welfare, agrarian reform, and political maturity, there remains the fact that much of the external debt is short-term rather than otherwise. On the basis of the 1961 outstanding external debt, it was estimated that over 50 per cent of it was due within the period 1962–5.[12] No doubt with the further increases in debt in 1962–4, much of it incurred by Argentina, Brazil, and Chile to finance imports indiscriminately, and some by Mexico to finance an accelerated public works programme, the percentage of the 1964 outstanding debt falling due in the next four years is even higher.

This problem is under constant review and steps have been taken to 'roll over' and refund, where appropriate, the short-term maturities in the most urgent cases, thus releasing foreign exchange to pay for current imports. But even allowing for these special transactions, the balance of payments burden of all foreign liabilities, obtained by adding to dividends and interest the scheduled amortization of medium and long-term loans, is high and has been increasing: 23 per cent of current income from exports of goods and services for all Latin America in 1956–60 to 26.5 per cent in 1963, amortization payments alone accounting for 9.5 and 13.3 per cent.[13] The extra burden imposed by amortization payments will only cease to be critical on the assumption that new disbursements on loans will more than offset current repayments and that the average maturity of new loan commitments will increase and suitable grace periods will be introduced. There is nothing in the whole complex mechanism of foreign borrowing that will automatically assure a given rate of disbursements. Some countries have been cut off altogether, others have had to undertake difficult negotiations, and project and programme preparations

[12] ECLA, *External Financing*, ch. iv, sect. iv/2, 7 Apr. 1963.
[13] ECLA, *Survey 1963*, tables 25 and 26.

have often lagged. It is easy for a country to fall back upon indiscriminate short-term financing.

The concern over the debt burden is not confined to financial experts in and out of government, but has certain political implications; first, in so far as excessive indebtedness may affect business confidence and contribute to exchange instability and inflation, and, generally, because foreign borrowing—'mortgaging' the country to foreign capital—may easily become a vulnerable flank, to an unjustified extent, in a government's economic programme. It may seem surprising, but the nineteenth-century experience in external debt and the foreign intervention accompanying it have not been forgotten, and are often regarded as the rule today. More subtle arguments abound, namely, to the effect that the World Bank, or the United States lending agencies, or the private lenders, as the case may be, impose conditions such as control of inflation, holding back of wage adjustments, reducing railroad deficits, raising electric power rates, improving government finance, etc., that are against the country's best interests, or affect national sovereignty. The accusation that the borrower 'sells out' to the lender is increasingly current, particularly from left-wing political groups. The policy and behaviour of the lending agencies has certainly not been unblemished, but the criticism can be carried too far. Sometimes all that the lender demands basically is adequate development programming, good project preparation, and a positive financial policy, with which progressive groups in any Latin American country should have no quarrel. In general, bilateral dealings between the United States and a borrowing country are more suspect of undesirable political pressures than in the case of loans from a European country. This source of friction over external borrowing could be eliminated by directing an increasing share of foreign lending through multilateral channels.

A different type of opposition to external borrowing frequently derives from right-wing groups, either over concern for the balance of payments burden or because the foreign loans are enabling a government to carry out the policies they are opposed to, particularly when, as under the Alliance for Progress, important structural changes such as tax and land reform are involved, or when the foreign loans strengthen the public sector *vis-à-vis* private business, or enable the share of public ownership in industry, transport, etc., to increase. The World Bank is envisaged as contributing to socialism! Here the local groups are transferring to the foreign and international lenders a purely domestic quarrel. Nevertheless, it is clear that as external borrowing increases over the next decade or two, it is inescapably going to have a bearing on domestic political struggles, for it will tend to be essentially part of the process of economic and social planning, and planning is primarily a political problem. Those who oppose planning and, through it, foreign borrowing for public sector programmes, may, however, have to give more consideration to the alternatives, one of which might be a slower rate of overall development and another a higher rate of taxation. There is no reason why the Latin American private sector itself should not gain more access to external long-term loans, all the more so if its expansion programmes are consistent with the comprehensive national development plans.

One of the most delicate aspects of foreign economic co-operation in Latin America is the question of grants-in-aid, which, although not of major significance in the total picture, have nevertheless contributed substantially in one or two countries. From $89 million during 1951–5, United States aid of this type increased to $429 million during 1956–61, and in 1962–4 reached a level of over $100 million annually.[14] Practically every country has been a recipient of such grants, mostly allocated to economic and social projects, but Bolivia, Central America, and other small countries have between them benefited most. In Bolivia the aid programme has been more in the nature of a general-purpose support of the economy. In many cases these grants have particular political overtones. Even where the grant may consist of a well-meant donation of some agricultural machinery to a small community, hospital equipment to a municipality, or a fire-engine, it is questionable whether in the long run this is a good policy, for it inevitably puts local authorities in the position of receiving charity from a foreign government, and may create conflict between a local authority and the central government. Grants have by no means been forced on the Latin American governments. On the contrary, many of the latter's public officials have been all too eager to obtain them for certain programmes and under various types of justification. A case could be made for special aid, on a temporary basis,

[14] ECLA, *External Financing*, ch. iv., sect. iv.–2, table v–6; also US, *Report . . . for third ann. meeting of Inter-American Economic and Social Council (1964).*

to help a very low-income country such as Haiti or Bolivia to set in motion her development programme; but it should be done preferably through multilateral assistance. Long-term, low interest, or soft loans, such as are now granted by the International Development Association and the Social Progress Trust Fund of the Inter-American Development Bank, would be more desirable than bilateral grants. If Latin American countries want to be free from bilateral grants, it is clearly within their power, through adequate development programming, to dispense with them and with the potential political corruption they sometimes imply.[15]

It may be expected, as noted earlier, that the amount of foreign direct investment in Latin America will be, on the whole, proportionately less important in the future than it has been in the post-war period. The significance of private direct investment in bringing about an importation of skills and technology is clear, and the contribution it could make to the development of many of the leading manufacturing industries is beyond question. However, even on a relatively limited scale and subject to the many conditions and restrictions that recent years have made common, and assuming foreign capital is willing to assist in the region's development, is Latin America receptive to such investment? Most observers agree that Latin America's attitude is ambivalent, which means in effect that a rational long-term policy towards foreign private investment has not been worked out successfully, or that it may be inherently impossible to do so.

In economic and political systems based on the right to private enterprise and property and equality before the law, such as prevail in all but one of the Latin American countries, outright exclusion of foreign private investment from all fields of activity is virtually impossible. Nevertheless, every Latin American country has at one

[15] Another source of grants to Latin America is the US Food for Peace Programme. A substantial part of this programme has consisted in sales of grain and other food in return for local currency which the US. may subsequently re-lend to the recipient country or otherwise use. These amounts are not properly speaking grants, although a form of aid. The remainder, a growing proportion, involving $57 m. in 1962 and $105 m. in 1963 (US *Rep. to IAESC*) represented emergency relief, child feeding programmes, and donations to voluntary relief agencies. These types of grant are in a special class and need not be questioned as to motives. However, the sales of food in exchange for local currency have occasionally given rise to grumbles from Latin American countries believing themselves in a position to provide similar supplies under ordinary commercial conditions.

time of another experienced the pressure and influence of foreign capital upon its pattern of development, its political and social institutions, and its historical path. Whether from a feeling of inferiority, from an actual position of weakness, from a sense of the injustice created by privilege, or from fear of frustration in carrying out national aspirations, Latin Americans have been suspicious of private foreign capital and generally disenchanted by their experience in dealing with it. Hence a wide assortment of methods has been followed to regulate its participation in national economic activity. These methods range from constitutional provisions that exclude foreigners from ownership of certain kinds of assets or reserve well-defined activities to the state, to requirements concerning the proportion of foreign and domestic capital in certain fields of business, or the employment of national labour and management personnel; and they include the use of various legal and administrative devices to give advantages to national over foreign capital. Much of the policy and the attitude of the Latin American countries is essentially defensive and lacking in clear purpose. Short-term economic or political expediency usually overrides serious attempts to evaluate the role of foreign private capital and lay new foundations for its collaboration in economic development. And yet it is becoming increasingly necessary to achieve consistency in ends and means, for Latin America is in danger of neither having its cake nor eating it.

If closing the prospective trade gap, or supplementing domestic savings, or spreading the use of modern technology requires some contribution, however limited, from private foreign investment, there is need to define a policy involving the use of such foreign capital in a manner that will render it effective in achieving the desired purpose. If Latin America were to become ready to solve its problems without foreign direct investments, its policies should be directed above all to making available to itself the totality of the skills and technology that it may require to increase productivity and living standards. At the present stage of economic, social, and political development such an alternative is clearly not viable; and it is doubtful that the use solely of international long-term loans and technical assistance, were it possible independently from private investment, would enable Latin America to attain that objective. What, then, are the chances of developing a positive policy to ensure a minimum flow of foreign direct investment of the type required in order to supplement and reinforce the more general policies and the present trends in international financial co-operation?

The question relates, naturally, to everything else that has to do with the forces of change in Latin America: the structure of power, the quality of government, the level of education, the urge to accept and discharge social responsibility, and, not least, the attitude and actions of the international community. There are, unfortunately, few signs of factors favourable to formulating a new approach. Latin American governments, under pressure of short-term considerations and partly as an admission of inability to resist or basically answer popular income and welfare demands, are apt to assume superficially nationalistic positions of scant lasting benefit; or they yield to local business interests whose motives are often far from innocent. Organized business and labour groups, with rare exceptions, are by the nature of their own privileges in the Latin American society unable to dissociate their attitudes to foreign capital from the prospects of their own particular advancement; and broad public opinion is misinformed, or uninformed, and, for good measure, resentful or openly hostile. Foreign capital itself, despite the multiple and repeated hard lessons it has received in its relations with Latin America, is in turn, despite some notable exceptions, lacking in the flexibility necessary to meet the changing mood of the region and the new requirements of development.

On a realistic basis, it would require much thought and study to steer towards a new approach. Prefabricated solutions, often supported by insistent argument, are only too readily available. 'Control' on the one hand, and 'guarantees' on the other, are excessive simplifications. The threat of control over foreign investment is enough to dissuade even the types most suited to national development; the granting or promise of guarantees is rendered inoperative because it involves treating foreign capital better than domestic enterprise. Investment codes would hardly be worth the paper they were written on; restrictions on profit remittances are biased against risk capital and, therefore, run counter to a good part of technological innovation. Rather than to methods, attention should, perhaps, be drawn to principles that might serve to build a policy framework acceptable both to Latin

American governments and to foreign capital. The main desiderata are, briefly, as follows:

1. The fundamental purpose of foreign direct investment should be to contribute to the development and well-being of the recipient country—extensive to the Latin American region through eventual free-trade or common market arrangements—by means of transfers of technology and skills that may raise productive capacity and productivity, income, and educational and welfare standards.

2. Ownership of domestic assets by foreign investors should carry with it a responsibility to ensure national participation in the decision-making process relating to the investment, its current operation, and its expansion.

3. Foreign investment should not predominate in the development of any particular natural resource. Wherever it does, mutually satisfactory arrangements should be negotiated to reduce its participation over an agreed period of time until it is balanced by public or private national investment.

4. Whenever foreign capital may be required for, or already occupies a dominant position in, basic industries or any activity in production, distribution, or services where political sensitivity may run high, arrangements should be made for an increasing participation of public or private local capital over a defined period of time.

5. Foreign capital should plan gradually to withdraw, in agreement with the country, from industrial activities in which technology is relatively stable or where there is ready access to untied technology that may require no more than advisory services to the local capital replacing the foreign-controlled investment.

6. In areas of dynamic technology, foreign capital should contribute to the development of local applied scientific research.

7. Joint ventures, with increasing incorporation of domestic management personnel, should be preferred to fully-owned foreign subsidiary or associated companies.

8. Foreign capital should contribute, through suitable financial intermediaries, to the development of local medium and small independent enterprises.

9. Foreign investments should unreservedly accept the jurisdiction of local courts and equality of rights and obligations with respect to nationals.

10. Latin American governments should attempt to harmonize among themselves their policies towards foreign direct investment,

but in any case should make explicit their broad lines of policy with regard to the areas of participation of foreign capital over a reasonable period of time and, within such limits and in accordance with principles accepted, allow sufficient freedom from detailed regulation, in any case not less than that permitted to local enterprises.

It would not be inappropriate to ask whether private foreign capital in the United States, Canada, and Western Europe that already has a stake in Latin America's development, or is able to lend its co-operation and is interested in doing so, is in turn ready to adapt itself to a new set of principles. The historical record is, perhaps, as uninspiring as Latin America's own lack of a clear-cut attitude, but some recent developments, such as the Atlantic Community Development Group for Latin America (ADELA), indicate willingness to try new approaches, even though the scale involved is for the time being limited.

One of the most dangerous illusions, as has been argued in this paper, is that the role of private foreign investment in Latin America's development could ever again be quantitatively decisive. But to assign to it a major qualitative part in the upsurge of Latin American industry is not beyond the pale of reason and hope.

[*Víctor L. Urquidi, formerly Director of the Mexico Regional Office of the ECLA and consultant on economic development at the Ministry of Finance and the Bank of Mexico, is now Research Director at the Centro de Estudios Económicos y Demográficos of El Colegio de México. His principal publications include* Free Trade and Economic Integration in Latin America (*1962*) *and* The Challenge of Development in Latin America (*1964*).]

Change and Frustration in Chile[1]

OSVALDO SUNKEL

If we want things to stay as they are, things will have to change ...
(GIUSEPPE DI LAMPEDUSA: *The Leopard*.)

AN examination of the literature on the social problems of Latin America or of the views that are frequently expressed by experts on Latin American affairs leads to the distinct impression that very little or no change has taken place, or is taking place in that region. Having accepted this view, interest is aroused in the reasons for the maintenance of the *status quo*.

As a logical consequence, the obstacles to change become the object of legitimate academic interest. However, after looking at what has happened in Chile during the last thirty or forty years, it is not possible to agree that there has not been any change. On the contrary, very rapid and intense change has taken place, but this has not produced certain expected social consequences, such as have resulted from the process of economic development in what are now advanced, industrialized countries. The reasons for this frustration are to be found in the persistence of the basic institutional structure of society which exerts a limiting and controlling influence over the process of social change.

An Analysis of Social Change

It has become customary to view the process of social change in terms of a dialectical interplay of two types of antagonistic social forces: one group of factors making for social change, and the other representing obstacles in its way. This type of approach automatically transforms the first group into the positive and progressive forces of historical development, and the other into the negative and reactionary forces.

[1] The opinions expressed in this essay are personal, and should not therefore be ascribed in any way to the institutions with which the author is connected. Gratitude is expressed to Sres Luis Ratinoff and Héctor Assael, who read the first draft and made many useful comments. Nevertheless, anything in this essay to which exception may be taken should be attributed entirely to the author.

This kind of approach, which is practical and useful when examining a static situation, has nevertheless serious drawbacks when used in the analysis of long-term change. There is a natural tendency to over-simplify in classifying the two groups of social forces. This may easily lead to a dogmatic division of the various actors of the social drama into good and bad, as neatly contrasted as black and white.

The tendency to over-simplify, combined with an ethical and political interest in change and a distinct impression that things remain, in fact, as they were, tends to produce an exaggerated interest in the obstacles to social change. Implicitly at least, it appears that many students of social change in underdeveloped countries have gained the impression that no transformation is taking place in these societies. One case in point is the assumption that so-called 'traditional' societies are like hardened shells, capable only of resisting or of breaking. Yet they have shown great flexibility in absorbing elements of modernization, without the need to alter their basic structure.[2] On the other hand many economists tend to equate economic stagnation with social *status quo*, believing that the combination of economic stagnation, demographic growth, and urbanization is producing explosive social pressures and tensions in Chilean society. Observation of what has been happening in Latin America shows clearly that both assumptions are incorrect, and that social change and economic stagnation are not incompatible.

On the basis of this evidence it is sometimes suggested that change is taking place in Latin America, but at a very slow pace, and that what is needed is to accelerate this process. This view also appears to miss the point. The question of social change is not one of rhythm or pace. The economic history of Latin America provides ample evidence of rapid social change over extended periods of time, even in economically stagnant societies. In fact, it is difficult to accept the proposition that any Latin American country could have survived through the last three or four decades without significant social change.

The only partial exception, important in certain countries such as Bolivia, Ecuador, Guatemala, Mexico, and Peru, is the large

---

[2] See ECLA, *The Social Development of Latin America in the Post-War Period* (Santiago, 1963).

Indian sector of population and culture, which occupies a substantial portion of the national territory. But even this segment of Latin American society, the most resistant to change, has experienced the impact of the universal expansion of the market economy, of the massive efforts to raise levels of health and education, and of the rapid development of non-written mass communication media such as radio, television, and cinema, some of which no longer require a direct supply of electric power. These and similar types of phenomena have reached the most isolated and primitive communities, and have introduced important changes in traditional habits and values.

Latin American countries have moved increasingly closer to the United States, whose gigantic economy and dynamic technology constitute an overwhelming and ever-present phenomenon. Most of the elements of modernization present in Latin America, particularly the technology of production and mass consumption habits, have been profoundly influenced by the economy and society of the United States.

Finally, many policies adopted to improve social conditions in Latin America have been present for some time, becoming institutionalized through a system of regional organizations. This has been true of health programmes in particular, but also increasingly of education and housing.

During the final decades of the nineteenth century and the first decades of the twentieth certain leading export sectors evolved in Latin America. They brought new forms of production, new technologies and techniques of organization, and have led to the development of close relations with overseas consumer markets and new groups of national entrepreneurs.

In some of these countries, as for instance, in Chile, the process of social transformation continued increasingly rapidly as a result of the intensified industrialization begun after the crisis of 1929. Industrialization and urbanization, a considerable increase in the functions and participation of the government in the economy, the growth of a middle sector, and the increasing participation of the population in the political process, are all evidence of the fact that Chile has undergone a period of social transformation during the last few decades.

Some social change must, therefore, have taken place, and it must have done so at a fairly intense pace, nor can it have been confined to one particular social sector. Why, then, the concern about obstacles to change? Because it is the quality, i.e. the results, of change which are important and it is clear that, however widespread the process of change has been, it has not had the expected impact and consequences.

While a relatively important and prosperous urban middle sector has developed, average standards of living in Chile have not risen much. The condition of the overwhelming majority of the population has probably not improved at all, even though a large part of it has moved from the countryside to the urban areas. Moreover, some important groups have suffered a substantial deterioration in their standards of living. Economic inequality, which has always been striking, has shown little signs of decreasing. Opportunities for improving living conditions, for wider participation in the political process, and for access to intermediate, technical, and higher education, continue to be almost non-existent for a large proportion of the population, and are open only to a minority which, though it has grown in absolute and relative terms, continues to be rather small. This discriminatory situation also exists in the treatment of the poor by the government agencies, by the administration of justice, and even by the social services, notwithstanding the fact that these are the outcome of social legislation which was originally designed to protect the lower-income groups.

These and other similar important symptoms of inequality persist largely as they were thirty years ago: although attenuated, they stand out more and are less acceptable. Until recently it was hoped that these conditions would inevitably be changed by the process of modernizing the economy and by the structural changes associated with industrialization, rapid urbanization, and the extension of the benefits of health and education to an ever greater proportion of the national population. But after almost three decades during which many policies directed towards these general aims have been implemented, there is no clear indication that the process of social change has in fact produced the expected results. Social conditions simply cannot improve while the Chilean economy continues to stagnate as it has done during the last ten years. But even if the economy started growing, as it did during the 1930s and 1940s, there is every reason to expect that, though the average material conditions of welfare might improve, a higher degree of social and economic equality would not be achieved automatically.

It has, therefore, been possible for Chilean society to change in many important respects, while at the same time this change has not produced the expected egalitarian results. Moreover, in the future it can be assumed that further transformations of this traditional type will also fail to produce a more equitable and dynamic society.

Three main complementary aspects of this problem may seem to call for analysis: (*a*) the nature of the various obstacles to change (on which excessive emphasis has been placed up to now); (*b*) the type of forces working in favour of change (extremely little has been said in the literature about this); and (*c*) the interplay over time of the conflicting forces of change and resistance (not much has been said about this either).

Obstacles to change may be an important element in explaining the process of change, but they are not the only, and may not even be the most important, factor in such an explanation. In the case of Chile, the inherent weakness and misdirection of the forces of change may be far more important.

Social Change since the 1930s

In 1930 Chile had 4.3 million inhabitants, 28 per cent of whom lived in cities of more than 20,000 inhabitants. The vast majority of these urban dwellers lived in Santiago, a city of almost a million inhabitants. The capital, therefore, accounted for nearly one-quarter of the population. Moreover, Chilean economic life was based almost entirely on mining, which contributed one-third of the national income. During the last decades of the nineteenth century the rich and booming nitrate fields of the northern provinces were incorporated into the economy, while immediately before the First World War a large and technologically advanced copper mining industry was also developed. The growth of important mining exports profoundly affected the structure of the economy and the living standards of the urban population. The export sector, with all its ancillaries, incorporated into the Chilean economy the modern technologies and forms of organization prevailing in Western Europe and the United States. But this process hardly affected the rest of the productive structure, which continued operating on the basis of traditional methods of high labour intensity, low productivity, and primitive forms of organization. This was particularly so in the case of agriculture.

With the expansion of foreign trade the government discovered an important source of additional revenue, which found its way into public services and the building of urban infrastructural facilities. The way of living and the values and attitudes of the urban population were affected, while new groups of urban wage-earners and of the lower middle class were coming into being with the development of these various activities.

The export boom made it possible for a limited segment of Chilean society to attain relatively high income levels on the basis of the improved rates of productivity developed in the exporting sector. The great slump of 1929 produced a dramatic contraction of world trade, and Chilean exports were reduced to a small fraction of their former value. As foreign demand for Chilean exports was drastically curtailed, mining activity stopped almost completely, and this resulted in serious unemployment. The crisis produced a sudden and substantial decrease in Chile's foreign trade reserves, and also reduced government revenues considerably, as the main economic activity was almost paralysed. Under such difficult economic and social conditions, the Ibáñez administration was overthrown and a period of grave political instability ensued, with a succession of governments trying to cope with the effects of the world depression. Unemployment in the export industries was followed by increasing unemployment in the cities, and the political situation deteriorated visibly.

Various measures were taken to stem unemployment, such as bringing gold-fields into operation, starting public works, and paying unemployment compensation. Simultaneously reserves were fast being run down and the government had to take protective action. Exchange operations were put under government control, the importation of many foreign goods was prohibited, tariffs were increased, and a far-reaching devaluation took place. This set of policies had the effect of isolating the internal from the international market, and substantially increasing the price of imported goods. A drastic change in relative prices, generally in favour of imported manufactured goods and against home-produced agricultural commodities, took place. Since at the same time an anti-cyclical employment policy was being followed, the level of internal demand was maintained and favourable conditions were created for expanding the internal production of manufactured goods. Not only was the national market being supported, but heavy protection was also given through import prohibitions, exchange control, and devaluation, while the limited resources of foreign exchange available were being used mainly to import capital goods in order to facilitate the development of industry.

The events of this period were entirely caused by external factors, and the favourable conditions for industrialization which resulted were largely the unexpected by-product of emergency policies. But in 1938, for the first time in Chilean history, a coalition of left-wing parties (*Frente Popular*) came to power and adopted a deliberate policy of industrialization. This meant in practice the encouragement of private industrial entrepreneurs through various devices of economic policy such as continued protection, tax exemption, special credit facilities, etc. Besides these policies, the national government, through an institution specially created for that purpose, the Corporación de Fomento de la Producción (CORFO), started an important investment programme in various sectors of the economy, such as electricity, petroleum, and steel. Moreover, this government, and those that followed, continued the policy of social legislation and reform started in the mid-1920s, enlarging or establishing the various social security institutions which were intended to assist the lower-income groups generally.

The period from the mid-1930s to the mid-1950s witnessed a dramatic change in the structure of the Chilean economy and society, reflected in three basic phenomena. The first was a rapid expansion of industrial production, which substantially increased the share of industry in the national economy in terms both of the income generated by this activity and of the proportion of active population employed in it. In 1930 15.7 per cent of the active population was employed in the manufacturing industry; this proportion increased by 1950 to over 19 per cent, and in 1960 had reached 24 per cent. Similarly in 1930 the proportion of income generated by the industrial sector—including the building industry—was 13.8 per cent, and had increased by 1960 to about 21.5 per cent.[3] Meanwhile the share of mining declined from 32.5 to less than 5 per cent.

[3] All the data given in this and the following paragraphs are taken from: Univ. of Chile, Instituto de Economía, *La economía chilena en el período 1950–63* (1963), and *Desarrollo económico de Chile, 1940–56* (1956).

The second phenomenon was the rapid growth of population, and particularly of urbanization. The total population in 1960 was 7.4 million, roughly double that of 1930. The increasing rate of demographic growth, which has climbed from 1.4 per cent in 1925–35 to an estimated 2.4 per cent in 1955–65, is mainly the result of a substantial reduction in the mortality rate, which was approximately 24 per thousand in 1935 and only 12 per thousand in 1960. In the same period the birth rate decreased only from 38 to 35 per thousand.

The country also witnessed an intensive process of urbanization. This had been going on since the beginning of the export boom in the last century, but gathered speed in the 1930s. Important contributory factors have been: (*a*) the reduction of employment opportunities in mining, mainly due to the development of synthetic nitrate and to technological improvements in the nitrate industry; (*b*) the stimulus given to industrialization in the urban areas; and (*c*) the decreasing opportunities of employment in the countryside, as little land has been brought into cultivation since 1930, and also because agriculture was considerably mechanized during the 1940s and 1950s.

Whatever the causes, the urban population represented about one-third of the national population at the beginning of the century, increased to almost half in 1930, and was estimated at two-thirds in 1960. Santiago, which in 1930 had over 1 million inhabitants, had almost 2.5 million in 1960. This represents one-third of the total population, while the equivalent proportion in 1930 was about one-fourth.

As an illustration of the changes which have taken place as a result of this urbanization, it is interesting to note, for instance, that the proportion of the active population in the total increased between 1930 and 1952 from less than 32 to about 36 per cent, and that, in particular, the proportion of female active population over total female population increased from less than 15 per cent in 1930 to 25 per cent in 1952. These figures show the extent of the incorporation into the market economy of a multitude of services traditionally performed within the family.

A third phenomenon characteristic of the change in Chilean economy and society since 1930 is the great increase in government activities and bureaucracy. A number of statistics reveal this process. Unfortunately no comparable figures are available for 1930, but even a comparison with 1940 will illustrate the trend. Total public expenditure increased from 14 to 19 per cent of the GNP between 1940 and 1961. Of this, current expenditure increased from 12 to 15 per cent, while the proportion of public investment expenditure almost doubled, from somewhere near 2 to nearly 4 per cent of the GNP. The total number of government employees increased from 72,000 in 1940 to 116,000 in 1955, i.e. from 4.1 to 5.4 per cent of the active population. These data underestimate the increase, since they refer to central government administration only, while it is precisely the autonomous public agencies and services, as well as the state enterprises, which have expanded most strikingly.

Not only has the government sector gained considerable absolute and relative importance, but its function within the Chilean economy and society has also changed significantly. If total government expenditure is classified in three categories—promotion of economic development; education, health, and other social services; and general administration, police, and defence—the relative proportion of these categories can be shown to have varied substantially between 1940 and 1954. Expenditures on the promotion of economic development increased from 18 to 25 per cent, and on education, health, and other social services from 28 to 37 per cent of total government expenditure. The third category, therefore, fell from 54 to 38 per cent. Government participation in the national economy has thus increased very rapidly, and it has done so specifically in order to promote economic development and to extend the scope of various kinds of social services. Among these, social security has been one of the fastest growing items, expenditure having increased from less than 7 per cent of total public expenditure in 1940 to 14.4 per cent by 1961.

During the last thirty years Chile has witnessed three fundamental transformations: she has become relatively industrialized, she has also become increasingly urban, and she has greatly expanded the economic and social activities of the national government. This transformation in the economic and demographic structure has been accompanied by important changes in the standard of living of different groups, reflected in fields such as education and health, in political participation and social

communication.[4]   Rapid industrialization produced an urban
working class. Later, when industrialization started to slow
down, and the urbanization process continued as before or even
accelerated, a large *Lumpenproletariat* was formed: today almost
one-quarter of the population of Santiago—500,000 people—lives in
the notorious *poblaciones callampa*—literally, 'mushroom villages'
—which encircle the capital.

The large increase in government activity has created many
employment opportunities for the middle class, and has provided
the basis for the growth of the Radical Party, until very recently
the largest Chilean political party. Higher expenditure on health
has helped to bring about the large reduction in the death rate,
and thereby the change in the age structure of the population, since
the general decline in mortality has been mainly achieved by the
reduction of infant mortality. The increase in the scope of educational services has made it possible to reduce illiteracy and has
improved the general educational standards of the population.

The effect of urbanization on the social structure and on social
change is the one subject that has engaged most attention from
sociologists. It is well known that with urbanization the size of
the family tends to decrease, the participation of women in the
working force increases, and the family becomes less important
in the upbringing of children.

Change and Frustration

Though no direct statistical indicators of social change are
available, it is clear that over the last decades Chile has been
undergoing a process of transformation of her economy which
must have had far-reaching effects on the social structure. Nevertheless, there also appear to be elements that have resisted change.
The process of industrialization and economic development raised
hopes which have not been fulfilled. In the first place, industrialization was supposed to lead to a dynamic economy with the capacity
to generate its own continued growth. This has clearly not

[4] The corresponding data will not be included in this essay as such statistics
are easily available in international publications such as UNESCO, *Social
Aspects of Economic Development in Latin America* (1962); UN, *Report
on the World Social Situation*; OAS, *Algunos aspectos salientes del
desarrollo social de América Latina* (1962); Pan American Sanitary
Bureau, *Hechos sobre problemas de salud* (1961).

happened. Since 1954 the Chilean economy has on the whole been stagnant, and this has been one of the main causes of frustration.

The process of industrialization was supposed to bring about a lessening of the great social and economic inequalities which have always characterized Chile. It is generally acknowledged, however, that there has been little improvement, except for an increase in the relative size of the urban middle group.[5] As regards wealth, while the concentration of landownership has apparently not been reduced, the creation of industrial and urban wealth has given rise to new forms of extreme concentration. As for equality of social opportunity, it was originally hoped that industrialization, urbanization, and the social policy of a Welfare State would produce substantial and inevitable improvement, but here again Chilean experience has been frustrating. As the statistics show, in spite of the great expansion of the educational services, an insignificant proportion of secondary and university students are of working-class origin. Illiteracy is highest in the rural areas and among the urban *Lumpenproletariat*, which are the largest low-income groups of the population. The highest rate of school drop-out also occurs in these groups. An examination of unemployment statistics shows that the highest concentration of unemployment, whenever it increases, is registered among the groups of less skilled workers belonging to these two sections of the population. The incidence of infant mortality is also highest among these groups. Many examples of this kind could be cited in order to show that the process of economic transformation and social change that has taken place during the last decades has not led to significant improvement in the situation of the majority of the people.

In the area of the political characteristics of Chilean society, evidence points to a very limited participation of the people in government at all its levels. The proportion of registered voters has been increasing rapidly, especially during the last few years, but political activity has been limited to participation in elections. With the exception of the Christian Democrat Party, relative political alignments have remained fairly constant, in spite of the increase in voters. Among the working class, trade union membership is very low and has not increased.

[5] There are various quantitative indicators of important regressive changes in income-distribution during the last ten or fifteen years. See, for instance, Aníbal Pinto, *Chile; una economía difícil* (Mexico City, 1964).

Political immaturity is mainly reflected in the persistent lack of rationality in the determination of economic and social policy objectives and the selection of the means to those objectives, as special interests usually prevail over the national interest. The clearest example is the incapacity of Chilean political institutions to deal successfully with her two main economic problems: stagnation and inflation. The country has consistently failed to produce the kind of policy that could bring about development and stability, the declared objective of every economic and social programme. This is the result of the failure to develop the kind of political structure and social consensus necessary for the determination of clear objectives, and for the implementation of the policies which lead to their achievement.

The political forces which have favoured economic and social change have found expression in the parties of the Centre and the Left, ranging from the Radicals and Christian Democrats to the Socialist and Communist Parties. Of these the Christian Democrat Party has only become important in the last few years, while at the beginning and during most of the period under discussion the principal political force was the Radical Party. The political base of these different parties has mainly consisted of the organized labour groups in mining and industry, the organized white-collar workers employed in public and urban services, the liberal professions, and to some extent the entrepreneurial middle class. Socialism, nationalism, and the social doctrines of the Catholic Church have been the main ideologies determining the political activity of these groups.

Only about 12 per cent of an active population of approximately 3 million are members of trade unions in Chile: perhaps most significant is the failure to incorporate the rural working class into an active and organized trade union group, as this means that over one-fourth of the population has practically no influence on the political process. There are several reasons explaining the failure of the political forces of the Left to organize powerful rural trade unions. In the first place, the distribution of landownership is such that over two-thirds of the arable land is accounted for by 4.4 per cent of the total number of landholdings, while 1.6 per cent is accounted for by over 50 per cent of the landholdings.[6]

[6] D. Baytelman and R. Chateauneuf, 'Interpretación del Censo Agrícola Ganadero de 1955', *Panorama económico*, no. 223 (1961).

Consequently most of the rural working population is employed in the service of the few large landowners, including a majority of smallholders who live on subsistence *minifundia*. Since the landowners keep a tight control over rural legislation, and over the provincial branches of the executive and judiciary, they have been able to prevent or delay the passage and implementation of laws which would permit the rural working class to organize.[7] As a result, trade unionism in the countryside is insignificant. On the other hand the ratio of rural population to land is relatively low in Chile, and a systematic policy of rural mechanization has helped to reduce employment opportunities in agriculture, thereby hastening the move of rural workers to the cities.

The penetration of reformist ideologies in the countryside has also been hindered by the extremely low educational standards of the rural population, where the largest proportion of illiteracy is found. The system of large landholdings produces a wide scattering of the agricultural labour force, making it extremely difficult to extend social services, including education, to this part of the population. Rural workers live largely in isolation, lacking the most elementary means of communication with the social and political activity of the country, except during election time.

During the 1930s there was some social unrest in the rural areas, and left-wing parties managed to secure strong rural backing in some important elections. But although a basis of political and ideological penetration existed, it was evident only on exceptional electoral occasions, while the more permanent conditions of political control and isolation prevailed most of the time.

The organization of the urban working class into effective trade unions has only been possible in the larger mining and industrial activities. Many other urban workers are employed in small establishments where they have no legal right to organize. Another important group, the craftsmen and artisans, also encounter rather unfavourable conditions for organization.[8] Then there is the large

---

[7] See ECLA, *Social Development of Latin America*, pp. 39–54, for an analysis of the way in which the traditional forms of political domination in the countryside were reinforced rather than weakened by the extension of state administration to rural areas.

[8] These craftsmen and artisans started an active and belligerent trade union movement in the 1920s, based on anarchist ideals. But later on this kind of professional union was taken over, and largely destroyed, by the great expansion of industrial trade unions, and also by the use of legal red tape.

mass of casual labour, which works mainly in the building industry and in some low-productivity services. These workers are basically unskilled and are usually employed only on a temporary basis; their opportunities for organizing in unions are therefore extremely limited.

The small proportion of the urban working class which has become efficiently organized is to be found in economic sectors with high levels of productivity. As a consequence, their living conditions, salaries, and social benefits tend to be more than adequate when compared to those of the rest of the urban and rural working class, so much so that they have been described as members of a workers' aristocracy. Since the supply of labour, particularly in the cities, has been growing rapidly, while industrial and mining activity has expanded only moderately and has incorporated modern labour-saving technology, the trade unions which have developed in these sectors are constantly faced with the threat of the ample availability of alternative sources of labour. This has led the unions to devote most of their energies to creating barriers limiting access to work in these high-productivity sectors. At the same time, in view of the strong inflationary tendencies of the Chilean economy, the unions have specially concentrated on defending their own real income level by exerting pressure for higher wages and more social benefits. The political significance of these groups as spokesmen for the working class as a whole has therefore been small and has probably been decreasing, especially since the stagnation of the Chilean economy during the last decade began to reduce the opportunities of employment and to endanger the standards of living which these groups had gained for themselves.

In the developed countries of the West, the rising industrial middle class is supposed to have been the main driving force of modernization and reform. Many authors seem to be under the impression that this process is repeating itself in some Latin American countries, and particularly in Chile, where industrialization and urbanization have apparently created a substantial middle class. However, this is not the case. The middle class in Chile is made up mainly of three elements: the industrial and commercial entrepreneurs, the middle ranks of public administration, and the professions. The origin and development of the industrial entrepreneur group is directly related to the process of industrialization and to the expansion of the economic functions of the state. Their existence and increasing economic power was initially caused by an external phenomenon: the World Crisis. It was then stimulated by the use of protectionist policies and the provision of state finance. Since, during the initial decade of this process, no significant change took place in the distribution of political power, it can be assumed that the traditional ruling groups, which controlled the government, did not feel particularly threatened by the rise of this new industrial bourgeoisie. In fact, later on they became closely associated with these new economic interests.

Over the last few years, a process of social fusion between the new and the traditional social groups has clearly been taking place by means of intermarriage and the access of the new industrial and commercial families to the institutions and social circles which characterize and give status to the traditional ruling élite. This may be observed not only in the case of the incorporation of these new rising groups into the exclusive clubs and organizations of the social élite, but also in the fact that an increasing proportion of the new industrial bourgeoisie is acquiring land, an important symbol of social status.

This process is particularly noticeable in the case of some groups of foreign immigrants who started with small factories and commercial establishments, and then built up large fortunes. The industrial capital thus accumulated moved into financial and banking ventures, and the second and third generations of these immigrants married into the traditional families, and started to take an active part in politics, sport, and various social prestige activities (horse-racing, wine-making, philanthropic activities, etc.).

The professions and the middle ranks of the public administration are of their very nature groups without an independent base of economic power. In fact, the liberal professions, as they exist in the United States and other countries, are fairly insignificant in Chile, since they are largely confined to the government bureaucracy. Medicine and education also are largely to be found within the sphere of the public sector, and the enlargement of government activity has required an increasing amount of professional talent. Engineers, architects, agronomists, etc., are, therefore, also employed in large numbers by the government. These various groups of the professions and civil servants have also followed, through their organizations, a policy of self-protection and improvement, by limiting entry and obtaining increasing social benefits for each specific group.

The traditional structure of Chilean society has allowed a limited degree of social mobility between the lower middle class and the middle class proper, and between this group and the traditional ruling élite. This social mobility, being limited and undoubtedly selective, has contributed to the strength of the traditional social structure, not only by incorporating new talent and wealth, but also by creating the illusion of an 'open' society. On the other hand the newcomers have not changed the traditional system, since subordination to the existing Establishment appears to be the very condition of entry into it. Moreover, the selection is made by the ruling élite—under the favourable conditions of a large excess of supply over demand—through the channels of education; employment in government, private enterprise, or the service activities; social acceptability; and traditional institutions such as the Church or the army.

Owing to the composition of the left-wing parties, and the particular interests with which each of the groups has been concerned, the policies of these parties have been turning away from their original socialist objectives to what is generally called 'populism' in Latin America.[9] This means that in spite of their socialist ideals of structural and institutional reform, these parties have in practice concentrated very largely on legislative measures to secure short-term social benefits and privileges for their supporters.

The new middle class and the organized urban workers, who lacked the ability of the ruling groups to circumvent the law, to avoid taxes, to isolate themselves in exclusive circles, to behave, in short, as if they enjoyed extraterritorial rights in their own country, have also been creating an elaborate structure of legal privileges the extent of which has depended on the power of their respective political pressure groups. The forty or fifty different social security systems, special pay clauses and benefits, tax exemptions, duty-free

[9] There is no such thing as an accepted definition of populism but this political phenomenon has a number of well recognized characteristics. It is generally supported by the urban masses and sometimes also by the peasantry; it lacks a clearly defined ideological structure, although their programmes and pronouncements make free use of socialist terminology; it usually follows a charismatic leader who bases his appeal on simple, almost irrational, promises of immediate redistributive changes; it is always nationalistic.

territories and ports, etc., are clear proof of this activity. The political ideologies of the Left are, therefore, no more than populist programmes designed to promote the granting of special privileges for certain middle-class and organized labour groups. It should be noted that this behaviour has not been a monopoly of left-wing parties and politicians. The right-wing politicians have frequently joined enthusiastically in this type of populism as a means of keeping or gaining popularity, and also of maintaining a certain degree of control over-'progressive' legislation. It is understandable that the populist politicians who have performed this function do not exhibit much reformist or revolutionary zeal, since that would mean the limitation of such privileges and could undermine their own political and electoral strength. On the contrary, they are acquiring an interest in the maintenance of the system, and, therefore, tend to develop into a formidable obstacle to the rationalization of the political structure and of economic and social policy.

It would be no exaggeration to say that the left-wing parties, including the Communist Party, as well as the trade unions, have in this way become increasingly incorporated into the political Establishment, and that their existence and influence depend on the maintenance of this system. The political influence of some of their leaders, and their respective bureaucracies, would probably vanish if these parties and trade unions were to be turned into real popular mass movements. This is suggested by the fact that a very low proportion of registered voters are members of any political party, and that an even smaller proportion of the labour force is organized.

Looking back over the last twenty or thirty years, the political action of the left-wing parties has followed two main lines: the enactment of laws and the creation of institutions which would expand the scope of social services and benefits for the middle and lower middle class and for the urban working class; and the support of legislation which would favour investment in the economic infrastructure and the development of industry. In other words, emphasis has been placed on the redistribution of income and on the conditions for industrial growth. Few of the objectives of redistribution have been attained because such redistribution as has taken place has been largely from the non-organized urban and rural groups to the urban middle classes and organized workers.

In fact, the expanded volume of government expenditures necessary for financing the social services of the urban middle class have not been matched by fundamental tax reforms which would have placed the burden of this financing on the wealthy. On the contrary, the redistributive policies have placed a burden on the lower income groups, who have had to pay through higher indirect taxation and the forced transfer of income through the inflationary process.

Both in the economic and social sense, policies directed towards extending the country's infrastructure and industrial potential have also been disappointing. They have failed in the economic sense, because income redistribution through fiscal policy has not been truly effective—as it cannot be so long as the concentration of wealth is not broken up—and consequently industrial expansion has been slowing down, due to the fact that the internal market did not expand. They have failed in the social sense, since a progressive income tax and taxes on property and wealth are either deficient or non-existent, and therefore the promotion of industrial investment within the limits of a small internal market has contributed to the concentration of economic power in the industrial sector. Further, many prominent members of the left-wing parties who did manage to reach the higher ranks of the expanding public services, and were therefore in a position to grant financial and economic protection to new industrial sectors, were in due course absorbed into the new industrial groups, and finally accepted into the most exclusive financial, commercial, and industrial circles. It is obvious that in these circumstances the revolutionary and reformist zeal of their parties has also suffered considerable attenuation.

While the former process has mainly affected the Radical Party, the Socialist and Communist Parties, which have not experienced prolonged participation in the government, have suffered from another kind of weakness. Particularly in the case of the Communist Party, political action has been largely determined by international developments. In many respects, the political line followed internally has been strongly influenced by the ups and downs of the struggle between the United States and the Soviet Union. Today one of the main controversies of the Left in Chile is the schism between the Soviet Union and China rather than the ideological challenge of the Christian Democrat movement.

This kind of attitude may be seen not only in the realm of political action, but also in that of political analysis. The political parties of the Chilean Left have conspicuously failed to produce an adequate theoretical interpretation of the historical process of development which could generate the kind of alternative revolutionary or reformist programme and policies that are required in a country with Chile's historical setting, traditions, and values.[10] This may also be the reason for the signal failure of these parties to produce any kind of strong nationalist movement.

One of the most important among the various factors which may explain the prevention of social change in Chile is the persistence, and probably the increase, of a high degree of concentration of wealth, income, and economic power in a small group of the Chilean population, and the corresponding creation of a set of values which emphasize money and power. The concentration of economic power in the hands of a small élite has pervaded all activities of social life, and has led to the growth of a system of control over the government, the press, finance, and middle-class employment. Instead of moving towards a system which rewards merit and effort, Chilean society, though changing and modernizing, has extended to the new urban activities and classes a traditional clientèle system of political domination which is structurally and functionally incompatible with the organization of a modern and effective democracy.[11]

The emphasis placed on industrial development during the last decades has left untouched the traditional system of landownership, while new forms of high concentration of capital have been created in industry. To this should be added the high degree of concentration of property in the mining sector and in real estate. As a result, income distribution has also remained markedly unequal, and savings have therefore also tended to be highly concentrated. This has, in turn, produced a tight control of banking and other financial mechanisms. Thus the funds available for capital formation are not easily channelled by government policy into the kind of activities required for economic growth.

The extent of the concentration of wealth in these sectors is indicated in the following statistics: (1) agricultural property: the

---

[10] See Espartaco, 'Crítica del modelo político-económico de la "izquierda oficial" ', *El trimestre económico*, no. 121 (1964).

[11] ECLA, *Social Development of Latin America*.

output of 3 per cent of the larger agricultural holdings represents 62 per cent of the total value of agricultural production; (2) large industrial enterprises: 1 per cent of the shareholders hold 46 per cent of the total value of shares; (3) real estate: in one residential quarter of Santiago 10 per cent of the number of dwellings represents 37 per cent of the total value of dwellings; (4) finance: 1 per cent of the shareholders of banks and insurance companies hold 35 per cent of the total value in shares.[12] According to a study quoted by ECLA, the top 2 per cent of income earners received 14 per cent of total personal income in Chile in 1960, and the top 5 per cent received 25 per cent of personal income. The average per capita income of the top 2 per cent income earners was seven times the national average and 22 times the average income per capita of one-half of the income-earning population, which received 16 per cent of total personal income.[13]

Because of this high degree of concentration of economic power, and the growing association of the higher echelons of the bureaucracy with the industrial and financial groups, the state has increasingly come under the control of private interests. The wider economic functions of the state, which were originally looked upon with suspicion by the traditionalist forces and private enterprise groups, and which—according to socialist ideology—were supposed to be the main instrument of institutional change, have been increasingly used for the defence of private interests. For instance, CORFO, a government agency created in order to stimulate industrial growth, has sold out its controlling interest in the various basic industries which it established. Even before this happened, this agency had been gradually changing from a pioneering promoter of basic industry to a traditional banking institution strongly influenced by private interests. Similarly, the government institutions charged with the task of transforming traditional agriculture have become less the expression of a national policy and more the instrument for pursuing the kind of policies that are directly in accord with the interests of the associations of large landowners. Parallel examples could be mentioned in mining, transportation, and other areas of government intervention. The state, the main

---

[12] Sergio Molina, 'Notas en torno a la distribución del ingreso', *Revista Economía*, no. 79 (1963).

[13] ECLA, *The Economic Development of Latin America in the Post-War Period* (Santiago, 1963).

instrument of economic and political power, grown large and influential as a result of the initiative of the left-wing parties, has in this way become an instrument for the preservation of the *status quo* rather than for the promotion of structural change.

The high degree of concentration of economic power and its influence on the government have also facilitated control of the main media of mass communication by private enterprise. Most of the principal newspapers, weekly magazines, radio networks, news and publicity agencies are owned by powerful industrial and financial concerns, and are largely in their service. It is noteworthy, for example, that Chile does not have a single daily newspaper of any importance representing the point of view of the political parties of the Left, nor does she have an independent, middle-of-the-road, liberal paper of the kind one finds in most European countries. The only significant exception to this situation is that of the two television channels, which have, after a long political struggle, been turned over to the two main universities. But in Chile this is still a very limited medium of communication.

The consequent bias in political information and reporting is not only noticeable in the information and comment about national events; it is even more striking in the case of foreign news coverage and comments. The sources of information on world events are almost completely under the control of the two or three main international news agencies, and Chilean newspapers and magazines are absolutely dependent on these sources even for information about other Latin American countries.

Another instrument which was thought to be an important factor of change and social mobility was education. The educational system was enlarged, and the number of students with access to primary, secondary, technical, and university education increased considerably. Nevertheless, the system has remained discriminatory and has functioned as a selective mechanism; it has allowed access to higher education mainly to the relatively well-off, and has not performed its function of democratic equalizer. The drop-out rates are high, so that of the children who start in the first grade, only 30 per cent reach secondary schools, and not more than 9 per cent reach the university; of these, less than 1 per cent graduate.[14] Given the enormous inequality in income distribution,

---

[14] Molina, *Revista Economía*, no. 79.

and the lack of any substantial scholarship programme, the drop-outs are largely the result of the inability of the low-income families to finance long years of schooling. A study made in the province of Santiago of the rates of maintenance of children in primary school, classified according to the income level of the family, showed the following results:

Years of primary school	Income level		
	Low	*Medium*	*High*
1	100	100	100
2	73	83	95
3	61	75	92
4	48	67	89
5	37	58	85
6	28	48	80
First year of secondary school	14	32	73

Source: Eduardo Hamuy, *Educación elemental, analfabetismo y desarrollo económico* (Santiago, 1960).

This situation has given rise to the formation of a discriminatory system of various types of schools for various social classes. The ordinary primary school is intended to provide education to the lowest-income groups of the population; frequently it offers only three or four years of schooling because of the high drop-out rates. This is particularly the case in rural areas or poor urban districts. The few that reach the sixth grade find it difficult to go on to intermediate schools, as the large drop-out between these grades shows. The primary schools which are attached to an establishment of intermediate education or *liceo*, however, provide schooling for the middle-income groups; the drop-out rates here are much lower, and the continuation of schooling is assured by the *liceo* of which the primary school is an integral part.

Moreover, the same kind of discrimination becomes apparent when comparing free state and paying private schools. The last are accessible only to the higher-income groups and show the lowest drop-out rates. They enjoy a substantial government subsidy, so that the cost of education per student—and therefore the quality of education—is normally much higher than in state schools. But since the intake of the universities is very limited compared with the demand for higher education, a system of examinations is used to select only the better qualified students who have graduated from secondary schools. The result of this is that there is a bias in favour of the children of high-income families, who attend better schools for a longer time and therefore receive a better education. In consequence less than 2 per cent of university students are of working-class origin, and these can be found only in the shorter and less traditional courses. Students of low-income origin are extremely rare in medicine, engineering, and other courses which take seven or more years to complete, and which maintain high academic standards.

The educational system, far from fulfilling a function of democratization and equalization, has therefore become organized in such a way that it segregates classes and discriminates heavily against the lower and in favour of the upper-middle and higher-income groups.

There is another point relating to education and employment which it is important to mention. As has been said before, although the Chilean economy has been stagnant for over a decade, a considerable degree of technological modernization has taken place. Employment opportunities have not therefore increased greatly. Meanwhile population growth has accelerated and educational services have expanded considerably, producing a substantial increase in the flow of skilled and professional manpower. Moreover, since the capacity of primary and secondary education has increased much faster than that of higher education, there are many young men about who have had secondary schooling but no special training. The excessive supply of educated, skilled, and professional manpower in relation to employment opportunities—to which the large outflow of Chilean technicians and professionals bears conclusive testimony—added to the fact that the employment opportunities in industry, commerce, the high-productivity service activities, and the government are controlled by the élite, has led to the development of a clientèle system of recruitment, where merit counts less than the patronage of conspicuous members of the upper class. This phenomenon has often been known to occur in government administration, with the politicians acting as employment agents, but it also happens in the private sector, which has itself developed top-heavy bureaucratic empires. Far from producing strong tensions and pressures, this situation tends to impose an attitude of conformism, which has become a necessary requisite for admission into these employments.

In the case of the professional groups, this conformist attitude is apparent rather than real, being essential for economic and social survival. But since these persons have a university education and a rational approach to social phenomena, deep dissatisfaction with the present state of affairs has ensued, and the need for structural change has therefore become increasingly accepted among them.

Enjoying strong ideological backing; able to keep and even increase their economic power; having almost complete control over the financial mechanisms; controlling a government machinery with enormously increased economic and social functions; having deprived the educational system of its normal function as a mechanism towards social equalization; and having control of employment opportunities and over the information and communication media, it is quite clear that the forces working against reform in Chile are in a very strong position to control the process of social change in such a way that, in spite of its scope and intensity, it has not brought about a radical transformation in the social and institutional structure of the country.

There are at least three additional factors of importance in the process of change which require analysis. One is the influence of the international situation.[15] A second factor is the influence of the Church, and the third is the role played by the army. It is not necessary to go into detailed examination of each of these factors to conclude that traditionally they have on the whole supported the forces which have resisted change.

The army and the Church have been the two principal social institutions concerned with the maintenance of the traditional values of society. Both have an important educational function at the adult level as well as among young people, and both have a far-flung national organization and bureaucracy, through which the exaltation of traditional values is inculcated. The army naturally has most influence among men, and reaches the rural population which has not attended school. The Church has a great moral influence on women, and this has undoubtedly been of political significance since women have been enfranchised. This is an important phenomenon because, at least in politics, women tend to be much more conservative than men. It has been observed

[15] This aspect is examined by Sr. Aníbal Pinto in his 'Political Aspects of Economic Development in Latin America', above, pp. 9 ff.

that in one of the most recent elections the votes polled for right-wing candidates were equally divided among men and women, while in the case of the left-wing candidates the proportion was of four or five men to one woman.

Nevertheless, the Catholic Church in Chile—especially in the last few years—has not been the rigid and extremely reactionary institution which is found so frequently in other Latin American countries. On the contrary, it has become a reformist influence which has tried to emphasize the social doctrines of the Church, and it has shown great flexibility and adaptability to change. The time is not yet ripe to evaluate the significance of this reorientation, but it should be pointed out that the Catholic Church has recently become an outspoken critic of existing institutions.

Looking back at the process of transformation that has been taking place during the last few decades, and at the interplay of the various elements of change and resistance, it would appear that the dynamic forces which emerged from industrialization, urbanization, and the extension of state action have slowly been undermined and eroded by the traditional forces and institutions of Chilean society. They have also been gradually and selectively incorporated into the upper class, and have tended to become increasingly conservative. The traditional structure has become adjusted to new functional requirements and has assimilated the new dynamic social groups, strengthening itself in the process.

The Prospects for Change

The preceding analysis may have given the impression that the possibilities for basic change in the structure of Chilean society are not only restricted but would even seem to have considerably diminished over the last decade. But this analysis is based on many generalizations and abstractions which may not be wholly justified, for every historical model based on certain constant factors and relationships is bound to produce a somewhat fatalistic outlook, since it cannot take into account new factors and relationships which might develop in the future. It is extremely difficult to anticipate the capacity and possibilities for social flexibility. The new forces of change which have been growing during the last decade or so, and which, under favourable circumstances, might produce great transformations in the social structure, are difficult to assess. For example, it is quite clear that the persistent stagnation of the Chilean economy has been producing strong social tensions and economic pressures which favour structural reforms. The large mass of urban and rural workers which are not integrated into Chilean society may constitute important areas of fermentation favouring change. Middle-class intellectuals have also been nursing a growing feeling of frustration.

The international political situation also reveals important changes. United States policy towards Latin America has oscillated between the Alliance for Progress and direct intervention; the interest of Europe in this region is increasing; and the relations between Latin American countries are being re-examined in the light of the movements towards regional economic integration and the pressure for co-ordination with the rest of the underdeveloped world in order to undertake common international economic action in the field of trade policy, as witnessed at the UNCTAD Conference held at Geneva in 1964.

The internal political situation shows one important novelty: the appearance of a strong and growing political movement with a reformist ideology and a progressive political programme. Though supported in the last presidential election by the right-wing Conservative and Liberal parties, the centre-left Christian Democrat Party has come to power with the declared intention of producing a democratic revolution in Chile. Looking at the present political situation without the benefit of historical hindsight, it seems as if a new phase in Chilean political history is being unfolded. It may therefore be interesting briefly to examine the possibilities of achieving the structural changes which are the declared objectives of the new party in power.

These will depend partly on the international political environment and the external economic conditions of the near future, and partly on the domestic policies of the government for internal policies are not independent of the external situation.

On the whole, the international political situation appears to be less favourable than in the recent past. The new United States policy towards Latin America which President Kennedy inaugurated so hopefully has lost its impetus, partly because of the enormous difficulties encountered both within the United States and in Latin America, and partly because of the change in direction after the accession of the Johnson administration. Yet it is also beyond doubt that the traditional premises on which United States hemispheric policy has been based have undergone considerable change and may still continue to favour reformist political tendencies in Latin America wherever these have solid international backing and are not contaminated by socialist ideology. The assumption is based on three observations. (1) The Cuban crisis and the Alliance for Progress produced a departure from the traditional American policy towards Latin America, which had left Latin American policy in the United States in the hands of private economic interests with large investments in that area. Even though economic groups in the United States continue to exert much influence, Latin America is now an area of national, and not simply private, United States interest. (2) The Cuban Revolution has now been isolated from the rest of Latin America, and its prestige as well as its intellectual and political influence among the progressive and nationalist groups has declined perceptibly. (3) The conflict between the Soviet Union and China has had a negative impact on the socialist and communist movements in Chile. This has not only meant an important loss of prestige, but it has also tended to disrupt the unity of the Communist Party, weakening it considerably.

New developments in the Soviet Union seem to be aimed at regaining the unity of the socialist camp. Even if this policy fails and there is no new period of acute Cold War policies, this may offer the possibility of strengthening a 'third position' based on the non-committed countries and the independent policies of some European countries. If this kind of rearrangement evolves out of the present rather confused international situation, Latin American countries will have more room for manoeuvre than they have had in the past. This would be particularly true in the case of Chile. The new party in power has some of the characteristics of an international movement, possessing ties with European Christian Democrat parties. Moreover, since it is not suspect as a pro-communist movement, it has not been frontally opposed by the United States although it has re-established diplomatic relations with the Soviet Union, thus regaining a measure of independence in foreign policy. The development of a new Chilean foreign policy may have an important internal effect, since it could deprive the left-wing parties of one of their most important political platforms. It may also make the Christian Democrat

Party look even more left-wing, since such a foreign policy is identified in Chile with left-wing and nationalist tendencies.

The transformation of Chilean society into a really functioning democracy requires the organization of a dynamic economy which must grow at a very fast rate in order to provide ample opportunities for a rapidly growing population. The very possibility of achieving the social and political objectives of the Christian Democrat Party will depend on the success of its programme of economic growth. In order that high rates of growth may be possible, and that this additional growth does not take the form of an additional concentration of wealth and a growing inequality in income distribution, it would be necessary to effect a drastic tax reform, aimed at a substantial increase in government revenue and at making the tax system more flexible and progressive, and an agrarian reform to redistribute property and income in the rural areas and simultaneously achieve an increase in agricultural production and productivity. The third basic aim must be a large expansion in exports to help achieve high rates of growth without undue reliance on foreign financing. This will require an important reorientation of national policy and also a speeding up of Latin American economic integration and a larger participation in world markets.

It is unlikely that the world economic situation will again produce, in the near future, the extraordinary periods of economic and financial booms which—together with very special internal factors—made the capitalist development of Western Europe, North America, and Oceania possible and successful. One cannot reasonably expect that very high rates of economic growth will be achieved in Latin America and in Chile through the traditional model of capitalist development propelled by some kind of exceptional international economic boom. Whatever the political shape the new development model may take, it would appear indisputable that the state will have to assume the leading role in it. It is true that there is general agreement that development is needed. But many forget that development in Latin America definitely implies structural change, and this type of change is prejudicial to many powerful interests. Policies aimed at bringing about these fundamental transformations will affect private interests and will demand new patterns of behaviour which are compatible with accelerated development. This will not be achieved simply by economic planning but will require a whole new philosophy of the functions of the state, and a thorough reorganization of the ways and means of government action.

For some years now, Chile has been confronted with a formidable challenge. The possibility of facing it successfully will depend very much on the capacity of the new political leadership to understand clearly the nature of that challenge, on its ability to produce realistic, modern, and purposeful answers, on its determination to bring about fundamental changes, and on the choice of a political strategy designed to undermine the pillars which support the traditional institutional structure. Otherwise, as Prince Fabrizio de Salina thought, ' all will be the same, just as it is now: except for an imperceptible change-round of classes'.

[*Osvaldo Sunkel is Professor of Economic Development at the University of Chile and is a member of the research staff of the ECLA Latin American Economic and Social Planning Institute. His main publications include* 'Inflation in Chile: an Unorthodox Approach', *International Economic Papers*, No. 10 (*1960*) *and* 'El fracaso de las políticas de establización en el contexto del proceso de desarrollo latinoamericano', *El trimestre económico* (1963).]

Political Obstacles
to Economic Growth in Brazil

CELSO FURTADO

To analyse the political factors impeding the economic development of Brazil is tantamount to identifying the reasons why that country has so far failed to formulate and consistently follow a policy of development. What particular conditions are necessary to allow development, as a supreme national objective, to prevail over class and group interests in the governance of fundamental political decisions? What exactly is meant by a policy of development?

According to liberal tradition, development results from the action of factors which are inherent in every society, being rooted in human nature itself, and more particularly in that instinct for change which Adam Smith claimed to have identified in men of every era, and which, according to him, causes peoples to find the road to self-development in spite of bad governments. The parameters of liberal ideology—a free labour market, free exchange, the gold standard—were gradually abandoned as a natural corollary of the need to seek more rational *modi operandi* applicable to economic systems of increasing complexity. The idea of an active policy of development only germinated much later as a by-product of the efforts made by various capitalist countries to attain greater economic stability, within the context of anti-cyclical policies. The attempt to determine accurately the conditions for equilibrium in a free-enterprise economy with a highly differentiated productive system and an extremely inequitable distribution of income demanded that a dynamic policy of full employment should be conceived in terms of expanding productive capacity. That is why in mature capitalist economies the so-called policies of stabilization progressively tended to take the shape of policies of development with centralization of responsibility for supervising the functioning of the economy as a whole, for planning its expansion, and for deciding how best to apply stimuli where necessary.

This type of development policy, which may be termed 'classic', is largely coextensive with what Jan Tinbergen has called a quantitative policy, which can be applied successfully where there exists an economic system structurally fit for development. Such is not, however, the case with most of the underdeveloped countries of today, and certainly not with Brazil. In this instance, a policy of development must mean laying the foundations of an economic system capable of expanding; the problem is therefore one of remoulding existing economic and social structures.

When conceived as a strategy for modifying an economic and social structure, the policy of development can only be pursued within a society fully cognizant of the problems that face it, which has worked out a project for its own future, and which has created an institutional system capable of effectively furthering such a project. Clearly, Brazil is a long way from enjoying the several conditions necessary for instituting a policy of development conceived in these terms. The growth of per capita product that she has achieved during the last thirty years is the result of a favourable set of circumstances rather than of policy, while during the whole of this period, the economic policy of the country has been controlled by groups directly concerned to defend their sectional interests.

Industrialization without a Policy of Development

Brazilian industrialization, child of the last three decades, is a typical example of what may be termed development on the basis of import-substitution. Its rapid and precocious growth during the period ushered in by the 1929 crisis is peculiar to Brazil within the Latin American picture. The great coffee plantations formed under the stimulus of the high prices prevailing in 1927–9 started production in 1931 and plunged the country into a crisis of overproduction just at a time when coffee prices had fallen by two-thirds on the world market. Thus Brazil found herself facing a dual crisis: one external, which forced her to cut her imports by half, and the other internal, resulting from the need to finance large stocks of unmarketable coffee. A good idea of the strain involved may be had by considering the value of coffee that had to be bought for stocking or destruction, which in some years exceeded

10 per cent of GNP. This was a policy inspired by the coffee interests, or designed to appease them.[1]

The more the government bought coffee for stocking or destruction, and thus inflated the internal economy, the more the Brazilian currency depreciated in relation to foreign currencies; this process also favoured the coffee-growers, because the price of coffee continued to rise in depreciated national currency even while the world price was steadily falling. The consequences of such a policy were, however, much more far-reaching than could be foreseen at the time. In seeking to maintain money incomes in the country under conditions of declining import capacity, the policy of favouring the coffee sector became, in the final analysis, one of industrialization. For, with the rapid devaluation of the currency, the relative prices of imported goods rose, thereby creating extremely favourable conditions for home production. Since profits in the coffee-cultivating sector were now declining, because the favoured treatment shown by the government only partly compensated for the fall in real value of exports, consumer-goods production for the home market became the most attractive field for investment in the Brazilian economy. In this way capital and entrepreneurship were deflected from the traditional export sector—principally that of the production and marketing of coffee—and channelled into the manufacturing industries. During the period 1929–37 total imports declined by 23 per cent, and industrial production rose by 50 per cent.

The second phase of Brazilian industrialization, that of the post-war years, is no less interesting from the point of view of the policy followed, and the results achieved. In order to protect coffee prices on the world market while there were still enormous stocks in Brazil, the government in 1946 maintained the wartime rate of exchange of the cruzeiro, in spite of the fact that the level of prices had risen far higher in Brazil than in the United States.

[1] With the revolution of October 1930, power passed from those elements directly associated with the interests of coffee into the hands of other, more heterogeneous groupings, supported mainly by the urban middle classes. The interests most directly linked to coffee unsuccessfully attempted a counter-revolution in 1932. Seeking to placate the coffee-growing interests, or at least to take the ground from under the feet of their leaders, the so-called revolutionary government instituted a policy of granting favourable credits to coffee growers and of buying their crops, a large proportion of which was destroyed. In less than 10 years 80 m. bags were destroyed in this way, equivalent at today's prices to more than $3 m.

By then it was known from experience that devaluation of the cruzeiro meant an immediate fall in the world price of coffee, with adverse repercussions on the country's balance of payments. In taking this measure, which meant low prices for imported goods, the Brazilian government completely disregarded the interests of industry, particularly as the Brazilian tariff was 'specific'—i.e. the import duties were fixed in money terms—and in no way geared to price rises on the world market.

The indirect consequences of this policy were unexpected. Imports rose rapidly, exhausting the reserves of foreign exchange accumulated during the war, and leading, as early as 1948, to the formation of short-term debt. Preoccupied with the price of coffee, particularly in view of its increasingly adverse trade balance, the government preferred to introduce a system of import restriction rather than devalue the cruzeiro.[2] In rationing the available foreign exchange, the authorities were in practice compelled to give general priority to the import, first, of raw materials and intermediate products in order to maintain the level of employment in existing industries, and, secondly, of plant and equipment. The import of anything 'superfluous' became extremely difficult. Thus, under cover of maintaining the external price of coffee, a dual protection of industry was created, whereby the import of foreign-made equivalents was virtually prohibited, and the necessary exchange made available for the import of raw materials and plant at subsidized prices. The government's firm adherence to this policy was one of the causes of the marked rise in world coffee prices that was a feature of 1949. Conversely, this rise in prices created conditions which encouraged the government to persist in this policy. In this manner a substantial proportion of the income generated by the improvement in the terms of trade available between 1949 and 1954 was transferred to the industrial sector in the form of deliveries of plant and intermediate products at relatively low prices. In these conditions, and in view of the fact that the demand for finished goods remained inflated, industrial investments were bound to show a rising yield.

[2] Between 1946 and 1949 coffee exports rose from 15.5 to 19.4 m. 60-kg. bags, although production remained stationary at around 16.5 m. During this period stocks held by the government were all used up, creating a scarcity which was in its turn to lead to a sharp rise in prices in 1949. The Brazilian authorities have admitted that by devaluing the currency they could have prevented this rise in prices.

Economic Aspects of Industrialization

It is evident from the above that Brazilian industrialization has been the indirect result of policies inspired mainly by circles closely associated with the interests of the traditional export economy. This type of industrialization was substitutive by nature, since it was supported by a market which had already been created by the export economy. Unlike 'classic' industrialization, which must initially establish itself by keeping down the prices of its products in relation to those of the existing craft products whose market it is designed to usurp, a substitutive form of industrialization has to deal with an economic vacuum created by the suspension of imports combined with a steady level of demand, and this allows it to proceed from the start at a fairly high price level.

The lack of a policy designed to guide the process of industrialization had serious consequences, whose stultifying effects are being felt today. For instance, no proper infrastructure preparations were made for transforming an economy based on the export of raw materials to one based on industry. This problem was rendered all the more serious by the sheer size of the country, and the semi-autonomous development which its principal regions had enjoyed hitherto. The preparation of an infrastructure of basic services requires comprehensive action on the part of national and local authorities, and this could have been possible only within the framework of a policy which laid down new responsibilities for the state in the economic field.

Another result of this lack of a consistent policy of industrialization was the concentration of investment in 'less essential' industries. The less essential a product, the more difficult was its import. It is small wonder, therefore, that sectors producing luxury goods had the greatest attraction for investors. The capital-goods industry in particular had its development delayed for a long time.

No less important was the tendency to over-capitalize and over-mechanize industrial concerns. The generous subsidy implicit in the import of plant and equipment, and the knowledge that huge capital gains could be made by the sale or use of such equipment in the event of this policy being discontinued, encouraged a general trend towards over-investment in plant. Since such investment was preferably made in the less important industries, those sectors developed large pockets of idle capacity, while investment in infrastructure and the basic industries (iron and steel, for example) was allowed to lag behind. In the event, the economic system was badly unbalanced, showing excess capacity in some sectors and inadequate capacity in others. A situation was created where, in order to keep all the available industrial capacity fully employed, the level of aggregate domestic demand (consumption plus investment) had to be kept well above the level of the real income generated by the domestic production; this was done by incurring a substantial margin of foreign indebtedness.

The tendency to over-mechanize had even greater consequences. Disequilibrium at the employee level must be regarded as the most serious problem in underdeveloped economies. It is the inevitable result of the assimilation of a technology borrowed from more advanced economies able to pay much higher wages in terms of capital costs. In underdeveloped economies the wages paid in the industrial sector are kept artificially high owing to a series of social and political factors. This creates a tendency to over-mechanize in accordance with the technology available, which in turn justifies the continuation of a policy of maintaining a much higher wage level than that enjoyed by the vast majority of the population, who are necessarily engaged in other forms of employment. When the relative prices of plant and equipment are artificially lowered (e.g. by foreign exchange subsidy, as happened in Brazil), the prejudicial effects of this tendency are bound to be further aggravated. The major industrial investments realized in Brazil between 1950 and 1960 therefore never helped to alter the occupational structure of the population. During those ten years the number of industrial workers rose by 2.8 per cent per annum, a rate less than that of the population growth as a whole, and less than half that of the urban population growth. Thus the chronic state of underemployment of labour severely worsened during a period of rapid expansion of production. This state of affairs was the outcome of a process of industrialization unplanned and unguided by policy.

Changes in the Social Structure

Industrialization in Brazil was thus a by-product of measures taken to favour the traditional agricultural export economy. However, industrialization produced important repercussions within those institutions upon which the traditional system of power was based.

Brazil's economic system and social structure in 1930 differed little from what they had been in the nineteenth century. Her economy was still based on the export of a narrow range of raw materials, chiefly coffee, and the state revenue was still mainly drawn from taxes levied on foreign trade. Production, whether of coffee, sugar, cacao, or other natural products, was organized on an estate basis, and the estate was still the basic social and economic institution of the country. Some four-fifths of the population was rural, and economically and socially organized around these estates, which were sometimes extremely large, supporting thousands of persons. About four-fifths of the population was also illiterate, and then as now such people were constitutionally without political rights. Those who effectively participated in the electoral process comprised scarcely more than 1 per cent of the total population of the country. For the great mass of the people, the state existed only in its most obvious symbolic forms, such as the person of the President, who to them had merely taken the place of the Emperor. Local authorities, even when forming an integral part of the machinery of federal government, were in effect controlled by the big landowners. There was no secret ballot and votes were controlled by trusty representatives of the local *grands seigneurs*. Finally, a mechanism existed whereby the electoral results could be altered by the central authorities. Thus those who were in power were equipped with all the necessary means to maintain themselves there.

From the point of view of the humble countryman living his whole life on a great estate the only meaning of 'power' was that exercised by the local estate owner. The state as a national political entity had hardly any meaning for the mass of the populace, since its prime function was to finance the military machine and the civil service. Control of the latter was for all practical purposes in the hands of local rulers forming a seignorial class, whose traditionally accepted authority was, as its name implies, based on the ownership of land. Brazil was an oligarchic republic on a seignorial basis. The struggles for power between regional oligarchic factions had been disciplined by the personal writ of the Emperor, who was the keystone of national unity. The republican régime installed in 1889 strengthened the hand of the local oligarchic groupings. However, at this stage, the coffee-growing section enjoyed undisputed pre-eminence, and continued to wield power uninterruptedly for the first forty years of the Republic.

Alongside this essentially stable society, whose system of power merely reflected its patriarchal structure, there grew up a source of instability in the form of an urban population engaged in activities connected with foreign trade, government work, and services in general. This section of the population had more opportunity for education, even higher education, and was much influenced by foreign ideas. It was this class that was most adversely affected by the exchange policy traditionally followed by the government to defend the interests of the exporters. Whenever the foreign market prices of Brazilian exports fell, the currency was devalued and a substantial proportion of the real loss of income was transferred to the importers. Since these urban populations relied quite considerably on imports, even for their food, prices rose sharply in all major cities and towns whenever the country was faced with lowered prices for their exports. Conditions such as these tended to create a feeling of unrest in the towns, which found frequent expression in local revolts. Nevertheless, the urban population was really no more than an appendage of the rural economy, from which, indirectly, it earned its living. The leading strata of urban society were composed for the most part of members of the great landowning families.

Stagnation of the agricultural export sector, concentration of investment in the main population centres, chiefly in manufacturing projects, and, finally, the rapid growth of state activities, combined to cause considerable changes in the social structure of the country whose most obvious outward and visible sign was a rapid process of urbanization. According to the census of 1920 (there was none in 1930), the population of Brazil was about 30 millions, of whom only 7 millions lived in the towns. Today the population figure is up to 80 millions, of which the towns account for no less than 35 millions. Since the urban population has a far higher percentage of literacy than the rural, it is clear that the political centre of gravity has undergone a radical displacement, at least in so far as the electoral process is concerned.

These important modifications to the social structure have not as yet been accompanied by corresponding changes in the political field. Since the process of industrialization has not involved conflict with the old vested interests in the sector of agricultural exports, the country did not give rise to an industrial ideology favouring effective political expression. In some parts of the country, industries arose within the framework of the old agrarian economy and inherited the latter's paternalistic outlook. Thus in the North-East the textile factories were often established in the rural sugar-growing districts or in small isolated up-country towns. In the São Paulo region the course of industrialization was strongly influenced by the large population of European immigrants, who looked upon themselves as being in a foreign country and kept aloof from politics. Thus the necessary historical conditions were lacking for the growth of a true industrial political outlook distinct from that of the other dominant sectors of the population. Industrialists were either linked by common interest to the agricultural economy or else willingly fell into line behind the old experienced traditionalist leaders. In contrast with the 'classic' type of capitalist development, Brazilian industry grew by import-substitution which had been restricted without clashing ideologically with agriculture. This was especially true during the phase of decadence of the coffee economy, whose policy of defending its own income standard and its foreign prices reacted, on successive occasions, to the benefit of the industrialists—either by assuring them a market, or by providing them with plant and equipment at low prices.

Another factor that helped to prevent the emergence of an industrial leadership with an independent political approach was the way in which the working-class movement developed. The social conditions in which industrialization proceeded in São Paulo, with major participation of European immigrant labour from the very start, enabled the establishment of a relatively high level of real wages. As internal communications improved, the labour market tended to become unified over the whole country, high-lighting the disparity between the real wages paid by industry in São Paulo and those paid in most forms of employment throughout the rest of the country, particularly agricultural wages in areas north of the state of São Paulo. Thus an extremely elastic supply of labour and relatively high real wages made the working class from the start moderate in outlook and the trade union movement very weak. Hence it was that, in the absence of any conscious antagonism between employers and workers, a social climate was created in industry similar to that prevailing in agriculture. There

was no need for industrialists to evolve a style of their own which
would have helped to distinguish them from the old class of
big landowners.

Political Consequences of Social Change

It is to this lack of an ideologically inspired and politically
active industrial class [3] that the slowness of progress in modernizing
the Brazilian political system must largely be attributed. Political
constitutions, including the latest drawn up in 1946, have always
been a powerful weapon in the hands of the old agrarian oligarchy
for preserving its own position as the dominant political force.
The present federal system, by granting extensive powers to the
Senate, where the small agricultural states and the most backward
regions wield decisive influence, for practical purposes places
legislative power in the hands of a minority of the population
inhabiting regions where latifundist interests reign supreme. In
the Chamber the number of deputies is proportional to the
population of each state. Thus the greater the proportion of
illiterates in a state, the greater the voting power of its enfranchised
minority; for example, the vote of a citizen living in a state with
80 per cent illiteracy is worth five times as much as that of his
fellow voter in a state that is 100 per cent literate. Since it is in
the most illiterate parts of the country that the landowning
oligarchy is most firmly entrenched, the electoral system obviously
serves to maintain its predominance. Being thus in control of
the legislature, which is the only body entitled to initiate constitutional change, the traditional ruling class occupies a privileged
position in the struggle for political control of the country.

A stranglehold over the main centres of power does not, however,
provide a just and adequate reason why authority derived from
it should be accepted as legitimate by the bulk of the population.
It is because this legitimacy was increasingly being questioned that
the exercise of power by the class consistently remaining in control
of the state was rendered more and more difficult.

The modification of the social structure brought about by
urbanization has created conditions favouring a dominant urban
vote. Although largely thwarted by the mechanism of the electoral

[3] This aspect of the problem has formed the subject of a recent analysis,
based on empirical data, by Fernando Henrique Cardoso in *Empresário
industrial e desenvolvimento econômico* (São Paulo, Edit. Difusão
Europeia do Livro, 1964).

process, the urban vote can still make itself felt in certain exceptional cases of majority voting. These exceptions are important, in the more advanced states, for the election of Governor, and, at the national level, for that of President of the Republic. In this way a state of affairs has been created in which the executive authority may represent the forces that seek to challenge the Establishment as represented by the old oligarchy still controlling Congress. Tensions between these two power centres have tended to grow, sometimes to the extent of virtually paralysing the conduct of government.

What is the nature of the forces from which the groups that have from time to time challenged the ruling oligarchy derive their strength? Circumstances never favoured the formation of an industrial class capable of leading a movement for the modernization of the country. The working class has tended to assume a complacent and compliant attitude rather than take the lead in changing the established structure. Brazilian urbanization was not the result solely of industrialization, nor was it identical with the traditional type of urbanization characteristic of 'classic' industrialization caused by the rapid absorption of factory labour. Industry has absorbed little labour in Brazil, especially since 1950.[4] Brazilian urbanization is a result mainly of rapid population growth, of an extreme concentration in the distribution of income, of the increase in state activities, of the saving in manpower caused by modern agricultural technology, and of sociological factors which operate particularly strongly in countries where there is a pronounced difference in living standards as between town and country.

That part of the rural population increment not engaged in agricultural labour (always a large proportion when export agriculture is not booming) tends to migrate to the towns, where there always seems to be a chance of getting work of some kind. It is in the towns that the bulk of the country's money circulates, including that spent by the ruling agricultural class. Where, as in Brazil, development is accompanied by extreme concentration of income, the market for professional and administrative services

---

[4] Comparing the census figures for 1950 and 1960, it may be seen that the agricultural labour force increased by 4.5 m. persons while that of the manufacturing industries showed an increase of only 435,000. Thus the annual increment was in the former case 3.5 per cent and in the latter only 2.8 per cent.

tends to increase sharply, directly and indirectly absorbing in the process a great deal of labour. Moreover, the great urban concentrations demand large and numerous public works and a disproportionately large growth of the state administrative machinery, which in its turn serves to intensify the process of urbanization. Clearly, such intensification can only be sustained where the production of goods, both industrial and agricultural, increases likewise, and in step. This was the case in Brazil. To give an idea in round figures: while the total population increased at a rate of 3.2 per cent and the urban population at almost 6 per cent, agricultural production increased at 4.5 per cent and manufactures at 9 per cent. It is interesting to note in this connexion that while the urban population increased at a rate of nearly 6 per cent, the corresponding increase in factory employment was less than 3 per cent. Thus the great mass of people concentrating in the towns was compelled to go into non-industrial employment or else remain unemployed, living in the conditions of misery for which large Brazilian towns are notorious.

This urban population, having no definite stratification to give it stability, and bereft of a class or group consciousness that would enable it to act as a coherent whole, came to represent the new decisive factor in the Brazilian political struggle. In this way unorganized masses made their premature appearance in Brazil and produced the kind of populism characteristic of the political conflicts of the last few decades.

Under the conditions prevailing in Brazilian politics in recent years, the very principle of legitimate government necessarily involves a contradiction. On the one hand, the government must, in order to legitimize itself, act in accordance with the provisions of the constitution. On the other hand the President of the Republic, in seeking to fulfil the expectations of the large majority vote which has elected him, will feel constrained to pursue objectives incompatible with the limits which constitutional law allows Congress to impose on his powers. The two principles of legitimate government clash, viz. the requirement to act within constitutional bounds and the requirement to obey the mandate of the public will, whereby the President is placed in the dilemma of either having to renounce his programme or else of finding an unconventional way out, which may even happen through resignation or suicide. One might well argue that a presidential candidate would be better advised to offer a more realistic platform, suitably tailored to take account of the power of those controlling Congress and a great part of the administrative machine. But if he did this, he would simply not be elected; someone else would always come along ready to promise the masses what they want. Because they are inarticulate, the masses have no real opportunity of participating in the political process, except at those moments when votes are exchanged for electoral promises. Considering that these masses, who are underemployed and permanently underprivileged, are impatient to attain the standard of living enjoyed by those earning high and medium incomes, it is not surprising that they are hard bargainers when the moment arrives to cast their votes.

Since the war a direct pact with the masses has been a necessary condition for attaining executive power in Brazil. However, the wider the scope of this pact, the more numerous the obstacles that will beset the maker of it in seeking to execute his mandate; in other words the more suspicious of him and his programme will be the traditional ruling class. The main reason for such suspicion is the ambiguous nature of any populist-based programme, an ambiguity made unavoidable by the heterogeneous nature of the masses which, aggravated by conditions of severe underemployment, forces the populist leaders to enter into compromises with contradictory or disruptive objectives. Unlike political movements supported by class or sectional interests with definite objectives, populism aspires to negotiate with the masses on the basis of promising them satisfaction of their immediate desires, regardless of the long-term consequences. In a situation such as this, any group wishing to proceed along organic lines, either to stimulate a historically determined development or to preserve a certain set of values, is bound to conflict with populist movements. Conflict of this kind has assumed various forms in Brazil, being at the very basis of that political instability which has been symptomatic of the whole phase of industrialization from the start, rather less than thirty years ago.

Power and the Armed Forces

The premature emergence of a mass society [5] opening the way for populism at a stage when as yet no new leadership group had

[5] Cf. the analysis by Francisco C. Weffort, *Estado e massas no Brasil* (Santiago, 1964).

formed that would be in a position to plan and carry out any project of national development, in opposition to the prevailing traditionalist ideology, has been the most important historical factor during the phase of industrialization. Up to a certain point, populist pressure may be regarded as a factor external to the political process; it is only brought to bear in elections for the principal executive offices. The control of government still remains in the hands of the traditional ruling class, which has shown itself capable of absorbing industrial leaders and elements representative of new interests linked to foreign capital. The federal structure and the huge size of the country enhance the importance of regional government centres, and so encourage survival of the old political structure with a paternalistic basis that is mainly latifundist in nature.

The struggle between the leaders of the executive, permanently subjected to pressure from the masses, and Congress, the centre of power of the traditional ruling classes, has been a constant feature of Brazilian politics in recent years and is only the most visible symptom of a deep internal conflict which vitiates the whole political process. Thus the 'developmentalist' pretensions of the executive are translated into plans for public works, investment targets, etc., reflecting compromise with the demands of the masses. In Congress, which has proved apt at assimilating the technique of populist rhetoric, these plans as a rule encounter no major obstacles, and are approved simply as 'authorization for expenditure'. But when it comes to financing the works concerned, Congress behaves very differently, refusing to countenance any tax reform which would effectively increase the government's financial capacity on the basis of a socially more equitable distribution of the fiscal burden. Any attempts at legislation designed to ease the institutional strait-jacket preserving the existing power system or to alter the distribution of income, whether coming from the executive or from a private member, are nullified by the Congress committees. Moreover, all appointments to key positions in the public service have to be discussed and agreed with the ruling political forces, in other words, with the traditional ruling class. In some spheres of decisive importance the executive's power to act is restricted by law. Thus it happens that the organization formulating coffee policy is effectively controlled by the coffee-growing interests themselves, either directly, or via the intermediary of state government representatives.

The federal administration appears at first sight to be an articulated system under unified command. However, closer examination will immediately reveal that this command is in fact divided and subordinated to regional government cadres. Since the regional political institutions are most strictly controlled by the old ruling class, the ability of the central authority to pursue its chosen lines of policy is consistently sabotaged by the obstructive action of local interests. To overcome these obstacles is a costly and difficult business. In 1959 the federal government, in attempting to solve the serious problem of the North-East, with its growing social unrest owing to chronic poverty and periodic droughts, felt it necessary to create a new administrative organization to replace the numerous federal agencies already operating in the area. These agencies were, however, all under the control of local political groups, and it proved almost impossible to wind them up.

The control of the federal administrative machinery by local political groups constitutes a serious obstacle to all attempts at rationalizing this machinery. Moreover, the degree of inefficiency thus induced in the organs of administration emasculates the effectiveness of central government and reinforces regional power centres. A vicious circle is thus created in which federalization of control of the country causes administrative incompetence, but administrative incompetence is a necessary condition for the continuance of the existing system of decentralized power. In some ways, central government can be looked upon as an apparatus for collecting taxes from the towns and the more advanced areas of the country, the revenue from which is used to maintain an administrative machine controlled by and designed to serve the interests of the old ruling class. By this means it has been possible to mobilize the resources of the more advanced parts of the country, primarily the urban centres, to maintain a power *status quo* based on the old latifundist system.

The fundamental conflict between the urban masses, without definite organization and under populist leadership, and the old power structure that controls the state permeates every pore of the body politic in present-day Brazil. The populist leaders, knowing the psychological state of the masses, constantly advocate a rapid modernization of the country by means of 'basic reforms' and 'structural changes'. Meanwhile, effective control of the state remains in the hands of the traditional ruling class which has astutely used populist pressure as a bogy to lure into its web the new vested interests that have arisen with industrialization. The struggle for power between the populist leaders and the traditional ruling class is the crux of a political conflict which tends to thwart every attempt at coherent planning by those who from time to time govern the country. Since all political negotiations are over-shadowed by 'the rules of the game', which all those aspiring to legitimate power are compelled to observe, it is only natural that this political struggle should tend to exacerbate conflict and reduce the area of possible consensus.

The existence of a fundamental schism which stalemates the proper functioning of the basic institutions in which government is vested creates favourable conditions for the armed forces to be the deciding factor, such as has recently occurred in Brazil. Such intervention does not in itself remove the causes of conflict, but it does make it possible to cut the Gordian knot—one way or another. It may serve either to consolidate the traditional power structure by anaesthetizing the masses, or be used to force change on that structure. The second hypothesis is, however, only valid where the prevailing political climate favours a military populism, i.e. where a military coup would involve the accession to power of a charis-matic leader. In such an event, the traditional ruling class, to whom nothing is more frightening than armed populism, is likely to react strongly. The problem therefore returns to square one, and the military leader in question must needs seek the direct support of the masses, since he will be unable to make his power acceptable under cover of intervention. In the first hypothesis, where pressure of the masses is staved off by some soporific device, or suppressed by violence, the intervention of the armed forces can be represented by suitable manipulation of public opinion as being in the true national interest, and defence of this interest easily becomes identified with maintenance of the *status quo*.

One may well ask: can a system of power designed to preserve the *status quo* be conditioned to formulate and pursue a policy of development in a country where development depends on the prior completion of changes in the existing social structure? If the conditions for realizing such a policy are lacking, will this power system be historically viable or will it lead to an impasse as before? In the latter case, is this impasse likely to last a long time, or to invite rapid corrective intervention? The course of Brazilian politics in the immediate future will answer these questions. Meanwhile the Brazilian community has not yet succeeded in creating an institutional system that would permit the transformation of its basic aspirations into positive and viable operational projects.

[*Celso Furtado was Minister of Planning during the administration of President João Goulart. At present he is Associate Professor of Economic Development, University of Paris. His principal publications include* The Economic Growth of Brazil (1963) *and* Dialética do desenvolvimento (1964).]

The Dynamics
of Brazilian Nationalism

HÉLIO JAGUARIBE

THE earliest appearance of Brazilian nationalism was in the guise of 'nativism' after Portuguese colonization of the new territory had become consolidated from about the middle of the seventeenth century. When Portugal was annexed to Spain from 1580 to 1640 the colony of Brazil had to fend for itself, both in financing internal administration and in repelling incursions by pirates and attacks by foreign powers, particularly during the struggles with the Dutch in 1624 and 1654. This state of affairs made the colonists aware of their own capabilities, and of the conflict of interests steadily unfolding between Brazilians (i.e. the settlers, as opposed to the indigenous Indian population) and metropolitan Portuguese.

However the 'nativism' resulting from this new-born consciousness cannot yet be considered as nationalism. Brazilians and metropolitan citizens still felt themselves equally members of the Portuguese nation and loyal subjects of the Crown. There was nevertheless a difference in that the Portuguese themselves looked on Brazil as a country of golden opportunity for rapid personal enrichment or promotion in military or government service, whereas the Brazilian colonists began early on to develop a feeling of patriotism for their new home. The war against the Dutch on the north-west frontier, sustained by the colonists practically without assistance from the mother country, emphasized this development. Furthermore, though firmly rooted in the country, the Brazilians were active in defending their status and their appointment to local posts against the unwelcome intrusion of nominees from Portugal who had the advantage of being within range of the Court, and used to arrive armed with rights and privileges, at the expense of the local inhabitants.

This 'nativism' was exacerbated in the eighteenth century by the conflict of interests between the gold miners and the Portuguese fiscal authorities. At the same time the constant growth of the colony, greatly accelerated by the discovery of gold, offered an increasing contrast to the gradual decline of Portugal after the Pombal renaissance and resulted in the centre of gravity of the Portuguese empire being transferred to Brazil. However, the Crown continued to exert a centralized metropolitan control that was quite incompatible with reality. The arrival of D. João VI in Brazil in 1807 during the Napoleonic wars, and his subsequent decision to remain there permanently and identify himself with the country's life and problems, did much to alleviate the antagonism existing between the former colony, now become the seat of government, and the metropolitan territory, now in effect a province. It was thus inevitable that, with the king's return to Lisbon in 1821 and the demand of the *Côrtes*—established in Portugal by the Liberal Revolution of 1820—to reintroduce a régime of colonial administration for Brazil, this country, which already had its own Crown Prince and complete administrative machinery set up by D. João VI, should rebel against the mother country and declare its independence in 1822.

Meanwhile the sentiments animating the Brazilian people in their bid for independence must still be classed as 'nativism', approximating more nearly to Bahian or Pernambucan local patriotism of the seventeenth century than to present-day Brazilian nationalism. The tensions that had existed between colonists and citizens of the metropolitan territory turned into bitter hostility between Brazil and Portugal. This anti-Portuguese feeling marked the early years of independence, and was to continue in gradually weakening form until the final transformation of 'nativist' patriotism into nationalism since the 1930s.

Nativism in Literature

This 'nativism', founded in a burgeoning feeling of patriotism for the new land that was now a home, and fanned by the conflict of interests existing since the end of the sixteenth century between colonists and mother country, soon found expression in Brazilian literature. The first major work of this kind was the *História do Brasil* by Frei Vicente do Salvador (b. Bahia, 1564), published in 1627, in which the author discusses the contrasts between the colony and the metropolis from a 'nativist' point of view. A century later, when the discovery of gold had brought the country to its apogee, Rocha Pita, born in Bahia in 1660, published his

História da América portuguêsa, a work of less literary and historical merit but characterized by a more accentuated 'nativism', in which Brazilian interests and sentiments are correlated with the vast natural resources of the country.

Glorification of the new country on the basis of its vast size, its natural riches and latent potential was the dominating theme of Brazilian 'nativism' as expounded by authors from Rocha Pita to Afonso Celso,[1] and it is to the latter that we owe the expression of this attitude in its ultimate form, namely, *ufanismo* or 'boastful self-confidence'. This is a form of pre-nationalism whose theme is the idealization of the natural resources of the country, regardless of social and cultural considerations, and divorced from any specific plans for realizing a future great destiny, since this would inevitably come to pass as a natural result of exploiting the country's physical wealth and inherent potential.

Idealization of the Indian as noble hero of the jungle, and esteem for him as ancestor of the modern Brazilian, form another theme of 'nativist' literature, first enunciated by José Basílio da Gama [2] (b. Minas Gerais, 1741) and Santa Rita Durão [3] (b. Minas Gerais, 1717) still in the colonial era. The theme is systematized by Magalhães [4] and Porto Alegre,[5] and reaches its literary and ideological climax in the poems of Gonçalves Dias [6] and the novels of José de Alencar.[7]

While 'Indianism' was a patriotic literary cult that was to evolve in a more modern form to regionalism, as it did in a romantic and idealized way in the work of José de Alencar, *ufanismo*, on the other hand, came to be a serious obstacle to the growth of Brazilian national consciousness. By imprisoning this consciousness within the narrow limits of 'nativism', and by the tendency to exaggerate and idealize the natural environment and resources

[1] Afonso Celso, *Porque me ufano do Brasil* (Rio, 1901).

[2] José Basílio da Gama, *Uruguai* (Lisbon, 1769), an epic poem describing the struggles of the Jesuit missions against the Indians.

[3] Frei Santa Rita Durão, *Caramurú* (Lisbon, 1781), a historical poem telling the idealized story of the love of one of the first colonists for an Indian girl.

[4] Domingos José Gonçalves de Magalhães, *A confederação dos Tamóios* (Rio, 1856).

[5] Manuel de Araújo Porto Alegre, *Colombo* (Rio, 1866).

[6] Gonçalves Dias, *Primeiros cantos* (Rio, 1846); *Os Timbiras* (Leipzig, 1857).

[7] José de Alencar, *O Guaraní* (Rio, 1857); *Iracema* (Rio, 1865).

of the country, for a long time it prevented the intelligentsia from forming a critical appreciation of the process of national economic and social development. Conversely, it led to the substitution of the external symbols of nationality, such as the flag and the national anthem, for the true task of nationalism, to foster and maintain the individuality and autonomous development of the nation, a state of mind still rife among the more conservative elements of the population, particularly in the armed forces.

The Process of Development

The economic and social development of Brazil up to the middle of the present century [8] falls into distinct phases of unequal duration: the colonial era lasting from discovery in 1500 to the abolition of the slave trade in 1850; the semi-colonial period from 1850 to the collapse of the one-crop system of coffee cultivation in 1930, and the period of transition from 1930 to the deliberate industrialization of the 1950s. To these must be added a fourth phase, beginning in 1961, which is characterized by the structural crisis of the nation.

During the colonial era the growth of the Brazilian economy followed the pattern typical of colonial structures, being externally governed by the European demand for its products: brazil-wood and other natural products in the sixteenth century; sugar and hides in the seventeenth; gold in the eighteenth. Moreover, since Brazilian production was at this stage based on slave labour and did not, therefore, generate any internal circulation of wealth, economic growth resulted not from the accumulation of internal revenues, but from mere aggregation from abroad, and from the export proceeds of new units of production which, in the final analysis, meant more slaves.

With the abolition of the slave trade [9] in 1850 the growing gap between the demand for labour and the available slave force was steadily filled by European immigration. The Brazilian economy,

---

[8] Cf. Celso Furtado, *A economia brasileira* (Rio, 1954), ch. iv and *Formação econômica do Brasil* (Rio, Fundo de Cultura, 1959), pt. 5; Jaguaribe, *Desenvolvimento econômico e desenvolvimento político* (Rio, Fundo de Cultura, 1962), ii. 143 and 195.

[9] The Eusébio de Queirós Act of 1850 made illegal the trade in slaves and their import while not, however, changing the status of those slaves already in Brazil. Slavery was not formally abolished in Brazil until 1888.

though still deriving its stimulus to growth from outside demands for its plantation products, began to be supported at home by a mounting population of wage-earners who, as consumers of goods, created a modest but increasing process of internal circulation of wealth.

The essential feature of the semi-colonial phase, from 1850 to 1930, was an exclusively one-crop and hence a narrowly-based economy. The natural productivity of Brazilian coffee cultivation was such that no other sector could show a comparable return. This led the country to concentrate on coffee production and import practically everything that it needed from abroad.

Two events proved fatal to this semi-colonial economic system. The first of these was the rise in Brazilian coffee production to a point where it exceeded the world demand, with a resulting fall in prices and accumulation of unsaleable stocks. The Convention of Taubaté (1906) established a definite hold-back quota binding on Brazilian coffee producers, and restricted export to the level of demand. These measures served to maintain prices, and ensured a few more years of precarious life to a system that was already moribund. The depression of 1930, with its drastically reduced demand, gave the system its *coup de grâce*. Coffee prices fell from 40 to 8 cents a pound, bringing the whole semi-colonial economy down in ruins. Coffee cultivation at the prices then obtaining no longer provided the most attractive sector for capital investment, and the drastically reduced yield of exports could no longer pay for the needed imports. There was thus a double incentive for Brazil to start her own production of goods hitherto imported.

Import-substitution was directed towards the light processing industries, textiles, clothing, and foodstuffs, and was concentrated in the region of São Paulo, which had attained the greatest economic density by the end of the semi-colonial era. The rapid growth of an import-substitution industry in São Paulo as part of a process which anticipated the real crisis of 1929 [10] led in the 1930s to the regional 'take-off' of this state, enabling it to give impressive evidence of its self-sufficiency during the insurrection of 1932.

[10] This anticipation was in part due to the previous effort at substitution occasioned by the dislocation of regular international trade during the First World War, and partly by the policy of investing the surplus from coffee production in local consumer industries, which were involuntarily protected from foreign competition by a series of devaluations of the national currency.

Controlled Industrialization

The corrective action introduced by the growth and development of these substitute processing industries necessarily involved a correspondingly increasing demand for imported intermediate products. After the rapid and ill-conceived exhaustion of the foreign credits accumulated during the Second World War, the country found itself facing a new and even more serious balance of payments crisis. The demand for imported goods could not now, however, be reduced, serving as it did the needs of the newly developed industrial complex.

Reacting to this new exchange crisis the country embarked on a fresh programme of import-substitution under a deliberate policy of industrialization, aimed this time at the manufacture of intermediate products. Through the Import-Export Department of the Bank of Brazil (CEXIM) a rigorous control was introduced over the use of such scanty foreign credits as existed, to the virtual exclusion of all consumer goods. Priority was given to the purchase of plant and equipment for the manufacture of intermediate products, and to measures for maintaining the flow of imported raw materials required for existing industry.

Meanwhile the country was becoming increasingly conscious of its economic problems, and this new awareness was shown both in the actions of its leaders and in the expansion and steady sophistication of economic and social studies. Brazil now realized that she was an underdeveloped country, that her structure was in transition, and still bearing the stigmata of semi-colonialism. Alongside this growth of economic sophistication there arose a desire to plan things properly, a will to adopt rapid, but soundly conceived, measures to overcome this underdevelopment by a policy of systematic and concentrated investment in the infrastructure and in basic industries. This was the moment of birth of conscious Brazilian nationalism.

The period from 1945 to 1960 constitutes a remarkable leap forward in the joint evolution of the nation and of the national self-awareness. From the traditional, naïve outlook which typified the Dutra government (1945–51) to the acute awareness and firm deliberation shown by the second Vargas government (1951–4) in reshaping the structure of Brazilian society, and to the decisive and systematic approach of the Kubitschek government (1955–61), was after all but a few years' span. Nevertheless, in this very brief period the country did more to develop an understanding of itself and to bring about a planned and effective change in its own structure than in the whole of its previous history.

Rise of the Middle and Industrial Classes

Politically, the period between the collapse of the semi-colonial system and the 'take-off' to development from the springboard of the Kubitschek régime can be divided into two distinct phases, spanning the periods 1930–45 and 1945–60 respectively.

Whereas on the economic side the first phase represented the unconscious and unplanned ousting of semi-colonialism as a result of the measures taken to substitute imports, the political hall-mark of this phase is the rise of a middle class. The product of an urbanization that preceded industrialization, it lived in a semi-colonial society composed of two prime divisions: one the ruling class of plantation owners and their urban counterparts, the import-export merchants; the other the rural subject class. The Brazilian middle class was essentially marginal in that the technical and administrative services needed by such a society were extremely modest; nevertheless, it was this class that constituted the enlightened and thinking element of the population, providing such public opinion as then existed. It was from its ranks that the officers of the armed services were recruited.

The system whereby the proprietary classes fitted the middle class into the scheme of things without in any way altering its marginal status was the policy of patronage exercised through, and as a buttress to, the *Estado cartorial*.[11] The essence of this system consisted in a bargain whereby patronage was accorded in return for the promise of support. The state served to foster and protect the existing régime, and at the same time provided the necessary number of sinecures to ensure the political support which the ruling class would otherwise have lacked, and which it needed in order to preserve its economic and political control of the country.

---

[11] The term is derived from the old colonial notaries public whose functions and status have remained almost unchanged to the present day, and who have a legal and sociological importance which goes far beyond that of their Anglo-Saxon counterparts. For a further analysis, see Jaguaribe, *O nacionalismo na atualidade brasileira* (Rio, ISEB, 1958), pp. 40 ff., and 'Política de clientela e política ideológica', in *Ensaios* (Rio, CNT, 1951).

The crisis of the semi-colonial system resulted in a basic disparity between the expectations of the middle class and the ability of the Brazilian patricians to satisfy them by dispensing patronage; a gap rather analogous to that which developed between the country's essential need for consumer imports and its ability to finance them with its coffee export earnings. The Vargas revolution of 1930 and the 'progressivism' of 1934 represented the political counterpart of import-substitution: the country, no longer able to import the consumer goods it needed, started to produce them at home. The middle class, finding its livelihood and well-being no longer assured by the old system, itself seized power and assumed control of the *Estado cartorial*.

This parallel process of substitution, both economic and political, was not conscious or deliberate. In assuming control of the state, the middle class considered that it was acting in good political faith, in support of electoral integrity and administrative morality. Official posts, regarded as a natural perquisite of the middle class, were increased in number to accord with the requirements of this class without in any way altering the structure and system of government or the country's general productive system.

So it was that a dual relationship developed between, on the one hand, the productive process and the proprietorial class which still controlled it on the traditional principles of a liberal economy, and, on the other, the political process and the middle class which had assumed control of the government by revolutionary means. The apparatus of government continued apparently to serve the class that controlled the economy, while in fact it looked after the needs of the middle class, which asked no more than guaranteed state employment.

This contradiction, which the Brazilian patrician order had failed to overcome by force of arms in the counter-revolution of 1932, proved in the long run detrimental to the middle class, which similarly proved itself incapable of resolving it. Had the Brazilian middle class of the 1930s had the social-historical sense exhibited, for instance, by its Egyptian revolutionary counterparts in the 1950s, it would have been able then and there to use the apparatus of government, suitably reorganized for the purpose, to bring about a deliberate and rapid transformation of the institutional structure of the country.

However, the generation of 1930 was the heir of a traditionalist semi-colonial past and was spiritually imbued with European *fin-de-siècle* liberalism. At the same time, with normal constitutional government re-established by the constitution of 1934, the ruling political class of the time fully realized that if it were to put into practice the political ideals for which it had itself striven— universal suffrage and secret ballot—the inevitable result would be the resumption of power by the patrician order whose rural dependants far out-numbered the urban middle class in voting power. Thus the middle class found itself in the peculiar position of wishing to control the state without altering the existing social and economic structure, and of being compelled by considerations of *Realpolitik* to jettison its political principles with the anti-democratic coup of 1937 and the setting up of the *Estado nôvo*.

It was during the second phase in the transformation of its semi-colonial structure that the country became aware of the revolutionary feeling that had been fermenting within its borders since the late 1920s and which received a fresh impetus after the Second World War. The Brazilian middle class, which had controlled the government during the first stage of this process without realizing its existence, faced the dilemma of trying to direct the destinies of the state without being able to take any positive steps to change the actual economic and social structure. Unable to reach a viable decision, it lost its revolutionary impulse. Viewed against this background, the socio-political perceptiveness of the leader of the middle-class movement, Getúlio Vargas, is all the more remarkable: during the final two years of the *Estado nôvo*, when the régime was ideologically and operationally bankrupt, he already understood the nature and scope of the Brazilian revolution before the new intelligentsia had even succeeded in formally analysing it.

Despite the unanticipated and rudderless course of its evolution, Brazilian society nevertheless discarded its semi-colonial traditionalist character during the 1930s in order to evolve into a transitional phase directed towards economic autarky and national development. Import-substitution had given the country the largest manufacturing capacity in Latin America and had caused the emergence, as its social concomitant, of a new urban working class. Moreover, the *Estado nôvo*, notwithstanding its petit-bourgeois limitations, had, without premeditation but none the less effectively, used its proto-fascism to promote the growth of national stature and to protect the country from foreign interference. The old Brazilian patrician class, bereft of political power and compelled by the crisis to give up its exclusive reliance on coffee exports, gave way under the influence of the pioneering spirit introduced by European immigration to an industrial bourgeoisie which was qualitatively different from the farming and mercantile bourgeoisie.

It was against this background that Getúlio Vargas, appreciating the lessons learnt from the Second World War and viewing recent internal developments from a fresh angle, reversed the policy of his government. The strong man of 1937, who had so nearly aligned Brazil with the Axis powers, realized that international fascism was moving towards irrevocable defeat. Internally he realized that the traditional Brazilian middle class, its revolutionary motive power spent, no longer enjoyed the conditions essential to its continued role in buttressing the machinery of state. He likewise appreciated that the future course of national development must henceforth depend on industrialization supported by the two newly emergent forces: the industrial bourgeoisie and the urban working class. Finally, he considered that the formal apparatus of government could well be made to serve a totally different policy from that hitherto pursued during the critical period of transition. It is clear that Vargas, astute politician that he was and determined at all costs to remain in power, must also have realized that his only chance of directing this next stage of his country's political advance was to take the initiative and anticipate events by changing the régime before such change was forced on him by public opinion and resulted in his own downfall.

Although Brazilian historiography is reluctant to appreciate this point of view, the fact remains [12] that during its last two years of existence the *Estado nôvo*, under the guise of constitutional continuity, was actually engaged in a revolutionary attempt to replace the traditional middle class as the foundation of the pyramid of state by the urban working class.

The military coup of 1945, though ostensibly aimed at doing away with fascism and establishing democracy, was in fact an instinctive defensive reaction by the more conservative elements of Brazilian society against a process of change, exemplified by the recent transformation of the *Estado nôvo*, of which they were

[12] Cf. 'O golpe de Agôsto', *Cadernos do nosso tempo* (Rio), Jan.–Mar. 1955.

not altogether aware. To the ranks of the innately reactionary landowning and mercantile aristocracy was added the middle class, which had itself become conservative with the passing of the years and was now the compliant satellite of its erstwhile foe. This alliance thought it was attacking the old Vargas; in reality it was attacking the new.

However, the extent to which Vargas's preliminary revolutionary measures were not unsuccessful is shown by the fact that five years after his deposition he was re-elected to power by massive popular vote. The subsequent course of events bore out the basic assumptions of his policy, which postulated the alliance between the industrial bourgeoisie and the urban working class, and the establishment thereby of the political supremacy of the nationalist progressive front resulting from it.

Nationalism and Development

The second stage in the process of accelerated industrialization, from the transitional interregnum of the Dutra régime to the second Vargas and the Kubitschek régimes, witnesses the victorious ideology of nationalism and development firmly implanted, supported socially by the alliance of the industrial bourgeoisie and urban working class, and economically by the establishment and growth of basic industries.

The conservative coalition· which had ousted Vargas in 1945 partly benefited and partly suffered from the Janus-like nature of the *Estado nôvo*, but its victory was extremely short-lived. Once Vargas had been deposed, the impact of his message on the mass of the people extinguished once and for all the proto-fascist image, which he personified, of the early *Estado nôvo*, and highlighted the new industrial and working-class outlook which he had come to represent at the end of his régime.

The election of Marshal Dutra in 1945, despite his conservatism, was made possible by the support of Vargas, exemplified in the famous slogan *êle disse* (literally: 'he said'), and effected in opposition to the specifically anti-Vargas candidature of Brigadier Eduardo Gómes. This was a trend that was to become more clearly marked later with the subsequent electoral victories of Vargas and Kubitschek.

The main feature of Brazilian society during this period of rapid change was its division into two very distinct groups completely cutting across class boundaries. On the one side were all those sectors of the population desirous of building up the nation as an independent and autonomous entity, and consciously and deliberately doing all they could to promote its economic development in the full understanding that this implied the end of the semi-colonial structure and its replacement by national self-determination. The ideology of these sectors was thus guided by the twin lodestars of nationalism and development. Ranged on the other side were elements having a vested interest in preserving the *status quo*, committed to maintaining the semi-colonial structure and underdevelopment of the country, and at the same time determined to keep Brazil dependent on the Great Powers of the Western world and in the Cold War.

The elements forming the first of these broad coalitions comprised the industrial bourgeoisie, the managerial and technical sectors of the middle class, and—rather incongruously—some peasant groups. The second included the farmers and merchants, the middle-class elements in the civil service, the 'populist' strata in the *Lumpenproletariat* which had not yet attained class consciousness, and the traditionalist groups among the peasantry.

It fell to the lot of the Brazilian intelligentsia to interpret Brazil anew in the light of historicism, post-Keynesian economics, and Mannheim's sociology, and, on this basis, to formulate a new theory of their country's development, and the ideology for putting it into effect—*o nacionalismo desenvolvimentista*, or the doctrine of developmental nationalism.[13] The discovery of the community of interests shared by all dynamic elements of Brazilian society in opposition to the protagonists of a semi-colonial and underdeveloped *status quo* was a powerful inducement to form a common nationalist-development front. This same awareness contributed decisively in the political sphere to the alliance between the *Partido Social-Democrático* (PSD) and the *Partido Trabalhista Brasileiro* (PTB).

The results of the effort for national emancipation and development that could be perceived towards the end of the 1950s were

[13] The most representative of these new intellectual movements was the Itatiaia Group, formed in 1952 and composed of sociologists, economists, political analysts, historians, and philosophers. In 1953 they founded the Instituto Brasileiro de Economia, Sociologia e Política (IBESP), which publishes the review *Cadernos do nosso tempo*, and in 1956 the Instituto Superior de Estudos Brasileiros (ISEB).

most satisfactory. With a population of 65 million and a 3.5 per cent rate of population growth—one of the highest in the world—Brazil had succeeded by her own efforts in almost surmounting the hurdle of underdevelopment and entering into the full 'take-off' phase. This she had done while preserving her democratic system, her ideals of individual freedom, and her sense of human values. During that period she was able to resist, virtually unaided, pressure from powerful international oil and power cartels. She had managed to transform her outmoded semi-colonial and dependent economic structure into one with a marked capacity for autonomous expansion. Her annual per capita income had risen to US$340, which was not far short of the symbolic figure of US$400 laid down by the United Nations as the boundary line of underdevelopment, and the development currently in hand in the infrastructure (such as roads, electric-power networks), in the basic industries (as represented by the USIMINAS, Ferro e Aço, and COSIPA projects already nearing completion), and in plant and machinery production, gave ample promise of a steady continuation of this process of economic growth, which was achieving an average effective rate of growth of over 6 per cent per annum, or approximately 3.5 per cent per head of population.

It is true that the Kubitschek government, after proving its capacity to carry out the *Programa de Metas,* (literally: 'target programme'), and enjoying its hour of glory with the inauguration of Brasília, went into a sharp decline. Financially, it showed itself increasingly unable to curb the inflationary spiral. Politically, it failed to produce from the ranks of the PSD-PTB coalition a candidate truly representative of the concept of national development and likely to inspire public confidence in its continuity. Meanwhile the predominant feeling in the country was one of well-being and of confidence in the nation's capacity and destiny. It was at this juncture—in 1961—that the election of Sr Jânio Quadros, scion of a political faction traditionally hostile to developmental nationalism but undeniably chosen by wide popular acclaim, struck a discordant note as perplexing as it was ambiguous. It seemed as if the Brazilians, with their national development not yet consolidated, were slipping back to the sterile adoption of moral postures or, even worse, sacrificing their hard-won victories in favour of a return to semi-colonial status and humble dependency on the Western powers.

The smug satisfaction of the reactionary circles who had supported and financed the election of Jânio Quadros did not last long. Once in power, President Quadros soon showed that he meant to put into effect his plans for reshaping the foreign policy of Brazil strictly in accordance with his electoral platform. The main deficiency of the developmental system built by the Kubitschek government lay in its foreign policy, where the spirit of mannered and subservient diplomacy had still persisted. President Quadros took the necessary measures to bring Brazil's foreign policy into line with the remaining aspects of national development, formulating and putting into execution an independent policy of co-operation with all states, free of commitment to any one bloc, and directed primarily to national development, to the closer integration of Brazil with Latin America, and to the determined defence of peace.

Furthermore, setting aside his preconceived aversion to economic development and to the techniques for its purposeful establishment, Quadros quickly saw the need to put this already ten-year-old policy of national development on a more systematic and better planned basis. To this end he set up a National Planning Commission. Thus it was that the first few months of President Quadros's régime saw his full conversion to the precepts of developmental nationalism.

In spite of all this, an analysis of the situation of Brazil since the Quadros régime shows clear symptoms of an impending crisis. Inflation, for instance, has reached proportions that make conventional monetary remedial measures ineffective or self-defeating. The economic barometer fell with a recession of the per capita national-product growth in 1962 and a further fall from 1963. Politically this was reflected in an increase of social tensions which resulted in the break-up of the alliance between the industrial bourgeoisie and the urban working class, and the failure, on the party-political level, of the coalition of the PSD and PTB.

Making due allowances for the influence of various contributory factors, such as political unrest culminating in the overthrow of the Goulart government and, in the economic sector, the further deterioration of the balance of trade in 1961 and 1962, the crisis now afflicting Brazil and temporarily halting her development is clearly of a structural kind. It also seems incontestable that this structural crisis in the developmental process stems from an aggravation, too great to be righted by spontaneous readjustment, of the more serious strains resulting inevitably from that process.

The strains in the social, economic, and political life of the country arise in the final analysis from a dual discrepancy. The first consists in the pronounced disequilibrium of development between the industrial-urban and the agricultural-rural sectors, and, conversely, between the Central-South region and the rest of the country. The second discrepancy lies in the lack of correspondence in the country as a whole between its economic development and the evolution of its political institutions.

The first discrepancy is marked by the growing and damaging disequilibrium between urban-industrial advance and rural-agricultural backwardness, as also between the rapid progress of the Central-South region, where industrialization has been concentrated, and the relative stagnation of all other parts of the country. The spontaneous industrialization that was a feature of the import-substitution period of 1930–45 and the controlled industrialization that followed were not accompanied by any corresponding movement in the rural economy. The Brazilian rural world thus remained at a stage of underdevelopment under a semi-feudal régime of land tenure and production. This prevented agriculture from reacting positively to the stimulus of home market prices, which were constantly rising owing to the widening gap between urban demand for foodstuffs and the available supply. This lack of flexibility in agricultural production began to hinder the development of the urban economy, first because rural consumption of industrial products remained static, and secondly because of the sharp upward trend in agricultural prices without any appropriate reaction from the suppliers.

The second discrepancy, between the economic advance of the country as a whole and its political evolution, proceeds like the first one in a vicious circle. This rural backwardness affects the body politic not only, as in most countries, by exercising a conservative and traditionalist pressure: in the particular case of Brazil it anaesthetizes the machinery of government with its policy of patronage, which is why the Brazilian state still remains a *cartorial* administration. This in turn ensures the immutability of the semi-feudal agricultural system which generates the conditions necessary for the continuance of the régime.

As has already been mentioned, the policy of patronage was a pre-ideological process of mobilization of interests based on the purchase or exchange of jobs in the public service for political support. Dating from the earliest beginnings of colonization, and with its roots in the social order of estate owners and landless peasants working for them, this policy in its primary form consists in the congregation around each *grand seigneur* of a following of dependants in a relationship rather like that obtaining between the Roman *paterfamilias* and his circle of protégés. The landowner receives the votes of his clientèle either for himself or, more usually, for his political candidates, and in return dispenses favours, mainly in the form of government employment, pulling the strings as required through his political contacts. In a secondary form of this process, local followings are co-ordinated to control the political machine of the state and, in a still more advanced tertiary form, the federal administration itself. The final result is a solid organizational pyramid, for which the bartering of political support in exchange for favours dispensed through the state administrative machine serves as the bricks and mortar. Hence the *Estado cartorial* functions on similar lines to the old colonial Chartered Companies. The purpose of its existence is not to carry out and provide public services, but to dispense administrative favours and provide for the sustenance of hangers-on as many posts, many of them sinecures, as the budget will stand.

The process by which rural backwardness serves to preserve the predominance of the patronage system in the general political governance of the country causes the gravest distortions throughout the whole life of the nation. One of the most important of these strains is caused by the structural disequilibrium between revenue and expenditure in the public sector. Hence the continuous condition of deficit of all states and municipalities and, on a still larger scale, of the Union itself. The direct consequence of this public deficit is structurally endemic inflation. From a figure of 20 per cent per annum during the Kubitschek régime, the cost-of-living index rose to 80 per cent in 1963, and in 1964 generated a monthly rise in the cost-of-living index of 5 per cent.

Another type of distortion observed, this time in the political sphere, has the effect of stifling the country's economic development in that its essential governmental and public duties are improperly performed. These duties fall into two distinct classes: those connected with the planning, promotion, and control of the productive services of society, and those connected with watching over the judicial system and the general administration of public services. What is required in the first case is that the right conditions should be created to assure future and continuing development and, in the second case, to give a guarantee of a general level of efficiency appropriate to an advanced society. In both cases the Brazilian administrative machine is prevented from giving proper attention to these two essential requirements by the anaesthetizing effect of its residual *cartorial* character.

The inefficiency of the state as a guardian of justice and purveyor of public services is shown by inadequate police protection for its citizens and by such tardy working of the judicial machine that there is now no point in seeking legal redress except in the gravest cases. The same sorry tale is true of all the routine public services: street-cleaning, public health, postal and telegraph services, and the like.

The ineffectiveness of the state in promoting and controlling its productive services, despite undeniable progress in the planning sector, is manifested by its failure so far to co-ordinate their activity and output in proper relation to planning. This produces a sharp divergence between production planning and practice with consequent loss of overall efficiency, and frequent under-capacity output from individual units of the planned production complex.

Disintegration of the National Front

The structural crisis just analysed exacerbated the internal contradictions that existed, as in any coalition of different classes, within the ranks of the national front. The urban working class, its bargaining position substantially strengthened by growing membership and superior trade union organization, began to demand larger and more frequent wage readjustments to offset inflationary erosion, and to seek a larger say in economic and social policy and even in the actual management of business and industrial concerns.

The national bourgeoisie was no longer benefiting from an inflation which had ceased to boost its investment capacity as rising costs had moved faster than prices, with the consequent reduction of profit margins. In this disagreeable situation, having to face competition with steady or falling foreign prices and embarrassed by an unrealistic rate of exchange and diminishing financial support from the public banks, this group was becoming increasingly unwilling to make concessions to the working class.

The middle class in its turn was subjected to two conflicting pressures. The traditional strata of the petty bourgeoisie—the small traders and the *cartorial* echelons of the armed forces and civil service—who had long resented the continual whittling away of their status differential as a result of economic development, and who were not equipped, as the urban working class were, with the necessary weapons for safeguarding their salaries against the effects of inflation, were driven to desperation and were ripe for insurrection. On the other hand the leading echelons of the middle class—qualified technicians and administrators—to whose benefit economic development had operated, while favourably placed as compared with the petty bourgeoisie, were none the less victims of the decelerating rate of growth and of inflation. The fact that this new technocratic middle class had only recently acquired a very superficial ideological consciousness made it the more receptive to the feelings of resentment of the traditional petty bourgeoisie; and in spite of itself it also found itself influenced by the revolutionary morality of the upper middle class.

With the economy slowing down and the schism in the national front growing wider, neither President Goulart nor the political and social leaders of the country's progressive forces were able to see a way out of the impasse in which Brazil now found herself.

The most important single factor preventing a regrouping and reorientation of the national front was the left-wing estrangement that involved the directing echelons of the trade union movement, the radical left-wing elements, and, with them, the Goulart administration.

Though his choice of terminology was polemical, the late San Tiago Dantas, when Minister of Finance in the Goulart government, produced a neat definition of the cleavage by describing as 'negative Left' that segment of the popular forces which, under the leadership of Deputy Leonel Brizola, had veered to the Left in a process of growing radicalization, and as 'positive Left' that other segment, of which he himself was the most representative leader, whose declared aim was to preserve and consolidate the alliance between the urban working class, the new technocratic middle class, and the national bourgeoisie on which triple foundation the national front was built.

The 'negative Left' was so named because it presented its social demands in terms inconsistent with the requirements of development: (1) increasing the consumer capacity of the masses at the expense of the national investment capacity; (2) demagogic disruption of proper work discipline to the detriment of efficiency in industry and state administration; (3) dogmatic and unrealistic insistence on nationalization of the means of production, so driving the national bourgeoisie into the reactionary camp. Conversely, the 'positive Left' was characterized by its attachment to policies designed, within a framework of nationalism and democratic reform, to reconcile social justice with economic expansion, allowing in the process ample common ground for the interests of the urban working class, the national bourgeoisie, and the new technocratic middle class.

If instead of the somewhat contentious appellations 'negative' and 'positive' Left, we were to use the purely descriptive expressions 'étatist Left' and 'developmental Left', we should be applying to the two wings of the bipartite Brazilian Left adjectives that fit them better.

The 'étatist Left' was supported by the better organized sectors of the people: trade unions, student bodies, the other-ranks and ratings associations of the armed forces, peasant leagues, newspapers and—despite the opposition of their leaders—the rank and file of the Brazilian Communist Party, and it achieved a clear predominance over the 'developmental Left', which was virtually stripped of popular support. Deputy Brizola, apart from his undoubted powers of organization and leadership, was also the brother-in-law of President Goulart, and in this capacity he was able to manipulate the machinery of state to his own personal ends.

Given such a set of circumstances, President Goulart, party leader but no statesman, excellent tactician but poor strategist, gifted with keen political intuition but bereft of practical know-how, showed himself incapable of controlling events and of reconciling short-term advantages—which he was always adroit in securing—with the longer-term interests of his government—which he was wont to sacrifice to the expediency of the moment.

Thus he was successful in his manoeuvres to assume power against the armed resistance of the former service ministers of the

Quadros régime after the spectacular resignation of its leader.[14] He was equally successful in the tactics that he subsequently employed to persuade Congress to advance the date of the plebiscite on the re-establishment of the presidential system from 1965 to January 1963. In spite of these successes President Goulart failed to produce a government that inspired confidence in its administrative capacity and political balance. He staked everything on a compact programme of major reforms involving constitutional amendments and complicated legislation against the mounting opposition of Congress, an opposition which he sought to overcome or by-pass by increasingly spectacular appeals to and preparations for ever more radical extra-legal manoeuvres.

This line of conduct on the part of President Goulart was not so much deliberate as spasmodically assumed in an effort to stabilize the administrative and political foundations of his government. It led him ever further towards the 'étatist Left'. His links with the forces of conservatism broken, Goulart was drawn irresistibly in the wake of Deputy Brizola despite his constant struggle with the latter for supreme leadership of the popular elements, and this only served to hasten his radicalization.

In his quest for popular support, without the compass of a party discipline, without the chart of an ideology to guide him, President Goulart was forced to be always farther to the Left than Brizola in a sterile and doomed attempt which rapidly overtaxed his powers of political endurance.

The next most important single factor contributing to the break-up of the national front in the conditions already discussed was the schism caused by systematic anti-communism, which spread from the more reactionary ranks of the upper class and the petty bourgeoisie to engulf the new technocratic middle class. The latter thus found themselves, as it were, reinforcing the interests and ideological viewpoints of the former.

Systematic anti-communism is a politico-social posture which identifies communism with absolute evil, by virtue, presumably,

[14] This resignation was *per se* a gesture of frustration made while in a state of depression but partly aimed at arousing a wave of national protest on whose crest he hoped to be re-elected with full powers. In fact, however, it did no more than anticipate a military coup which was already well under way. On this point see the present writer's study on the resignation of President Quadros in the *Revista brasileira de ciências sociais*, Nov. 1962.

of the historic atheism and materialism of Marxism and of the Bolshevik doctrine of revolutionary violence. A second feature of systematic anti-communism, which it shares with anti-Semitism, is to overestimate beyond any reasonable bounds the capacity for action and co-ordination of 'international communism'. Most of the ills of contemporary existence are, hence, attributed to communist infiltration. Finally, systematic anti-communism nurtures the belief that all things which run counter to the interests and beliefs of the propertied classes are the work of communism, and all people who oppose the perpetuation of class privilege, imperialism, and colonialism, must necessarily be communists or fellow-travellers.

In semi-colonial and underdeveloped countries, where by virtue of such structure the ruling classes necessarily act as the proconsuls of dominating foreign interests, so forming what we may term a 'consular bourgeoisie', the doctrine of systematic anti-communism is almost bound to flourish as the only way by which this class may rationalize the social-historical function it exercises. It provides an indispensable ideological support for the *status quo*, whereby all attempts at re-channelling the economic process to the nation's own benefit and away from the coffers of the mother or tutelary country and of the local consular bourgeoisie must unquestionably be labelled as communist-inspired. The stagnation-inducing effect of systematic anti-communism may, however, be neutralized if there grows up within the ranks of the ruling classes a new and distinct sector which does not concern itself with the export of raw materials or the import of manufactured goods but which produces for the home market and so becomes solidly identified with national development. This new sector is the national bourgeoisie, and its petty bourgeois counterpart is found in the technical and administrative echelons staffing the new enterprises whose establishment is an integral part of development, a sub-sector which we know as the 'new middle class'. The formation of this new sector and its associated sub-sector introduces a growing distinction between communism and the nationalist popular movements, which are treated as if they were the same thing by systematic anti-communism. As the nation gradually develops and its leadership moves from the 'consular' to the national bourgeoisie, the former begin to appreciate this distinction to the point at which it is apparent even to them that their anti-communist views are no more than a rationalization of the defence of foreign interests.

This stage of the unmasking of systematic anti-communism was reached in Brazil immediately following the suicide of President Vargas. The emotional impact of Vargas's sacrifice, victim as he was of a typical systematic, anti-communist intrigue during a phase of Brazilian development in which the national bourgeoisie was in the process of taking over the reins of leadership from the traditional ruling classes, made it crystal-clear to all sectors of the population that the accusations of subversion and corruption made against the Vargas government were no more than the arts and stratagems of the forces of reaction seeking to block the process of national emancipation and development.

It was thanks to this exposure of systematic anti-communism in its true colours that President Kubitschek was enabled to quell the insurrectionary attempts made during his régime (Jacaré-Acanga and Aragarças) and to continue his policy of development throughout the whole of his term of office. This also made it possible for President Quadros to put an end to Brazil's traditional position as a satellite and launch an independent foreign policy. Finally, it conditioned the circumstances in which the attempted coup, after President Quadros's resignation, by his service ministers against the accession of Vice-President Goulart failed to rouse public support and proved abortive.

All the more striking, therefore, is the exhibition of immaturity on the part of the national bourgeoisie and the new middle class and of incapacity on the part of their leaders in permitting themselves to be so much upset by the foolish left-wing radicalism rampant in the Goulart régime that they were led to readopt the discredited platform of systematic anti-communism. It was this estrangement of systematic anti-communism in the panic caused by 'étatist Leftism' that prevented the opposition to this latter doctrine from being correctly formulated, that is, within the context of national emancipation and development plus political and social democracy. Instead the opposition to 'étatist Leftism' became identified with the interests of the 'consular bourgeoisie' and tainted with the stigma of reaction and satellitism.

The Alternatives before Brazil

The studies of economic development conducted since the 1930s on the basis of the macro-economic principles of the classical economists and Marx were carried far beyond the boundaries of economic science. They covered an area in which all the social sciences overlapped. It was beginning to be realized that development is a total social process whose political and cultural aspects are no less relevant than the economic aspects. The construction of models of economic and political development [15] based on the analysis of the process of development resulted in the growth of a well-nigh unlimited confidence in the ability of man to programme the development even of societies—such as those found in Latin America, Africa, and Asia—still remaining in a state of marked economic backwardness. If to the optimistic notion that development can be deliberately promoted is added the new attitude adopted by the highly-developed countries—albeit within the context of peaceful East-West competition—whereby increasing efforts are made to assist the economic progress of backward countries, the algebraic sum so obtained represents the measure of confidence felt internationally in the probability of a rapid economic and social evolution of the world's more backward regions.

However, it would seem that recent events should make us view this social-humanistic optimism with considerable reserve. For the creation of the means for deliberately promoting the development of backward countries is coinciding with an irreversible trend towards a new international rigidity deriving from the widening gap between ordinary national societies and the super-powers which are enjoying tremendous relative advantages in their ability to profit by the second industrial revolution, based on cybernetics and nuclear power. The United States, the Soviet Union, and Common Market Europe, into which Great Britain and the countries of EFTA must inevitably be drawn, already constitute three centres of economic, cultural, political, and military polarization tending to share world leadership between them. China, despite the tremendous gulf at present separating her from super-power status, and the increasing Soviet resistance to her development, seems already assured of becoming a fourth super-power before the present century is out.

In these circumstances two prime considerations would seem valid. The first is that the development of the world's backward areas will from now on increasingly tend to be influenced by the

15 Cf. Jaguaribe, *Desenvolvimento econômico*, vol. i.

pressures generated by each super-power within its own geopolitical sphere of influence, making it impossible for such areas to develop autonomously and independently. The second point is that potential candidates for super-power status have only a limited time in which to achieve it. There is a more or less fixed historical time-limit that must be observed under penalty of absorption into the spheres of influence of the super-powers already consolidated.

Historical precedent shows that it used to take Great Powers of any era two or three generations to attain that status: bearing this in mind and allowing for the much faster pace of modern historical change, it is clear that countries like India and Brazil have little time left in which to prepare themselves for graduation to super-power status. It is likely that the last two decades of this century will decide the relative positions of the various countries during the first half of the twenty-first century. If, therefore, India and Brazil have not by then reached the minimum indices of economic, cultural, social, and political development necessary to resist the pressure of existing super-powers, and so to preserve the conditions for subsequent endogenous and autonomous progress, they and their fellow societies of South Asia and Latin America will inexorably be drawn into the spheres of influence of the present super-powers: like other countries before them they will cease to exist as national entities, economically and politically.

Problems and Perspectives

The main conclusions to be drawn from the present study of Brazilian nationalism, the problems by which it is presently beset and the future courses open to it, are as follows.

The first concerns the present crisis of nation and nationalism in Brazil, which arises from the incompatibility of the institutional structure of the country with the demands of national development; from the internal contradictions of the national front aggravated by the recrudescence of inflation and the slower pace of development, which has caused the urban working class and the national bourgeoisie to adopt diametrically opposed and mutually irreconcilable positions. The ascendancy achieved by the 'étatist Left' towards the end of the Goulart régime dealt the death-blow to national front unity, and drove the national bourgeoisie and the new middle class into the arms of the 'consular bourgeoisie', under the banner of systematic anti-communism and in defensive alliance with the forces of imperialism.

The second conclusion to be drawn is that nationalism, which only makes sense when it serves to promote national emancipation and advancement, is also a necessary condition for economic development. Without the impulse of nationalism and the framework of a national state as prime mover and controller respectively of the national society, the latter's internal contradictions will act as a brake on its development, and render it helpless against the external pressure of the Great Powers.

The third conclusion is that the supremacy enjoyed by the interests and ideology of the 'consular bourgeoisie', upheld by military support, has inevitably a degrading effect and makes for stagnation. There exists no conservative or rightist solution for the development of a society emerging from a semi-colonial form in a world divided among super-powers possessed of limitless cybernetic and nuclear resources because Rightism and conservatism imply the preservation of privileges incompatible with the universalization of political and social democracy or with national self-determination. Consequently the traditional ruling class can neither effectively harness the country's internal economic potential nor base its exercise of power on the political and social consensus of the nation.

The fourth conclusion is that keeping Brazilian society stagnant and bereft of autonomy under a régime of open or veiled political and military oppression must lead (but has not yet led) to the creation of a significant revolutionary movement of the extreme Left. The possibility of such a movement erupting into violent popular revolution is directly related to the degree of economic and social stagnation prevailing and of the amount of political and military oppression exercised. It would, however, be naïve to imagine that social tension in Brazil will be allowed to rise indefinitely without foreign intervention. After the lesson of Cuba, it is difficult to imagine that the United States will allow the formation of another extreme left régime in Latin America without intervening directly and openly.

Even assuming that the revolutionary forces were aided by the Soviet Union (despite the latter's tacit agreement with the United States for non-intervention in each other's spheres of influence) this would make Brazil the battlefield of yet one more local war, and utterly destroy her chances of national survival.

The only way to extricate the country from its predicament is to reconstitute the national front in such a way that the causes that produced its break-up are removed, and to allow a fresh alliance to be formed between the national bourgeoisie, the new technocratic middle class, and the urban working class.

For this there are three prerequisites. The working class must be assured of a continuing share in the national wealth and the widening of opportunities for education and advancement to the top levels of the society. The national bourgeoisie must be assured of a continuing freedom of enterprise, certain sectors of the economy being reserved to them free from the threat of nationalization and immune from foreign control. As regards the new middle class, the fundamental condition for reconstituting the national front is the reincorporation into it of the armed forces, who are at present estranged by systematic anti-communism and converted by the loss of their historical and social *raison d'être* into a sort of praetorian guard in the service of imperialism and the 'consular' bourgeoisie. Only by a radical change in the present *cartorial* outlook of the armed forces through the establishment of a system of effective national defence comprising a small but highly trained military force, armed and equipped by Brazilian national industry and in no way dependent, even for training, on imperialist aid, will it be possible to restore the national ethos of the Brazilian armed forces and reconvert them to the tenets of the nationalist movement. Ultimately, the national destiny of Brazil will be determined by the ability of her statesmen to achieve these basic prerequisites rapidly, while there is still time to do so by popular consent.

[*Hélio Jaguaribe de Mattos, formerly President of the Cia Ferro e Aço de Vitoria, founded the Instituto Superior de Estudos Brasileiros. He is now Visiting Professor of Government at Harvard University. His principal publications include* O Nacionalismo na atualidade brasileira (1958), Desenvolvimento econômico e desenvolvimento político (*1962*).]

Violence and the Break-up of Tradition in Colombia

ORLANDO FALS BORDA

THE stubborn nature of Latin American conservatism has often baffled social scientists as much as those primarily concerned with seeing the promotion of progress and reform. It is discouraging to note how relatively few real changes have taken place in the region during the last decades, and how the superficial change produced has, as a rule, served to reinforce traditional and often obsolete structures. Colombia has been singled out as a concrete case of such conservatism, and it is worth while examining more closely the nature of Colombian institutions, especially in historical perspective, in order to discover any intrinsic causes for this. Is the stabilizing mechanism to be found in the peasantry, or in the system of land tenure? Must political action for reform started in the city spread inevitably to the countryside in order to ensure its lasting success?

The success of domestic political action appears to be intimately related to the social values and attitudes of the people in whose name such action is taken, or at least to their latent or manifest collective goals. Political acts such as the promulgation of laws are not, therefore, enough to ensure their being implemented or understood, something learned early during the Spanish conquest and occupation of the Latin American continent. The nature of beliefs, the local traditions and ways of life, and the informal structures of society actively condition the actual working of politics, furnishing in this way a framework for statesmen; in theory, at least, the more political action acknowledges and adapts itself to local customs, the better it succeeds.

Tradition may, on the other hand, become a burden, and the existence of such historical predicaments usually generates social processes of different kinds. Successful political action must also be attuned to these new trends. Two such processes in Latin America are industrialization, which has found ample support in existing economic structures, with many laws favouring its development, and secularization, which has found expression in various circles and which, though it has enjoyed little overt support from political bodies or from the law, constitutes a powerful engine for change under the surface, thanks to its capacity for permeating basic institutions.

This essay will document the survival, in Colombia, of colonial attitudes and conceptions of life that can be included under the idea of 'the sacred' (as used by Howard Becker—not in the religious sense). More specifically it will focus on (1) the interference of 'the sacred' in certain contemporary social processes, and (2) the continued existence of an ethic of 'other-worldliness'. It will be suggested that these elements present important obstacles to political action of a secular nature, aimed at promoting modernization and development. 'Modern political action' will be used here for collective attempts to gain or use, through wider social participation, the control of power to promote change in harmony with contemporary views of the secular order.[1]

The essay will also explore the hypothesis that the appearance of violence in the countryside in Colombia since the late 1940s has been an irrational but effective political response to efforts to preserve essential aspects of the same old 'sacred' order, but that the effects of this response have been vitiated by the tendency to institutionalize violence. This has warped further modern development, and has, possibly, laid the foundation for a counter-movement of potentially great strength.

The Interference of 'the Sacred'

The social structure that emerged from Spanish colonial policy was, as a whole, of the closed type. This is understandable in the context of contemporary Spanish society which was authoritarian

---

[1] The 'sacred-secular continuum' theory, elaborated by Howard Becker, is based on the different structure of values found on the one hand among traditional, isolated, family groups in rural areas, and on the other among urban peoples where social relations are more complex and take on a secondary nature with a tendency towards self-reliance in man. Values in 'sacred' societies revolve mainly around beliefs and attitudes towards the supernatural and the ordained. See Howard Becker and Alvin Boskoff, eds., *Modern Sociological Theory in Continuity and Change* (1957), pp. 133–85. For the concepts of political development and modernization see S. P. Huntington as cited by Merle Kling in *Social Science Research on Latin America*, ed. by Charles Wagley (1964), pp. 194–6.

and hierarchical. All communities in the Spanish colonies hinged on the Church and the *ayuntamiento*, or municipality, as foci of activity. Most of them were mission centres for Indians, called *reducciones*, where the final word on behaviour and control was that of priests and *corregidores*.[2] Even though they were appointed and paid by the *encomenderos* (persons who received from the King of Spain the right to levy tributes from the Indians, in exchange for which they were required to catechize and 'civilize' them), the priests in practice dominated the local communities, gaining undivided loyalty and often the affection of the Indians. This is important to understand, for, in the subsequent conflicts between *encomenderos* and missionaries, the missionaries won. The *encomienda* system began to be abolished as early as the second half of the sixteenth century.

According to accounts, in many parts of Colombia *encomenderos* and priests became powerful lords whose word often carried more weight than that of the civil officials. One outcome of this was the emergence of a theocracy in which the priest's policies were as a rule more readily acknowledged and carried out than those of the civil authorities. Another result was the establishment of channels of political power by landowners. At the regional level, this development helped to bring about the alliance of Church and state which was the basis of the whole New World venture, and produced momentous consequences in colonial times. In the case of Colombia it proved to be effective in times of crisis, such as the *Comuneros*' revolt of 1781, when the Archbishop of Bogotá personally intervened to prevent rebellious peasants from overthrowing the civil government; two years later the Archbishop himself was appointed viceroy, thus formalizing those theocratic arrangements that appeared to be important for the colony's normal development.[3]

In many communities where such values survive, especially in the Andean mountains, the citizen often finds himself torn between the authoritarian tradition of the colony and the framework of his relatively new political institutions which require a fuller basis

---

[2] Fals Borda, *El hombre y la tierra en Boyacá* (Bogotá, 1957). The *corregidor* was one of the highest civil officials in the Spanish colonial bureaucracy.

[3] Cf. José Manuel Groot, *Historia eclesiástica y civil de Nueva Granada* (Bogotá, 1889); Fals Borda, *Campesinos de los Andes*, 2nd ed. (Bogotá, 1962), pp. 236–8.

of so
find
attitu
is m
'missi
comm
serva
the g
or th
innov
institu
vested
the la

The
policy
and p
ideolo
justific
well-in
tection
run, h

on big names or *caudillos* for their smooth fur
efforts could perhaps have been more success
with this colonial survival.

The paternalistic syndrome is also affe
ment campaigns in Colombia, a polic
in 1958 to foster basic democratic
people through co-operative in
movement must create self-reli
of constructive self-govern
which shifts from the C
started. The conclus
of the changes
Colombia:

The most i
and behavi
peasant
salute

élite; the Indians were given protection against members of the
élite, but the élite was vested with the final authority in all matters
civil or religious.[6]

Owing to cultural inertia, certain modern groups tend to behave
in the same paternalistic and condescending way towards the
mestizos who today constitute the majority of Colombia's population. Examples of this include: the organization of important
enterprises headed by eminent persons to tackle the educational,
housing, and trade union problems of the country; or the survival
of paternalistic traits in modern factories in Medellin, Cali, and
Bogotá; or the imposition on rural communities of school-
construction blueprints designed by urban-based national federa-
tions; or the obsolete organization of political parties that depend

---

[4] Andrew Pearse, 'Estudio de Tenza', unpublished monograph (1964) in the
Social Research Section, Faculty of Sociology, National Univ. of
Colombia, Bogotá.

[5] See, for instance, Juan Friede, *Problemas sociales de los Aruacos* (Bogotá,
1963); B. Haddox, 'Religious Institutions of Colombia', unpublished Ph.D.
dissertation (1962), Univ. of Florida, Gainesville.

[6] Fals Borda, *Campesinos*, pp. 233 ff.; the same author on 'Education in
Colombia', in A. C. Wilgus, ed., *Contemporary Colombia* (1962).

ctioning. These
ul if unencumbered

cting community develop-
started by the government
procedures and to educate the
centives. To be effective, such a
ance in local leaders and a new sense
ment in the communities, the centre of
hurch to the school once the process is
ons on a significant case may be indicative
sought through community development in

mpressive changes are those related to peasant personality
our. The farmers are no longer those resigned and ignorant
who took off their hats when the master met them and who
d with reverence and fear. Now they are men in the total and
structive meaning of the word, men who know how to act with
dignity as well as to request and to command. Because they become
convinced that they can shape their own destiny, that they are capable
of doing things, that they do not have to depend any more on
arbitrary *gamonales*, masters or government officials.[7]

Naturally this transformation is viewed with suspicion or
resisted by leaders of the traditional type, who would rather
maintain their cultural and economic monopoly and behaviour
control than see the rise of a new type of local democratic leadership that might compete with them. Thus social and economic
development and modern political action are not fostered in
communities where the paternalistic syndrome is still in force.
Present-day *mestizos* do not have the same mental and social
outlook as their Indian ancestors and they have gone some way
towards absorbing a secular Western culture in which man is
increasingly self-reliant and able to handle technical and scientific
concepts. The insistence on treating *mestizo* workers, clerks,
and peasants as primitive Indians to be saved, or as minors,
is a survival of the attitudes of colonial aristocratic rule. Community leaders, especially politicians, who still adopt such an
attitude unwittingly create barriers between themselves and the
people, and weaken their own power to give an impetus to change.

[7] Fals Borda and others, *Acción comunal en una vereda colombiana*
(Bogotá, 1961), pp. 60–61.

The Ethic of Other-Worldliness

The second survival from colonial 'sacred' attitudes militating against modern political action in Colombia is the ethic of other-worldliness. This constitutes a formidable problem in many regions, where it prevents the emergence of an awareness of the importance of economic problems and of the achievement of better living conditions in the present world.

It is not necessary to dwell on the Weberian thesis about the relationship between religious beliefs and economic attitudes. A puritanical ethic was not introduced into Colombia until after Independence, and it then found its best exponents not among a Protestant minority but among the deeply Catholic Antioqueño group.[8] Yet in most areas of the country the 'sacred' society went on to insist on the importance of life in the hereafter, which served, as a by-product, to make people resigned to suffering, passive before life's opportunities, and politically subdued.

According to some scholars, passivity as a philosophy of life in Latin America came with the Conquerors, who brought with them not the redemptive, positive Christianity of the Spanish mystics but the resigned suffering of the Christ of Tangiers, a marginal saint that was to fill many niches in Colombian churches.[9] This insistence on the acceptability of suffering as something to be rewarded by God explains in part the traditional resignation of some social groups, especially of peasants, in religion and politics. Such an attitude is one result of complete trust in God. 'The Lord giveth, the Lord taketh away.' A good crop this year, a bad one next, all fits the wondrous pattern of the will of the Lord. The consequent behaviour is that of negative stubbornness, a lack of desire to improve conditions, especially if this effort goes beyond a very low limit of physical, mental, and financial capacities. Instead, *campesinos* are content to leave such matters to God's supernatural forces, and they find it easy to evade specific issues. For example, they believe that epidemics are sent by God, and for that very reason man should not try to prevent them. This was the prevailing attitude during the foot-and-mouth scare of

[8] See especially Max Weber's *The Protestant Ethic and the Spirit of Capitalism* (1930), where he attempts to isolate the religious components that stimulated the development of capitalism in Europe, and particularly through Calvinistic teachings. For Colombia see E. C. Hagen, *On the Theory of Social Change* (1962), pp. 363–78.

[9] J. J. Mackay, *The Other Spanish Christ* (1933).

1950 when the national government ordered all cattle to be vaccinated, but the peasants of certain regions did not take the trouble. As they explained, 'This disease may be the will of God'. After all, is not the whole problem in the hands of God? Epidemics are not threats that can be averted; they are simply a matter of course, almost sacred.

Owing to this combination of the 'threat of hell' with practical earthly guidance from the Church, many peasants have become a docile flock of believers. By surrendering responsibility and initiative to the Church, they give the appearance of being lazy and exhausted. Fortunate peasants, perhaps, these *campesinos*, for they are quite clear about how to get into the other world on the right side, and are sure that they will be eased into it by the Church and its ministers. This feeling of assurance should make them among the happiest peoples in the world, probably on the same level as the Tibetans. Yet the path to salvation presented to them is thorny and winding, heavy like the very Cross of Jesus. The amazing aspect of this spiritual development is that the peasants have accepted almost cheerfully their obvious earthly suffering. This is their cross; it is part of the bargain of life. Suffering is life, and life is suffering. And thus the peasants, anaesthetized by religion, put up with their physical distress.[10]

Needless to say, the breaking of this passive rural ethos is of strategic importance in starting a cycle of social, economic, and political change. Fortunately, there are signs in Colombia that it is being broken—in spite of traditionalist opposition—through the incidence of social factors such as technological innovation, the revolution in communications, and the spread of an integrated market economy. Here again, Spanish society has done much by fostering the important economic development of colonial times that converted primitive cultures into truly peasant civilizations. But the changes which resulted were limited. The basic institutions remained identified with the past, and consequently they remain rather ineffective at the present time. Modern political parties and action are difficult to organize and maintain within social structures where such a passive mentality is still paramount.

Violence and the Passing of 'the Sacred'

The break with tradition can take dramatic turns, especially when the structure of society is rigid and the channels of social

[10] See Fals Borda, *Campesinos*, pp. 224–7.

mobility become clogged. The 'closed society' was part of the heritage of colonialism in Colombia. It survived the Wars of Independence, and was not seriously challenged until the turn of the century, when the industrial revolution found a sure foothold in Medellín and a new entrepreneurial class with political potential began to be formed. During the 1920s the technological and secular trends gathered momentum, and their full impact on Colombian society was felt at the time of the Liberal take-over in 1930. The Liberal Presidents Enrique Olaya Herrera, Alfonso López, and Eduardo Santos promoted a number of reforms in important aspects of national life, including education, university organization, Church and state relations, labour movements, social security, fiscal policies, and land use and ownership. These new policies were of such importance as to provoke serious resistance among Conservative groups, and the political atmosphere of the nation became charged.[11]

The political conflict between the relatively left-wing Liberals and the Conservatives became acute during the presidency of Mariano Ospina Pérez. Then the Liberals found a genuine leader in Jorge Eliécer Gaitán. In a sense, Gaitán personified social change and the secular revolution, and his challenge was widely feared by those who felt that the best course of action for Colombia was to keep her cherished traditions, including political, economic, and ecclesiastical relationships. The situation was frankly pre-revolutionary, with much mass agitation, even in the rural areas—which was unusual—and with an intelligentsia actively engaged in examining and criticizing the state of the country. The people increasingly saw in Gaitán a leader who could achieve the desired transformation, especially since he did not belong to the traditional aristocracy. In this way he became a political symbol of the new Colombia.[12]

The Gaitán movement grew stronger almost daily in the face of the opposition of the Conservative government. By 1948 it was evident that the Liberal leader would be elected President of the Republic in the 1950 elections, thus returning the Liberals to power and opening the gates to the much feared flood of reforms. Enthusiasm and discipline were maintained until Gaitán was

---

[11] J. D. Martz, *Colombia: a Contemporary Political Survey* (1962).
[12] Cf. Antonio García, *Gaitán y el problema de la revolución colombiana* (Bogotá, 1955).

killed on 9 April 1948. His assassination has remained a mystery. Not even a special commission of Scotland Yard specialists invited to Colombia for the purpose was able to solve the mystery. Many people sought to solve the problem by asking themselves who benefited most from Gaitán's death. Not the Liberals, although the centre and the old guard were not entirely pleased with his programme. Judging by the results of the upheaval that followed the assassination, the plan to impose the election of the Conservative Laureano Gómez as President, and the consolidation of a minority as a government party, it can be argued that those who reaped the greatest immediate benefit from the murder were those persons and groups who were trying to stop the Gaitanista movement. After 1948 counter-revolutionary measures to neutralize the Liberal secular drive and restore the previous socio-political balance were the order of the day.

The momentum of the Gaitanista movement was nevertheless so strong that the futile attempt to restore this previous balance led to rural and urban unrest. It was countered by the use of violence by government forces, including the police; this soon stimulated the formation of the first guerrillas. These groups were primarily concerned with self-defence, particularly among the peasants, but many of them also had the political aim of taking over the government and implementing Gaitán's policies.

Thus violence was first used by the anti-reformist forces, as an instrument of repression. The Liberals replied with violence. According to the authoritative Guzmán report, a mistaken political strategy had brought the parties to a head-on collision. It led to an electoral campaign in 1949 in which the main issues were the entrenchment of the Conservative Party in power with the violent exclusion of the Liberal opposition; the use of the police in a systematic campaign of persecution, undoubtedly conceived and executed by the inner government circle; and the declaration of civil resistance by the persecuted Liberal Party. The logical and inevitable consequence was the *Violencia*.[13]

In a sense, the use of violence in Colombia, and in some other Latin American countries, had acquired respectability as a necessary element in informal politics. Violence, as the exercise of

---

[13] Germán Guzmán and others, *La Violencia en Colombia* (Bogotá, 1962–4), i. 43. See also Fals Borda, 'The Role of Violence in the Break with Traditionalism; the Colombian Case', *Trans. 5th World Congress of Sociology* (1964), pp. 21–31.

physical coercion to achieve personal or group ends related to the use of power, had been acceptable by reference to so-called 'patriotic interests', or ideological or religious aims. Hence violent uprisings or revolutions could be justified within this informal framework. The last violent cycle in Colombia started in this traditional manner, but soon the use of violence could not be held within reasonable bounds and it got out of the control of the political leaders who had sought to use it and became a monster of malfunctioning based on unanticipated structural faults and cleavages. A new political phenomenon was in the making: the violent rise of a people without ideology or vision, with petty motives, emotional, cruel, and blind, leaderless and disorganized, caught unprepared in the midst of transition. This new kind of violence has been termed 'total conflict' or 'conflict of annihilation' —the *Violencia*.[14]

Several issues were at stake: the enjoyment of power and the use of public finances, the use and control of land, the defence of local and regional political chieftainships and organizations, the traditional supremacy of the Church—in a word, the survival of vested interests with deep roots in the 'sacred' past. Most of the people had favoured change in such social institutions whilst Gaitán was still alive. They had been moving away from the traditional heritage: a new nation was in the making. But with the charismatic leader gone, with frustrated hopes and expectations, those accumulated energies went wrong, leaving a wake of destruction. Colombia's contemporary strife thus appears to be a spontaneous—and in part undesirable—outlet for the social revolution frustrated in 1948 by the assassination of Gaitán. Despite the efforts made to rationalize and organize the revolt, it remained formless, becoming a confused expression of predominantly personal conflicts: an irrational weapon of distorted politics.

In effect, the *Violencia* that followed 1948 was made or directed by people lost in the pursuit of the immediate, with only a dim vision of the great changes that could have been achieved, and without the mystical support of a patriotic ideology. They were people who remained as they were, poor and ignorant, because they brought little but poverty and ignorance into that undignified conflict. With their energies spent in vendettas and sex crimes, the

[14] Ibid. p. 26; Guzmán and others, i. 376–81.

peasants, bereft of competent leaders, were unable to take the next step towards the social revolution that they unconsciously desired. The revolution was frustrated, in spite of stimulation from outside groups, by the use and abuse and, finally, by the routinization of brute force.[15] The common people, by some sort of fiendish action, had been led to identify their enemies among their own neighbours and relatives, not among the members of outside groups, and mainly on the basis of political allegiances. Nevertheless the latent socio-economic issues that had cracked the traditional structure soon erupted, though in devious and abnormal ways.

It is difficult to establish at what point the routinization of violence displaced the mystique of the Gaitanista movement among peasant groups. Field research, difficult to undertake on this subject, has unearthed some interesting facts which demonstrate the power of survival of their previous reformist aims. For one thing, displaced communities tended to reorganize themselves on a socialist or communal basis, with mutual aid and common use of land predominating. This pattern, however, slowly reverted to the general system of private ownership, especially when the conflict abated and the peasants sought legal title for their plots. Nevertheless these groups attached great importance to collective action, to the point of formalizing its expression in the 'laws' promulgated by several bands and groups of guerrillas.[16] Previously, individualism had been stimulated in traditional peasant society. Today co-operatives of a new type have emerged to pool local resources for the transportation and marketing of agricultural products in the affected areas.

Persecuted rural groups initially turned to paternalistic leaders to ensure survival, but soon this traditional leadership was displaced by younger elements not burdened by too many memories of the 'sacred' past. On the contrary, most of them had grudges against the old system and became guerrilla fighters. In due course they gave way to a third type of leader, emerging from the so-called 'children of violence', who grew up since the *Violencia* started. Their emergence merits some attention. According to the Guzmán report,

the new type of criminal is above all uprooted. He starts by substituting the norms which ruled his conduct before for others adapted to

15 Guzmán and others, i. 371.   16 Ibid. ii. 71–74 and 92–96; i. 138–9.

the new conditions of violence. Thus in the first place he breaks the binomial man-and-land relationship which is vital to the peasant. He does not cultivate the land. . . . Consequently he loses the idea of the farm as something capable of anchoring him or of giving him internal peace, security, or permanency. He turns itinerant, vagabond. His extra-legal situation makes him unstable. . . . In the third place, the criminal turns to precarious environments, very different from his home environment, that induce him to become instinctual . . . with sexual anxiety and pathological tendencies. . . . He loses also the conception of the road as an integrative element of peasant life, and turns to . . . unsuspected, hidden paths. . . . He loses the traditional religious attitudes . . .[17]

These children of violence considered themselves victims of traditional society, which had paid little attention to their needs. Initially they had suffered the impact of the disaster in their own families or communities. Some of them have been of the Robin Hood type, implementing a rudimentary redistribution of wealth and imposing taxes on the rich to help the poor, which in itself is unusual in Colombia.

This new leadership of rural violence also found a way to break the rigidity of the 'sacred' society to which they had belonged, and instituted their own special channels of social mobility. For instance, they established their own ranks of officers, issuing titles of generals, colonels, captains, and the like, a development inconceivable in normal times. Through the *Violencia* these persons achieved new ways of governing or of controlling their own destinies, impossible in traditional society. Displaying an impressive amount of resolution, some of them were even able to establish 'independent republics'.[18]

Conditions of conflict, particularly those stemming from guerrilla action, and certain types of activity such as social welfare and public relations, which were incompatible with the basic pattern of previous society, served to promote a more complex division of labour. In many areas the mechanistic type of social solidarity was duplicated by social solidarity of the organic type, heralding the passing of 'the sacred' and the coming of the secular and modern order of society.

[17] Ibid., ii. 327–30.
[18] Camilo Torres Restrepo, 'La Violencia y los cambios socio-culturales en las áreas rurales colombianas', in Asociación Colombiana de Sociología, *Memoria del Primer Congreso Nacional de Sociología* (Bogotá, 1963), pp. 124–6.

The *Violencia* also ended the isolation of many rural communities, bringing them deeper into the stream of national life. The old traditions could not hold after the ecological boundaries were down, and migrations and displacements were essential for survival. Such hitherto unprecedented mobility enabled peasants to compare their situation with that of other—often more favoured—socio-economic groups. New ammunition was thus provided to implement old Gaitanista precepts, and a class consciousness which would have been unthinkable in 'sacred' times began to develop.[19]

In their unusual role of perpetrators of violence, the government and some civic and ecclesiastical institutions fostered in the peasantry a deep mistrust of their intentions and programmes. These institutions were the formal representatives of traditional society and direct conflict with them could only hasten the transformation of their image in the eyes of the peasantry. One aspect of this, already referred to, was the weakening of traditional leadership, now viewed with suspicion and often hatred. Support of leadership could no longer be based on sentiment or tradition but had to be based on a more rational motivation of common interests and needs.[20] Moreover schools and libraries counted for a great deal in the minds of guerrilla fighters and other aroused groups. The first thing they built in their new domains was not, as formerly, a church but a school; and one of the group usually volunteered as a teacher. Education soon became a most valued goal, a cultural symbol of the new era of which Gaitán had spoken.[21]

In this way the foundations of traditional 'sacred' society were once again made to undergo the kind of transformation initiated in 1948. Change has been brought about in unusual circumstances, in an atmosphere of war, conflict, and crime, with strong organized opposition by Conservative governments anxious to maintain the *status quo*. Under these circumstances change could hardly fit into the existing framework of Colombian society, and would produce incongruities and abnormalities. This fact may be at the root of the aggressiveness with which the process of change appears to be associated in Colombia, aggressiveness likely to

[19] Ibid. pp. 104–6.
[20] Ibid. p. 111.
[21] Guzmán and others, i. 139 and 267; ii. 338–9.

erupt when it is recognized that aspirations which are considered normal under different circumstances are frustrated.[22] The peasants found a means of expressing their desire for social transformation only in these, often aberrant, practices. Their action was, in a sense, political, but their lack of organization and their numerous petty motives served to turn their initial dynamism into an irrational expression of collective behaviour. The absence of a national leadership capable of giving the movement articulate direction by turning it into a modern political group may be one reason for the immense amount of frustration. Many peasants, however, who had previously existed on the margin of Colombian society have now been socially assimilated. This fact in itself would appear to be evidence of a transition hastened by violence.

The Institutionalization of Violence

The process of rural strife in Colombia since 1948 clearly represents a mode of achieving social change, albeit in abnormal circumstances, which was not possible in the previous closed type of society. We should now look at the other side of the coin: the institutionalization of violence as a justified means to govern the country, made possible partly because of the time that has elapsed since the *Violencia* was unleashed. After sixteen years, this strife still has not found any visible rational or modern political outlet, yet it has acquired sufficient weight to be turned into a vested interest, a peculiar tradition, possessing the same tendency to prolong its life and to maintain the *status quo* that it helped to create, just as happened with the 'sacred' order.

Traditional values may serve to justify violence as much as passivity. It is clear that the past sixteen years of conflict in Colombia are indicative of a moral crisis of very great proportions. No national institution was found capable of arresting its devastating effects. On the contrary, some of these institutions are guilty of stimulating the use of violence to arrange their internal affairs. A relatively peaceful country has had to live with a new type of permanent violence in its backyard. Some groups have profited from it and have become important obstacles to further development discouraging new and more constructive ventures in social transformation.

[22] Torres Restrepo, p. 117.

One such group of profiteers is formed by the bandits themselves, especially the generation which grew up since the start of the *Violencia*. They still exist in many rural areas of Colombia, in spite of raids by government troops. In such areas the peasants resemble living dead, hypnotized by the dread of violence, mistrustful of outside help, incapable of moving ahead. The damage done by the organized bandits—and some guerrillas—is incalculable. Quite apart from the destruction of property, these bandits are preventing potential social development in their own regions. No entrepreneurs dare make investments there except in the infamous trade in arms in which both local and national groups of the two traditional parties have been engaged. With such rural markets virtually closed, urban industrialists are discouraged from expanding their production, causing an economic stagnation of which the country is now painfully aware.[23]

Moreover, local bandits and guerrilla leaders have often turned into vote-getting agents for politicians. It is plain in several regions that certain members of Congress could not be elected without the support of banditry, which, in turn, expects protection and a minimum of security. Even priests are known to be implicated in this machinery, and some ministers of state, ambassadors, and other public officials have antecedents that connect them with the *Violencia*. It is not surprising, therefore, that a number of influential persons should be trying to prevent the trial of bandits in Colombia's courts of justice.[24]

Other groups that have benefited directly or indirectly are the landless peasants of some regions who illegally occupied *haciendas*; the *mayordomos* and farm managers who counter-exploited their landlords; the number of people who took advantage of the occasion to purchase properties at ridiculous prices from frightened owners; and those who took over lands previously owned by their political opponents, when the latter had to leave in the wake of bellicose bands or, often, equally criminal police.

The cost of reducing banditry had to be paid. This has meant the organization and maintenance of a modern army and police at the expense of other items necessary for development, such as education, health, and public works. At present military

---

[23] Guzmán and others, ii. 10–11.

[24] More pertinent information is found in the Guzmán report already cited. Periodically, such data appear in newspapers; for instance, *El Tiempo* (Bogotá), 26 Jan. 1965, with reference to the bandit Efraín González.

expenditure ranks high in the national budget, but cannot be justified solely for the defence of national boundaries. It is needed mainly to repress internal movements. Some high military officers are acutely aware of the social cost of their organization and have tried to return a part of the investment to society in the form of 'military-civic action'. However, the military cost of suppressing violence is so high that it is itself becoming an obstacle to further development in Colombia. It is claimed that one single operation against bandits cost US$30 million. The cost is dearer still in purely social terms since the chief method of combating violence is renewed violence—a technique which has proved futile often enough. Underdevelopment cannot be solved by this type of repressive investment, yet it tends to become the accepted, normal 'solution' for rural violence.

Even the two traditional political parties have adapted themselves to violence. At first they encouraged it, then they produced a treaty to stop it and devised new rules for the political game, but never did much to foster socio-economic change. This is what might have been expected from entering into tortuous compromises. The masses were led to believe that with the political alliance not only would the *Violencia* end but a peaceful revolution would be effected to satisfy rising needs and expectations. Neither hope has been fulfilled after six years of agreed alternation of government. Instead, the system is once more showing weakness and sterility in handling national problems, and violence is spreading to the cities, to the universities, and elsewhere. In their present form, such political arrangements as have been devised to stop rural and urban strife may turn into obstacles to change, because they evade and obscure the basic social and economic issues.

At the same time tradition produces its own system of balance that intrudes even into the most explosively violent situations. Undoubtedly there have been changes in Colombia, but no real transformation has taken place; at least not one in harmony with present-day urges and needs. One is left wondering whether Latin America is capable of ruling its own destiny until such time as it is prepared radically to modify its traditional structures. The case of Colombia—where social costs in terms of life and suffering are out of all proportion in relation to the results achieved—may be illustrative. Moreover, the advent of violence may be symptomatic: similar outbreaks should not be altogether ruled out in the remainder of Latin America, which shares with Colombia a common cultural background and basic patterns of social structure.

At the present time we may be witnessing the final test of the capacity of Colombia to leave behind the heritage of the colonial past. Too many persons and institutions have been profiting from the routine of violence. Perhaps they have been courting violent destruction, like the sorcerer's apprentice, by conjuring up little understood potent forces. The groups affected by the *Violencia* are producing a new set of values to take the place of those that have been destroyed but it is still too early to determine what this new scale represents since it seems to vary considerably according to groups and levels. The transition towards secularism is far from complete, although trends in this direction are evident. Instead, we find a conglomeration of traditional and modern values which have been juxtaposed and fused to the point of being contradictory and confusing—leading to a condition in groups which is frequently referred to as 'anomic'. Perhaps the new scale of values could be described as 'anomic', as a reflection of the insecurity of the transition, possibly as a symptom of a still undefined stage through which the more developed countries have had to pass.[25]

This 'anomic' stage through which Colombian society seems to be passing impedes the complete realization of the thoroughgoing changes envisaged in the 1940s. Nevertheless, new foundations for the fundamental institutions are now being laid. This stage is no more than a transition requiring care and perseverance to produce something 'better'. 'Better', in this sense, may refer to the creation of a new social structure based on the actual application of recognized ideals, such as justice, respect for life, and encouragement of the creative impulse—a combination of values which could easily be made to serve as a political platform.

There seems to be an increasing awareness that the *Violencia* is a burden that must be shed if the country is to progress. The common people, the workers, especially the rising bourgeoisie and the industrial class, are all expressing discontent with the present state of affairs, and their protestations have shaken the government

[25] See also Fals Borda, 'The Role of Violence', p. 30.

on several occasions. Even the peasants themselves are co-operating in tracking down bandits, something unheard of even two years ago. It would appear that the time is ripe for a new type of modern and rational political action to tie up the loose ends of previous efforts and to achieve some sort of orderly but profound national transformation. Colombia is no longer an entirely closed society. She has emerged from these years a different nation. Politicians who persist in employing methods of action and control of pre-*Violencia* days soon find themselves swept away by the tide of social change. In a way, the *Violencia* and 'the sacred' are passing away together. The great historical predicament today is to turn the abnormal weapons used to achieve this momentous change into constructive tools to achieve the goal of a better society.

[*Orlando Fals Borda, Ph.D. (Florida), Professor of Sociology and Dean of the Faculty of Sociology of the Universidad Nacional de Colombia, was formerly Director-General of the Colombian Ministry of Agriculture. His principal publications include* El hombre y la tierra en Boyaca: bases sociologicas e históricas para una reforma agraria (*1957*) *and* La Violencia en Colombia (*1964*).]

Mexico:
The Lop-sided Revolution

MOISÉS GONZÁLEZ NAVARRO

THE Mexican Revolution was meant to benefit the growing urban middle class, the landless labourers in the countryside, and at the same time the urban workers—all within an economic system in which there was room both for state intervention and private enterprise. In the sphere of agrarian reform the Revolution made provision for both smallholdings and *ejidos*.[1] The latter was at first considered as a provisional institution, pending the eventual participation on equal terms of the Indian population in the economic life of the country, but with the advent of Cárdenas the *ejido* became an end in itself, while the urban workers pitted their forces against those of the bourgeoisie.

From then onwards the country's industrialization, complicated by the rapid growth of population, proceeded at the expense of the lower income classes, above all the peasants. The urban workers, organized in powerful trade unions, managed to do much better for themselves. However, the appearance in the cities of a growing *Lumpenproletariat*, representing an abundant reservoir of labour, has in certain respects nullified much of the social legislation passed.

On the eve of the Revolution land tenure fell into four main categories: (1) state-owned land, (2) large estates (owned both by Mexicans and foreigners), (3) smallholdings, and (4) communal land owned by the villages. According to one of the most reliable estimates, the 200 million hectares of national territory were distributed as follows: 10 per cent state-owned land, 54 per cent

---

[1] *Ejido* is a system of communal tenure modelled on the ancient Indian communities. *Ejido* lands are held as the property of a town or village, either for collective use or for distribution among *ejidatarios* for cultivation in small plots to which an individual has the right of occupation and use but not of sale or mortgage. The overwhelming majority of the *ejidos* are of the individual type, in which crop lands are worked individually and pastures and woodlands are used collectively.

large estates, 20 per cent smallholdings, 6 per cent communal land, and the remaining 10 per cent waste land. Mexican estate-owners held 44 per cent of the total, while the surveying companies, mainly owned by foreigners, held about 10 per cent.[2]

Under the régime of Porfirio Díaz, the communal landed property of the towns and villages of Mexico was virtually abolished.

Information from official sources shows that 40 million hectares of land, i.e. a fifth of the entire national territory, changed hands for various reasons during the period from 1867 to 1910, and this figure is twice as high as that previously estimated.[3] According to other sources, a quarter of the country's landed property was in the hands of foreigners.[4] Perhaps the most difficult point to establish concerns the number of communities which, despite the Disamortization Law (1856),[5] were able to retain their communal property. Francisco Bulnes estimates this at only about 15 per cent.[6] The estates in the central plateau benefited mainly from the foreclosure of mortgages on land owned by the Indian communities and those in the north and south gained from the disposal of uncultivated land (*baldíos*). The latter was used, in the main, for cattle rearing and the cultivation of produce for export, while the non-irrigated central regions were, as a rule, mainly in the hands of Mexican landowners engaged in subsistence farming, i.e. the traditional production of grain. The most notable exception was the state of Morelos, where a prosperous capitalist sugar industry developed, profiting from the boom created by the Spanish-American War, and where a higher proportion of communal land was expropriated. In the north a capitalist economy developed, based mainly on cattle-raising, in which the ranchers

[2] F. Gonzáles Roa, *El problema ferrocarrilero y la Compañía de los Ferrocarriles Nacionales de Mexico* (1915), pp. 66–67.

[3] M. González Navarro, *Estadísticas sociales del Porfiriato 1877–1910* (1956), p. 42.

[4] González Navarro, *La colonización en Mexico* (1960), p. 93.

[5] The Disamortization Law (*Ley de Desamortización*) of 1856, which broke up the estates of civil and ecclesiastical corporations, was also applied to the communal holdings of the Indian villages. Each Indian became the owner of the plot he worked. The main result of the law, as far as the Indian villages were concerned, was to hasten the transfer of their land to speculators or the local landlord.

[6] F. Bulnes, *The Whole Truth about Mexico; President Wilson's Responsibility* (1916), p. 85.

were both creoles and foreigners, especially North Americans; in the south-east both Mexicans and foreign planters produced sisal, coffee, and tobacco for export.

Each type of land tenure was characterized by a particular type of crop and labour system. Share-croppers and tenant labourers predominated in the north; forced labour in the south. The Yúcatan sisal farmers, the Valle Nacional tobacco producers, and the Chiapas coffee growers obtained their labour by recruiting vagrants and criminals and the recently-conquered Yaqui Indians. In the central regions the worker's lot was, as a rule, easier. Debt servitude for tenant labourers was on a smaller scale and less frequent, probably owing to the more plentiful supply of labour in comparison with the rest of the country, where it was scarce. There was a relatively large number of free workers, as some of the communal holdings still remained, thus enabling them to work only part-time on the estates. Share-cropping and leasehold arrangements were frequent in the central regions, but share-cropping in particular was subject to much abuse, since the owners tended to get the lion's share.

Finally, official records of the state of Yúcatan for the 1880s show that there were 20,767 peons indebted to their masters, i.e. 8 per cent of the total population of the state.[7] According to the 1910 census there were 3,123,975 labourers, i.e. 88.4 per cent of the agricultural population, 830 estate owners, or 0.02 per cent, and 410,345 farmers (small and medium owners, lessees, share-croppers, communal owners, and free workers), or 11.6 per cent of the total agricultural population.[8] However, this census is obviously inaccurate, since it lists 830 estate owners but 8,431 estates, and includes owners and free workers under the heading of farmers; this, in turn, would mean that those classed as labourers must be considered as tenant-labourers, which would amount to a very high figure indeed.

Whatever the true figures, the Porfirio era was characterized by latifundia, by an emergent industry which was beginning to supplant an artisan economy, and by a mining industry depending principally on international investment.

[7] González Navarro, *El Porfiriato, la vida social* (1957), p. 223.
[8] González Navarro, *Estadísticas*, pp. 40, 217.

Violence and the Birth of Reform

Porfirio Díaz made a belated attempt to settle the agrarian problem peacefully by offering to accelerate the distribution of *ejidos* and community-owned lands, and to make allotments of state-owned land in return for payment. His agrarian policy thus followed the liberal tradition, and the only new feature it offered was that of using state-owned land to create a group of smallholders.

Francisco Madero initiated the revolt against Porfirio Díaz by submitting his San Luis Plan in protest against small owners, mostly Indians, being wrongfully deprived of their land under cover of the Colonization Law of 1894. He offered to restore such land and to pay compensation for the loss they might have suffered. Possibly because Madero and his family were estate owners themselves, the San Luis Plan contained only timid proposals for agrarian reform. But these were later stepped up by the peasant movement and they did have the effect of opening the door to popular demand and of raising a banner, moderate though it might be, in the struggle for land. In fact, the hint of agrarian reform in the San Luis Plan was enough to spark off a spontaneous and disorganized rebellion among peasant groups, one that was, as often as not, inspired by an instinctive desire for revenge.

The agrarian proposals contained in the San Luis Plan were construed in many different ways. Some saw in them the foundation of a radical policy never advocated by Madero. He had always called for a peaceful solution to the agrarian problem, to be based mainly on the recovery of state-owned land, the purchase of certain estates in order to form a class of small landowners, and the allocation of *ejidos* to the villages. He also ordered the return of the Yaqui Indians who had been sold as slaves to work in the south-east. For the rest, he left it to each peasant to make the requisite personal effort. As a result, his agrarian policy did not conflict with the basic principles of latifundism.

Congressmen, on the other hand, submitted numerous proposals to settle the agrarian problem by increased taxes on uncultivated land or by its compulsory purchase; others advocated the abolition of duties on the division of large estates and the distribution of uncultivated land (*baldíos*). Luis Cabrera's proposal, submitted on 3 December 1912, was the most comprehensive and radical of them all. It held that the restoration and allocation of *ejidos* to the villages was in the public interest as a means of supplementing agricultural wages.

Despite his timid social policies, Madero was assassinated during a counter-revolution. When Victoriano Huerta seized the presidency he declared his intention of 'settling the agrarian problem gradually'. To this end he submitted two bills, in one of which the government was to play the part of mediator between the landlords and the peasants, and, with a view to enabling the latter to purchase the landlords' estates, was itself to guarantee the bonds issued by the land-allotment agencies. In the other bill he proposed abolishing payment of estate duty in any form by small owners and by those who entered into share-cropping or leasehold agreements.

In actual fact neither Madero nor Huerta went far enough to meet the aspirations of the peasants. Emiliano Zapata became their spokesman when, in November 1911, he put forward his Ayala Plan, in which he demanded the return of land taken from the villages, the allocation of communal land to those which were without it, and the nationalization of estates belonging to the opponents of the plan. This document, perhaps by its very simplicity, was strongly supported by the peasants, who transformed it into one of the main slogans which kept the cause of the Revolution alive.

When Venustiano Carranza took up arms against Victoriano Huerta, he did not at first intend his action to be viewed in a social but merely in a political light. Indeed, his agrarian policy reflected the fact that he was an established landowner and old supporter of Porfirio Díaz. However, several of his army commanders took it upon themselves to order the distribution of land, an order which Carranza promptly cancelled. They also took the initiative in issuing a decree abolishing debt servitude and truck shops; limiting the working day to 8 or 9 hours; requiring double time to be paid for night work; declaring Sundays and holidays to be days of rest; establishing a minimum salary, payable in legal currency; giving free use of pasture land and wood for fuel; and allowing free hunting and fishing to tenants, settlers, and day-labourers.

Compelled by the impatience of his own military chiefs and by the need to weaken the power of the combined peasant forces of Villa and Zapata, with whom he had fallen out as much over disagreements over questions of leadership as over reluctance to accept the agrarian provisions of the Ayala Plan, Carranza issued the decree of 6 January 1915. This Act, drawn up by Luis Cabrera, was based on the principle that since, because of their backwardness, the Indians had not adapted themselves to private ownership, their claim to communal ownership had to be acknowledged for the time being. This was to be implemented in two stages, the first being the restoration and allocation of land to the villages, not in order to revive the former Indian communities but to ensure that the villages were freed from the state of servitude in which they were living as a result of having lost their land. The second stage was to regularize the situation with regard to these lands and decide when and how they should be divided among the peasants, who would, in the meantime, continue to work them on a communal basis. The law authorized the temporary taking over of land, with immediate effect, although this was subject to later confirmation by the federal executive. Soon, however, Carranza became alarmed at the drive and speed with which the villages recovered their land, and on 19 September 1916 he ordered provisional occupation to be suspended.

The 1917 Constitution

After defeating Villa and Zapata, Carranza convened a meeting of Congress in September 1916, composed exclusively of his own supporters, an overwhelming majority of military personnel and professional men representing the urban middle class, and only three workers. The Congress, however, was divided into two groups: those who supported Carranza, mainly professional men, forming the right wing, and a younger generation of military radicals leading the left wing. Thus what had been essentially a peasant revolution in which peasant armies had triumphed, remained in the hands of people who could only represent the peasants indirectly, since Zapata and his supporters were never present at the debates although the more radical Congressmen continued to be inspired by him.

The 1917 constitution was drawn up in accordance with the bill for reforming the 1857 constitution, which was submitted by Carranza in his capacity as supreme head of the revolution. Carranza proposed that the liberal constitution of 1857 should only be slightly amended, and it fell to the left wing to give the new constitution a truly revolutionary character. This was accomplished through Article 27, which stated that land and water were originally owned by the nation as a whole, which had, and continues to have, the right to transfer the ownership thereof to individuals. Private ownership was to be subject to such conditions as it might be found necessary to impose in the public interest. The essential point was that Article 27 made it possible to expropriate land without the prior payment of compensation, whereas the 1857 constitution had demanded compensation in advance.

Article 123 is the other outstanding innovation in this constitution. In the original bill only passing reference had been made to the rights of workers in the article concerning freedom of labour, apparently because Carranza intended that these should be covered by an ordinary law. However, left-wing Congressmen managed to introduce into the constitution a comprehensive charter of workers' rights, the first in the world to be included in a constitution. By Article 123 the working day was limited to 8 hours, night work to 7 hours, and work by children between 12 and 16 years of age to 6 hours; one day's rest was granted per week. The article also laid down the principle of equal pay for equal work, without distinction of sex or nationality. Employers were obliged to provide suitable and hygienic accommodation and were made liable for industrial accidents and occupational hazards. The right to form trade unions and to take strike action was also acknowledged.

A comparison between the capitalist system in its early stages and the constitutional framework of revolutionary Mexico shows some interesting similarities and differences. Private ownership was absolute in the former but limited in the latter; while the former promoted private enterprise, the latter promoted state intervention; liberal capitalism permitted the exploitation of labour, while the 1917 constitution prohibited it. On the other hand in the Western pattern there existed a capitalist agriculture, whereas the Mexican constitution provided for a mixed agricultural system: capitalist by virtue of its protection of the small landowner, and pre-capitalist or socialist by the common ownership of the *ejidos*. The Western capitalist countries became imperialist, while Mexico, a semi-colonial country, became emphatically nationalistic, encouraged by an emergent domestic bourgeoisie allied to the peasants and workers. In the West the population explosion had two outlets: neo-Malthusianism and emigration. For Mexico the answer was emigration to the United States.

The Agrarian Revolution

Once installed as constitutional President, Carranza initiated the agrarian reform. His policy centred mainly on the recovery of alienated uncultivated land, and by 1 September 1918 he had recovered almost 15 million hectares out of a total of slightly over 22 million hectares, comprising tracts of over 100,000 hectares each which were in the hands of foreigners and were located in the prohibited frontier zones. However, when it came to dividing the large estates, the development of the fallow land, and the allocation and restitution of *ejidos,* he was not only cautious but suspicious, objecting that there was no legislation regarding agrarian debt. He actually went so far as to revoke the constitutional law which provided for expropriation without compensation in advance. Thus after ten years of violent strife, which had, directly and indirectly, resulted in a loss of over 1½ million people (those who died in the civil war and the Spanish influenza epidemic and those who emigrated to the United States), although the liberation of the peasants represented a profound change, particularly since the estate owners lost political control over the country, the social structure of Mexico remained virtually unchanged.

The first decree regulations for the law of 6 January 1915 was promulgated on 28 December 1920. It acknowledged the definitive but not the provisional allocations, and confined the beneficiaries of land distribution to the supporters of the Carranza administration. It provided that the extension of *ejido* land should be sufficient to ensure a daily income equivalent to twice the average local wage; but since farm wages were extremely low, even this was not enough to provide a suitable solution. President Obregón later repealed this act on 22 November 1921. He acknowledged the legality of provisional possession and set up a land registry to promote, without payment, the restitution and allocation of lands.

Agrarian regulations issued on 17 April 1922 fixed the area of *ejido* allocations at 3–5 hectares of irrigated or watered land; 4–6 hectares of land with an abundant and regular rainfall; and 6–8 hectares of other types of land. These regulations gave the agrarian procedure a judicial character and made it possible for landowners to intervene in it. In order to overcome the difficulty arising from certain political categories of the community alone having the right to receive land, a decree issued on 23 April 1927 granted to every community with more than 25 inhabitants the right to receive land if it had none.

The estate owners had successfully resisted the agrarian reform by resorting to legal proceedings and the communities, after prolonged lawsuits which often lasted up to five years, were obliged to return the land. To obviate this, a decree issued on 23 December 1931 ruled that landowners affected by land settlements were not to have any legal right of appeal. The law of 19 December 1925 on the allotment of *ejidal* lands and the establishment of individual title to *ejido* plots ended the system of 'possession in common' which for ten years had led to land being allotted for the benefit of the *ejido* managers and their favourites. Two years later the Ejidal Patrimony Law for the first time declared *ejidos* inalienable.

On 22 March 1934 the first Agrarian Code was promulgated, which co-ordinated the existing piecemeal and general legislation. The granting of land to villages was made conditional on their being in existence before the date when they applied for it, since it often happened that communities were formed expressly for the purpose of acquiring land. The size of individual *ejido* plots was fixed at 4 hectares of irrigated land, or its equivalent in other types of land. In addition, the code re-established the *ejido* of the colonial period in the sense that besides the arable land to be shared out among the *ejidatarios* (an *ejido* in the modern sense of the word), land was set aside for hill-grazing in summer, forest, and communal pasture. Another basic innovation was that tenant-labourers were granted the right to hold land in neighbouring villages and in newly formed agricultural settlements.

During the Cárdenas administration, even though land distribution was at its height, the Agrarian Code was revised on 1 March 1937 to protect the cattle-raising industry, which was in a critical condition as ranchers feared that they would lose their land if they increased their herds. Cattle ranches of 300 to 50,000 hectares might now be exempted from expropriation for fifty years. This would only be granted in places where the agrarian requirements of the villages had been adequately satisfied, or where there were no communities entitled to *ejidos*.

Smallholdings

All this agrarian legislation was specifically concerned with *ejidos*, this being one of the two objectives of the agrarian reform. The other was the smallholding. From the very outset preferential consideration was given, in one way or another, to the individual smallholder as against the communal owners of the *ejidos*, and the main purpose of Article 27 of the constitution was to break up the large estates in order to create smallholdings.

On 2 August 1923 all Mexicans over eighteen years of age were granted the right to acquire up to 25 hectares of irrigated land, 100 hectares of first-class non-irrigated land, 200 of second-class and 500 of third-class non-irrigated land or of state-owned grazing land, the only condition being that such land must be personally occupied by the new owners and demarcated by them. A comparison between the amount of land allocated on an *ejido* basis and that obtainable on the basis of this decree will show the extent to which preference was given to the individual smallholding. Before the advent of President Cárdenas, the *ejidatarios* were considered to be inferior beings, as it was claimed that they were still too backward to be able to compete with the smallholders, and that the consequences of the Disamortization Law of 1856 had shown how unfit they were to succeed in the battle for life. The authors of the Revolution were confident that protective legislation would be able to put *ejidatarios* on a more even footing with smallholders.

After the establishment of a capitalist system of smallholders, the agricultural workers relied on the protection afforded by Article 123 of the constitution and, in 1931, by the Federal Labour Law. The 1928 Civil Code revised the share-cropping contracts so as to unite the interests of the owner and the share-cropper, making both of them dependent on the success of the harvest. The share-cropper was allowed to make use of the natural resources of the land he occupied as a contribution towards his livelihood. In accordance with the concept of property as a social function, which permeates this mode, properties left uncultivated by their owners might be compulsorily let out to share-croppers.

The Trend of Agrarian Policies

During the years 1910 to 1920, the principal leaders of the Revolution, Madero and Carranza, were themselves landowners and therefore inclined to favour political rather than social reforms. During the next fifteen years the leaders of the Revolution were drawn from the middle class. Lázaro Cárdenas was the first and perhaps the only President to give the Revolution a predominantly peasant character. The end of his administration marked also the end of the agrarian and the start of the agricultural and industrial revolution. This is clearly shown by the agrarian allocations. By 31 August 1962 almost a quarter of the country had been distributed as *ejidos* but in a very uneven manner: 0.3 per cent from 1915 to 1920 and 13.6 per cent from the fall of Carranza to the advent of Cárdenas (1920–34, i.e. while the governments emanating from the anti-Carranza rebels, De la Huerta, Calles, and Obregón, were in office). During the 1930s the agrarian problem was considered to have been settled in many parts of the country.

That this was far from being the case is proved by the fact that 37.1 per cent of the total allocations effected up to the present time were made during Cárdenas's term of office. Since then, circumstances arising from the Second World War, a vigorous political campaign directed against Cárdenas, and greater emphasis on industrialization have apparently brought the Mexican Revolution to its Thermidor. The percentage of agrarian allocations has, in fact, progressively decreased; 11.5 per cent under the presidency of Manuel Ávila Camacho; 8 per cent under Miguel Alemán; and only 6.6 per cent under Adolfo Ruíz Cortines.[9]

As evidenced in Miguel Alemán's 1946 reform, such changes were not only quantitative but also qualitative. According to him, the first stage of the agrarian reform was intended to break the power of the large landowners, whereas the second or technical stage was designed to raise the economic and moral status of the agricultural labourer and to increase production. To attain the first of these objectives, the area or individual unit allocated in each case was increased to a minimum of 10 hectares of irrigated or watered land, or, where this was not available, an equivalent area of other types of land. To attain the second objective, the owners of agricultural or cattle ranches who held certificates of

[9] Mexico, Presidencia de la República, *50 años de revolución mexicana en cifras* (1963), p. 46.

exemption were granted the right to obtain injunctions against unlawful dispossession of their land or water. The term 'small-holding' was applied to an agricultural unit not exceeding 100 hectares of first-class irrigated or watered land, or 200 hectares of non-irrigated land or of grazing land, 150 hectares in the cotton-growing areas, and 300 in those devoted to the cultivation of bananas, sugar-cane, coffee, sisal, rubber, coconuts, vines, olives, vanilla, cacao, or fruit.

A further method of assessing the rate of development of the agrarian reform is to compare the sizes of holdings: in 1930 those of over 5 hectares still accounted for 93 per cent of the total agricultural area. In 1940, after the Cárdenas reform, this figure was reduced to 76.7 per cent, then to 72.4 per cent in 1950, and to approximately two-thirds in 1962.[10] The figure relating to individual holdings of under 5 hectares has remained virtually unchanged: 0.7 per cent of the total in 1930 and 0.9 per cent in the other three years. On the other hand, *ejido* land increased considerably, from 6.3 per cent in 1930 to 22.5 per cent in 1940, 26.7 per cent in 1950 and 31.1 per cent in 1962. Although the 5-hectare limit does not appear to be very significant, it is evident that the area of *ejido* land has increased considerably, at the expense of the individual holdings of over 5 hectares.

Moreover, the average area of holdings of over 5 hectares has fallen progressively from 441 hectares in 1930 to 340 in 1940 and 292 in 1950. The trend applicable to holdings under 5 hectares is somewhat uneven: from 1.54 hectares in 1930 their average area fell to 1.25 in 1940 and increased slightly to 1.36 in 1950. As against this, the average area of the *ejidal* holdings increased from 1,192 hectares in 1930 to 1,970 in 1940 and to 2,213 in 1950.[11]

It is evident that the total number of *ejidos* and *ejidatarios* has increased in absolute terms. From 7,049 in 1935 the number of *ejidos* doubled to 14,680 in 1940 and increased further to 17,579 in 1950. The number of *ejidatarios* also doubled, from 898,433 in 1935 to 1,601,479 in 1940, but in 1950 it dropped to 1,552,926. The area and value of *ejido* arable land diminished

[10] The agricultural-livestock and *ejidal* census for 1960 has not yet been published. *Ejidal* data for 1962 have been taken from *50 años de revolución mexicana en cifras*. The figures relating to holdings of over and under 5 hectares are considered to have remained unchanged.
[11] Mexico, Dirección General de Estadística (DGE), *Tercer censo agrícola ganadero y ejidal* (1950), pp. 7–12.

between 1935 and 1950, whereas pastures, woodlands, and uncultivated productive land increased.[12]

The *ejido* itself has undergone important internal changes, one of which is the progressive reduction in collective farming and growth of individual farming. The percentage of *ejido* collective farming was 6.62 in 1940 and 3.34 in 1950,[13] but the percentage of *ejidatarios* with individual land holdings rose from 76.36 in 1940 to 88.76 ten years later.[14]

The *ejidos* have not, however, been equally successful throughout Mexico. The decisive factor is not the institution itself but the social environment which produces wealth or poverty. For instance, an analysis by zones shows that both the North Pacific and the northern area had the largest proportion of *ejidos* providing school facilities (81 and 75 per cent respectively), while the South Pacific area had the smallest proportion (64.41 per cent). Almost the same applies to medical services: in 1940 7.31 per cent of the *ejidos* in the North Pacific area had a permanent medical service, and 6.57 per cent in the northern area against only 1.19 per cent in the South Pacific region.[15] The same is also true of seed drills; in 1950 in the northern area these accounted for 4.87 per cent of the total amount of machinery, implements, and vehicles, while the North Pacific area had 2.27 per cent and the South Pacific area only 0.18 per cent.[16] Similarly, tractors accounted for 0.71 per cent of all agricultural implements in the North Pacific area, 0.45 per cent in the northern area, and only 0.04 per cent in the South Pacific area.[17]

It is therefore obvious that the economic success of the *ejidos* depends on the type of land involved. While *ejido* lands increased between 1935 and 1950, those on the non-irrigated land decreased from 81.71 to 78.49 per cent of the total area, whereas those on irrigated land increased from 11.42 to 13.78 per cent. The wealthiest *ejidos* are naturally to be found in the irrigated regions and where farming is carried on for export. Thus in the North Pacific area the percentage of irrigated land increased from 15.91

[12] Mexico, DGE, *Primer censo ejidal, resumen general* (1935), p. 105; *Segundo censo ejidal* (1940), p. 284; *Tercer censo ejidal* (1950), p. 62.

[13] *Segundo censo*, pp. 145–6; *Tercer censo*, p. 6.

[14] *Segundo censo*, pp. 123–6; *Tercer censo*, p. 5.

[15] *Tercer censo*, p. 62.

[16] *Segundo censo*, p. 283; *Tercer censo*, p. 62.

[17] *Tercer censo*, pp. 10–13.

per cent in 1935 to 36.13 per cent in 1950; in the north the increase was from 14.42 to 17.49 per cent. However, in the South Pacific area, despite a large relative increase, the percentage of irrigated land rose only from 1.62 per cent in 1935 to 2.38 per cent in 1950. In the central regions there was an actual reduction from 17.43 per cent in 1935 to 16.11 per cent in 1950, the proportion of non-irrigated land increasing from 77.85 to 88.78 per cent over the same period.

The Industrial Revolution

Although ever since colonial times there has existed a primitive textile industry, which was modernized after Independence—it was under the Porfirio era that the first important steps towards industrial development were taken by laying the foundations for the production of iron and steel, cement, sugar, beer, and textiles. But in fact the industrial revolution came to Mexico in the last quarter of a century, with the creation of the *Nacional Financiera* in 1933, the tremendous impetus given to the agrarian reform by Cárdenas, the nationalization of the petroleum industry, the creation of the National Polytechnic Institute, also inspired by Cárdenas, and the opportunities afforded by the Second World War, which were exploited by the governments of Manuel Ávila Camacho and Miguel Alemán.

The manufacturing industry was developed with the aid of direct foreign investment channelled through official agencies. This was how development was effected in such industries as iron and steel, paper, chemicals, textiles, metal products, electrical goods and appliances, sugar, motor-vehicle assembly, fertilizers, rubber goods, building materials, bottling plant, etc. In fifty-five years the whole face of the nation has been transformed from a rural and agricultural to an urban and industrial pattern.

The fiftieth anniversary of the Mexican Revolution was celebrated by a display of official euphoria about the progress made by the country which, thanks to modern publicity techniques, surpassed the loudest boasting of the Porfirio era. According to official sources, contemporary Mexico exhibits the following positive features. A population explosion: an increase in the country's population from 15 million inhabitants in 1910 to 35 million in 1960, Mexico being the country with the highest rate of population growth during the decade from 1950 to 1960. This growth was due to a high birth rate and a drop in the death rate owing to an effective health policy. Industrialization and increased agricultural productivity led to a greater percentage of the population settling in urban areas (13.4 per cent in 1910 as against 37.5 per cent in 1960), which in turn led to a rise in the standard of living. One of the most conspicuous manifestations of national progress was the increase in life expectancy, more than doubling from 27.4 years in 1910 to 62 years in 1960, although this increase took place mainly from 1940 onwards.

As regards the employment structure, the overwhelmingly large agricultural population drifted towards industry and the public services. Indeed, the agricultural population, which in 1910 accounted for 72 per cent of the total, had fallen to only 52.8 per cent in 1960, while on the other hand the industrial population increased from 11.3 per cent in 1910 to 15.5 per cent in 1960. The increase is in effect much more important since on the eve of the revolution the crafts were also classed in the census as industrial activities. In addition, mention should be made of the constant rise in the percentages of civil servants, from 1.3 per cent in 1910 to 4.2 per cent in 1960, as this indicates the increase of state participation in the economy.

The gross national product has increased fivefold in real terms since 1940 as a result of industrialization. The participation of industry in GNP has risen from 20 per cent in 1910 to 36 per cent in 1960. The productivity of labour doubled within fifty years and real per capita income increased threefold. The gross national investment has also risen in the past two decades as a result of the growth in the public sector.

As the agrarian reform was one of the most important aspects of the Mexican Revolution, official sources make much of the fact that by 1960 48 million hectares of productive land had been made over to the peasants. Throughout the period from 1928 to 1960, $2\frac{1}{2}$ million hectares were irrigated. As a result, agricultural production increased fourfold, and was able to provide the raw materials required for industrial expansion. The outstanding success of the irrigation policy is borne out by the fact that between 1933 and 1963 the value of the harvest in the irrigated zones is stated to be five times the amount invested. The irrigation policy, together with agricultural credits, technical education, and the favourable situation of world markets, has trebled agricultural production during the last twenty years. Maize, wheat, beans, and rice, the basic elements of the national diet, are now produced in adequate quantities and efficiently distributed through national organizations, which guarantee adequate remuneration for the growers while ensuring low prices for the consumers. Cattle raising too has recovered from the ravages sustained during the decade of revolutionary strife, and poultry breeding also plays an important part.

Despite its historic importance, the mining industry no longer constitutes the country's main source of wealth. With the exception of the iron-ore mines, it is virtually stagnant. Although the oil industry has never again reached the production levels of its Golden Age (1921 to 1925), the nationalization of this industry made a major contribution towards industrialization, since it supplied the needs of the home market, increased currency reserves, and encouraged the development of the petro-chemical industry. The production of crude oil has increased almost uninterruptedly since the time of Mexico's participation in the Second World War. The state also nationalized the sources and distribution of electric power, in order to accelerate its development.

With regard to transport, there has been only a slight increase in the railway mileage constructed since the Porfirio era. The emphasis has mainly been on modernizing rolling stock, particular importance being attached to freight services. In marked contrast with the railway system, the road network has increased considerably, from 695 kilometres in 1925 to almost 50,000 in 1960, i.e. more than double (23,487) the mileage of the railways. Road haulage is mainly used over short and medium distances, and the railways for long distances and heavy loads. The number of motor vehicles on the roads has similarly increased from 44,858 in 1924 to 902,029 in 1961, and petrol-driven vehicles have increased to 33 times the number existing thirty-five years ago.

Again according to official sources, the country's economic development has been achieved without imposing an excessive burden on the working classes. Inflation is kept to the minimum, thanks to government intervention. Although from 1936 to 1962 the purchasing power of earnings fell by a tenth, minimum wages rose in the same proportion, and thus the purchasing power of less skilled workers has been maintained at a fairly constant level. In rural areas the minimum wage is lower, but the farm labourers supplement their income by doing other work. In the cities the wages earned are generally above the minimum, and increase more rapidly than the minimum wage. This does not take into account the fact that social insurance provides a substantial and effective additional emolument. At present, social insurance caters for more than a tenth of the working population, and an eighth of the entire population of the country. It was first established in 1942, although provision for its establishment had already been made in the 1917 constitution. In 1954 it was extended to farm workers and in 1960 to *braceros* (seasonal workers).

The Institute for State Workers' Insurance and Social Welfare gives aid to over 600,000 people, while the Institute of Social Security for the Military Forces is mainly concerned with the army. The National Institute for the Protection of Children covers 43 per cent of all municipalities throughout the country, and provides school meals in all of these.

According to official estimates, the proportion of members of the upper class has remained virtually unchanged, increasing only from 0.6 per cent of the total population in 1900 to 0.7 per cent in 1960. The rural upper class decreased from 0.4 to 0.2 per cent, while its urban counterpart increased from 0.2 to 0.5 per cent during the same period, this being a natural sequel to the breaking-up of the large estates. The former estate owners have turned into 'dynamic' and 'active' business men, 'conscious of their social responsibility for the general progress of the nation'.

The working class experienced an overall decrease, from 91.1 per cent in 1900 to 82.4 per cent in 1960, a change particularly noticeable in the countryside, where it involved a reduction from three-quarters to one-half of the population during the period mentioned. On the other hand the urban workers doubled, from 16.3 to 32.3 per cent, during the same period. The middle class also doubled as a result of better economic and educational opportunities. According to these estimates, the rural middle class increased only from 6.6 to 9.9 per cent, while the urban middle class rose from 1.7 to 7 per cent over these sixty years.

As has been stated, the provision of better facilities for education provided the basis for the country's social development. In 1960 the federal government's appropriation for schools accounted for 21.7 per cent of the national budget, and was twice as high as the amount provided for the army. In 1900 the reverse was the case, 21.4 per cent of the national budget being earmarked for the army as against only 3.6 per cent for education. As a result of this increase, literacy among Mexicans over 6 years of age rose, in spite of the population explosion, from 23.1 per cent of the total population in 1900 to 59.9 per cent in 1960.[18]

This optimistic official view of contemporary Mexico is accurate in what it states, but partly inaccurate in the way this is stated, and above all in what it has omitted to state. A comparison of the official figures with the criticisms put forward at the Agrarian Congress held in Toluca in 1959 reveals that in various instances, thanks to fictitious distribution, large estates continue to exist, even in places very near the capital. In other areas those who apply for government land are still victimized. They are refused work or permission to obtain property on a share-cropping basis. In many places the farm worker has no legal protection and is paid a wage far below the minimum legal figure. One speaker at the Toluca Congress estimated that there are still 2 million unprotected day-labourers. In certain central areas the wage is so low that the peasants can eat only once a day. It was also maintained that false returns are made to give the impression that the land is divided into smallholdings. Another speaker asserted that over half of the *ejidos* are not in the hands of the titular holders, that even in rich areas such as the Valle del Yaqui half of the *ejidatarios* lease their land, and that in the Valle de México itself about 70 to 80 per cent of them are employed as manual workers in the numerous factories surrounding Mexico City; they then lease their land or make it over on a share-cropping basis, and thus exploit their fellow peasants.

The Toluca Congress was also told that there is a steadily increasing number of peasants whose claims are upheld, that is to say whose right to *ejido* plots is acknowledged, but who are not given the land either because there really is none available or because it is held by protégés of the new oligarchy, an occurrence which is denounced daily in the press. Innumerable protests also arise from the expropriation of *ejido* land in favour of the developers of the new residential zones in the large cities on a basis of mutual favours. All this happens because the *ejido* system is a tool in the hands of the new oligarchy. To overcome this evil it has been proposed to prohibit the re-election of *ejido*

[18] *50 años de revolución.*

committees. The present system gives rise to the perpetuation in power of a small group.

It was said at Toluca that, to judge by the number of landless peasants, the state of poverty in which many of the *ejidatarios* live, and the fact that, lacking protection, they have become the slaves of their leaders, the Mexican Revolution does not yet appear to have reached the countryside. Someone actually stated that in 55 per cent of the *ejidos* the agrarian problem still persists, as the plots allotted are either not big enough or not good enough. Apart from the country's limited agricultural resources, the poverty of the *ejidos* is explained by the lack of credit facilities. True, in 1926 the National Agricultural Credit Bank was founded, and in 1936 the National Ejidal Credit Bank (*Banco Nacional de Crédito Ejidal*); but in fact only slightly over three-quarters of the *ejidos* receive bank credits. It is not surprising therefore that many of the *ejidatarios* should find themselves in the clutches of land-sharks, or that capitalist agriculture should, generally speaking, be far more efficient than *ejidal* agriculture.[19]

Although some of these criticisms may appear to be exaggerated generalizations, they serve to damp the optimistic reports emanating from official sources. A recent survey carried out by an experienced investigator, who was also a civil servant, corroborates the criticisms. He maintained that in various parts of the country the wealthy farmers employ the poor *ejidatarios* as labourers on their own property, particularly on the large sugar estates, misleadingly termed co-operatives. Some *ejidatarios* who have received land work in factories in Mexico City, where they earn 3 to 4 times as much as in the fields, while at the same time exploiting landless *ejidatarios*. Although *ejidos* may not be sold, many allotments in the Bajío region were taken over by the local farmers, by entering into fictitious sales or leasehold agreements. In Zamora only a third of the *ejidatarios* cultivate their plots themselves, the rest lease it or hand it over to share-croppers. Thus some of the wealthier farmers are able to gain control of up to two dozen *ejidal* allotments. Out of a total of 106 such land-sharks, 28 own over 50 hectares apiece and 9 own over 1,000. Even in the rich Valle del Yaqui, 30 per cent of the *ejidal* land is subject to share-cropping or leasehold agreements.

---

[19] *Memoria del Congreso Nacional Agrario de Toluca; Mesas redondas, sesiones plenarias, conclusiones y ponencias* (1961).

One of the reasons for this absenteeism is the insufficiency of the *ejidal* allotment for supporting a family. Earnings are not of course in accordance with the legal minimum, and in any case their purchasing power has fallen. In 1963 the price of 53 kg. of maize was the same as that of 80 kg. in 1934 when the minimum rural wage was first established. This wage is smaller than in colonial times, and corresponds to only three-quarters of the minimum wage customary at the end of the last century. The Ejidal Bank has only partly achieved its purpose, among other reasons because it has created a superfluous bureaucracy and because its funds have often been dishonestly administered. Private properties have a much higher output than the *ejidos*. Certain branches of the *Ejidal* Bank have revived some aspects of the truck shop. However, in other areas, such as Nayarit, the Ejidal Bank operates satisfactorily as the beneficiaries are collectively responsible for loans.[20]

On the other hand, it was decided on 22 January 1963 to abolish the Federal Settlement Law which encouraged fraudulent claims to have established officially sponsored settlements. In marked contrast with these, spontaneous settlements have opened up the virgin lands of the south-east and Veracruz, without any cost to the nation.

To sum up, the Mexican Revolution, as seems to be the case with all industrial revolutions, has sacrificed agriculture to industry, and the countryside to the city. The Mexican Revolution is based on the capitalist pattern, except for the *ejido,* which is an institution foreign to the capitalist régime now increasingly gaining ground in Mexico. The *ejido* is, however, firmly anchored in a romantic agrarian tradition which tends to preserve symbols and slogans.

Moreover, the population explosion has complicated the social problems arising from the country's underdeveloped economy, although there has always been the outlet of seasonal emigration of unskilled labourers to the United States. Not all these, of course, are peasants. Some of them come from the cities, but even these are really drawn from the mass of peasants who have moved into the urban slums. They have not been absorbed by industry,

[20] M. T. de la Peña, *El pueblo y su tierra; mito y realidad de la reforma agraria en Mexico* (Mexico City, 1964).

and their underemployment in services amounts to barely disguised unemployment. Although no precise figures are available, because so many *braceros* cross the frontier illegally, a rough estimate for a peak year in the middle of the century put their number at 1.16 per cent of the total population and 8 per cent of the agricultural population. But the *braceros* play a dual social role. On the one hand they help to correct the adverse balance of payments, together with tourism and foreign investments. On the other hand they act as a safety valve by offering better paid work to important sectors of the overpopulated central region, which would otherwise exert pressure on an inadequate labour market.

One of the ways of appreciating the difference between town and country is to compare urban and rural mortality rates. The former fell from 30.2 per thousand in 1937 to 11.3 in 1960, while the latter fell from 21.6 to 11.8 during the same period. (In many developing countries, of course, the rural death rate is even higher than the urban.) In other words, the urban rate has been reduced much faster than the rural rate, which is now the higher of the two.[21] That the cities are better off than the countryside is also shown by the housing programme which, with a few exceptions, is virtually centred on the cities.

Apart from the important peasant group of Zapata's followers which remained politically marginal until the assassination of Carranza, the Mexican Revolution from the outset had middle-class leanings. On 1 September 1917 Carranza declared his intention of promoting the creation of small industries to form an independent middle class which, he hoped, would attenuate the class struggle.[22] Twenty years later Lázaro Cárdenas declared that the place of the middle class was, historically speaking, at the side of the workers.[23] Under Cárdenas an equilibrium appears to have been achieved between the political forces of the middle class and the workers and peasants. The hard-fought elections of 1940 provided the starting point for a change of heart on the part of the middle class which, convinced that it could not dislodge the governments born of the Revolution, gave up the frontal

[21] México, DGE, *Anuario estadístico* (1942), p. 225; *Anuario estadístico* (1963), p. 56.

[22] México, Camara de Diputados, *Diario de los debates*, 1 Sept. 1917, p. 20.

[23] Ibid. 1 Sept. 1940, p. 23.

attack and decided to work instead through its pressure groups: chambers of commerce, industry, bankers' associations, etc. The reconciliation between working class and middle class followed the pattern of Porfirio Díaz's compromise with the conservatives and the clergy: the government maintained the façade of a peasants' and workers' revolution, whereas the country's economic development confirmed the capitalist nature of the Mexican Revolution.

This led to a series of mutual concessions: formally, the government retained a secular and anti-clerical outlook in its legislation, but tolerated or disregarded the violation of these principles in practice. Revolutionary phraseology continued to include workers' and peasants' slogans, but in practice the lion's share of the national income went to the capitalist pressure groups, even though at the same time state intervention in the economy increased considerably.

As a token of its closer understanding with the revolutionary government, the new upper classes have abandoned their only opposition party, *Acción Nacional*, and, though not formally joining the government party, they have openly supported its candidates and programme.

The peaceful incorporation of the upper class into official politics is partly to be explained by the fact that the Revolution has created its own élite. Revolutionaries who have grown rich strengthen the leadership cadres of the traditional upper class, some of them as the heirs of the landed gentry of the Porfirio era, and some as a natural product of the Revolution itself. The financial oligarchy dominates the private sector of the Mexican economy, in return for which it gives a free hand to the members of the revolutionary political oligarchy, heirs of the actual makers of the Revolution, who are too young to have taken an active part during the revolutionary wars. Thus the political oligarchy, akin to but not identified with the financial oligarchy, retains the monopoly of political power through a conformist and self-contradictory *Partido Revolucionario Institucional* (PRI).

The middle and working classes enjoy the prestige of a Revolution carried out in their name. Thus the organized urban workers are treated with great deference by the government. Certain groups in particular are so much better off that they now belong to the middle class.

In agriculture the smallholders have strengthened their position, mainly through the irrigation projects in respect of land used for export crops. *Ejidatarios* on non-irrigated land, or without land, bear the brunt of the country's economic development. In other words the self-same people who made the agrarian revolution, or their descendants, have little but poverty for their reward now that the revolution has passed into the industrial stage because it has been channelled through the capitalist system. The Mexican Revolution certainly freed the peasants from the semi-feudal servitude of the Porfirio era, but it has subjected them to that which is inherent in the capitalist régime of an underdeveloped country.

Even the inflationary spiral since 1940 has favoured the employers.[24] From 1939 to 1946 the participation of wage-earners in the national income fell from 30.5 to 21.27 per cent. Later it recovered slightly and reached 29 per cent by 1955.[25] The Mexican working class has made most of the sacrifices needed to achieve the extraordinary advances of the period from 1939 to 1950, when the country's economic development was considerably speeded up.[26] According to official pronouncements, this sacrifice was necessary for Mexico's economic evolution, as it made possible the establishment of numerous industrial, commercial, and cultural undertakings.[27]

It is only natural that those who look at Latin America as a whole and conclude that its foremost problem is the agrarian one, should be led to believe that Mexico could serve as a model to the other countries of the region. Apparently, the Mexican Revolution has created an open society without any institutional obstacles to hinder further development. However, there exists a basic incompatibility between the institution of the *ejido* and the continued economic and social development of the country. In spite of its economic rigidity and its administrative corruption, the *ejido* remains the best protection for the weaker and most neglected peasant groups which, in a pure capitalistic economy,

---

[24] S. A. Mosk, 'La revolución industrial en México', *Problemas agrícolas e industriales de México*, Apr.–June 1951, p. 216.

[25] E. López Malo, *Ensayo sobre localización de la industria en México* (1960), p. 60; Mexico, Secretaría del Trabajo y Previsión Social, *Memoria de labores* (1957), p. 142.

[26] G. Rivera Marín, *El mercado de trabajo* (1955), p. 139.

[27] México, Secretaría de Economía, *Memoria* (1954), p. 9.

would have perished long ago. As these form the bulk of the agricultural workers who are shouldering the burden of the industrialization of the country, this situation has added new obstacles to development, different from those already removed by the revolutionary agrarian reform, itself now in need of reform.

[*Moisés González Navarro, former President of the Sociedad Mexicana de la Historia and Professor of the History of Social Doctrines and Institutions at El Colegio de México. He now directs the Seminar on Contemporary History of Mexico at El Colegio de México. His main publications include* El pensamiento político de Lucas Alamán (*1952*) *and* La vida social en el Porfiriato (*1956*).]

Disunity as an Obstacle to Progress

FELIPE HERRERA

LATIN American regional integration may be defined as the collective effort of the Latin American states to ensure their individual progress through the development of the region as a whole. Their common historical and cultural background predisposes the Latin American countries to integration, but if they now seek it with all possible dispatch, it is not merely as a consequence of that background. Their mutual affinities alone would be insufficient to compel them to make the transition from regional co-operation to regional integration. It is the urgent need for development and the limitations imposed by present world conditions on the ability of underdeveloped countries to develop beyond a certain point that are the basic reasons for integration.

Any suggestions for remedying the defects (whether political, economic, institutional, social, or cultural) in the internal structure of Latin American countries must take into account the fact that expansion from a national to a regional basis will inevitably stimulate and support necessary internal reforms. This holds good even for relatively well-developed countries in the region.

Integration and internal development are complementary. In contrast to the process of development in the great industrial centres of the nineteenth century, material growth and the safeguarding of domestic markets for domestic production cannot today be left to the free play of economic forces. On the contrary, a deliberate and planned effort must be made to overcome inefficiency in the economic and social structure, to channel resources towards activities that are basic to industrialization, and to accelerate the growth rate by all available means. Planning is necessary to make the formulation and application of this policy as effective as possible. Opening up new lands, diversifying natural resources, expanding markets, and consolidating economic relations with other areas will bring greater and swifter advances within reach.

Unless a determined effort is made to narrow the gap as quickly as possible, Latin America's relative backwardness will increase as the new scientific and technological revolution progresses in the more industrialized countries. The effort must be a concerted one, because all the Latin American countries face largely the same problems. Their economies have similar characteristics and needs, and their individual potentials are subject to the same limitations. Moreover, the greater backwardness of some Latin American countries in comparison with others is harmful to the region as a whole, just as the general economic situation of the larger countries is affected by the imbalances arising from variations in development between industrial and less favoured areas within their own borders. An ECLA report has this to say about the problems the Latin American countries have in common:

Latin America, however great the external assistance it receives, however high the rate at which its exports expand—and they cannot do so very rapidly—will be unable to carry out its development plans, will be unable even to regain the rate of growth it achieved in the ten post-war years, unless it makes a sustained effort to establish within its own territory the capital goods industries of which it is in such urgent need today, and which it will require on a large scale during the next quarter of a century. . . . In order to produce the capital goods and develop all the intermediate goods industries required to launch these highly complex dynamic industries . . . Latin America needs a common market.[1]

The Historical Process: The Centrifugal Tendency

According to one interpretation of Latin American history, the winning of emancipation in the nineteenth century meant the breaking up and dispersal of the great colonial empire of Spain. However, a more thorough scrutiny of the political, cultural, economic, and social characteristics of the colonial period shows that, despite its outward semblance of unity, Latin American society in reality lacked underlying geographical and structural cohesion.

Western culture—a new language, religion, and legal system, as well as a new system of economic activity and trade—was brought to Indo-America in Spanish and Portuguese ships. The economy was reoriented to satisfy the needs of the mother countries rather than local needs, thus bringing about an upsurge

[1] ECLA, *The Latin American Common Market* (1959), p. 1.

in the mining industry but a decline in the efficient systems of agricultural production of the Andean region.[2] Trade took on a centrifugal tendency. The old Indian roads fell into disuse, and communication between different parts of the colonial empire was hampered. The principal economic function of roads was to transport minerals to sea-ports for shipment to Europe, or to provide access to the coastal communities which were the centres of the new political power.

The sites the *conquistadores* chose for their towns and cities were typical of this centrifugal tendency. The great Indian capitals, like Tenochtitlán in Mexico and Cuzco in Peru, had been established in the interior and served as centres of their respective geopolitical areas for gathering and transmitting cultural and economic exchanges. The new Spanish and Portuguese cities— Lima, Cartagena, Panama, Havana, San Salvador de Bahía, Rio de Janeiro, Santa María de los Buenos Aires, Valparaiso, Valdivia, Buenaventura, Veracruz—were established on the coast, where they were more readily accessible to the metropolis with which the colonial administrators were required to maintain constant contact, and from which no European wished to detach himself.

This 'radial' organization of the Spanish American colonies, whose epicentre was the distant metropolis, accounts for their isolation from one another.[3] The colonies lacked geographical integration, and, in the vivid words of a Chilean historian, 'the cultural landscape of the Spanish Empire up to 1810 was a series of islands set in a vast, unexplored and perilous ocean'.[4]

There is no dearth of modern writers who try to demonstrate that intercourse among the colonies was much greater than this statement might lead one to suppose. That, however, is a question of degree which does not substantially alter the picture.

Moreover, the community of language, religion, institutions, law and authority went no more than skin-deep, and this was the origin of the superposition of appearance on reality—of the 'apparent' nation on the 'real' nation—that characterized almost

---

[2] José Carlos Mariátegui, *Siete ensayos de interpretación de la realidad peruana*, 5th ed. (Lima, Amauta, 1957).

[3] Victor Andrés Belaúnde, *La realidad nacional* (1945).

[4] Francisco A. Encina, *Bolívar y la independencia de la América española* (Santiago de Chile, Edit. Nacimiento, 1964).

the whole of Latin America until very late in the nineteenth century, and that still persists in some countries. Except as embodied in the Laws of the Indies, which were 'respected but not obeyed', the cultural patterns introduced and officially adopted by the Iberian immigrants made no attempt to blend with the geographic and economic reality to which they were applied. Thus, just as different parts of the colonies were geographically isolated from one another, the alien culture was isolated from the indigenous culture because it was superimposed on it and was not integrated with it. America was a mere projection of the Iberian peninsula, and it was through the eyes of the Iberian peninsula that it looked out upon the world.

By contrast, the Anglo-Saxon migration to North America in the seventeenth century was based on the wish for permanent settlement and identification with the new environment. After an initial period of settlement along the coast, trade among the colonies created a drive towards integration that grew in strength as trade pushed inland. Consequently external trade was a factor of importance in the internal development of the North American colonies, and not a centrifugal tendency, as in Spanish America.

During the Spanish colonial era the visible, 'official' nation felt no such impulse towards integration. The factors, forces, and interests that made for regional coalescence were missing, and in the 'real' nation, no longer purely Indian and slowly becoming *mestizo*, conditions were still not ripe for the emergence of political and economic interests conducive to interdependence, because the political and economic structure was organized in favour of the metropolitan countries. Thus the Iberian colonies lacked economic interdependence to link their component geographical sectors, they lacked communication, and they lacked integration in depth.

Nevertheless, the outward form of a cultural identity that may be likened to a shell, enclosing the 'real' nation from one end of the Spanish colonial empire to the other, served to unite the creoles, the American-born Spaniards who gave the colonies their independence.

This explains why, though the leaders of the independence movement were standard-bearers of the ideal of integration, the young American republics, far from achieving integration, were compelled by harsh realities to fall in step with the fragmentation of the colonial empire that accompanied the breakdown of a purely formal colonial authority.

The emancipation of the colonies did not stem from profound economic or social interests of the 'real' nation. It might rather be described as a revolutionary movement generated in the 'outer shell', in the thin social strata of the governing élite. It was the work of Spanish Americans who drew their inspiration not from the American scene, but from the French Revolution, and the more enlightened among them understood this. In consequence, once rid of the peninsular Spaniards representing the reigning absolutism of the mother country, they copied constitutions and laws which, though liberal, were even more inappropriate than those imposed by the colonial empire.

This, too, was why the role of the 'real' nation—the Indians and *mestizos*, the Negro minorities imported to work the fields as slaves, and the Spanish Americans of humble birth—in the independence movement was confined to serving as cannon fodder for the opposing factions. The 'real' nation continued to be a passive bystander while the new forms of political organization were shaped.

Nevertheless, the ideal of integration espoused by the leaders of the independence movement was not a purely romantic one. There was a common enemy, and each part of the colony faced the same adversary. 'Among those who directed public affairs during the revolution', said Monteagudo, the Argentine leader who collaborated with Bolívar in his plan for a confederation of nations, 'no design was older than that of forming a league against the common enemy'.[5]

For the same reason that there had been no integration in depth, there was no more than an extremely timid blossoming of nationalistic feelings. With few exceptions, the leaders of the independence movement were the sons of Spaniards, who thought of themselves as Americans rather than as Argentinians, Venezuelans, or Chileans.

The chief political reason for integration disappeared when the wars of independence ended. There was no longer an external enemy to fight, and the ideal was shipwrecked in the sea of

[5] Bernardo de Monteagudo, 'Contra el enemigo común', in *Hispanoamérica en lucha por su Independencia* (Mexico City, Cuadernos Americanos, 1942).

'national' ambitions that surged out from the new governments. Because there was no economic interdependence among the new-born republics, which inherited their respective colonial areas; because there were no genuine economic and social pressures to sweep them out of inherited isolation to interdependence, incipient nationalism took root and the delimitation of frontiers became the principal concern of the new ruling classes.

The Congress of Panama (1826), where Bolívar aspired, if not to integrate an independent America, at least to organize it as a confederation, was destined to fail, as it did. Bolívar himself foresaw this when, in his 'Letter from Jamaica', he said:

> To attempt to mould all the New World into a single nation, with but one bond to bind its parts each to each and each to all is a grandiose concept. Since by origin, language, customs, and religion it is one, it should have but one government to confederate the several states that will come into being; but this is impossible to realize, because different climates, diverse situations, opposing interests, and disparate temperaments divide America.[6]

The genius of the Liberator naturally could not overlook the real obstacles to integration. Like all prophets, he was ahead of his time, and was attempting to impose his ideal on a society not yet ready for it. Ironically, he succeeded only in exacerbating nationalism, which in Argentina, Bolivia, Peru, Ecuador, and even in Colombia and Venezuela, had become an anti-Bolívar movement, that is to say, an anti-integration movement.

The economic and social structure of the Latin American republics did not differ substantially from that of the colonies in which they had originated. The defects of the colonial system persisted under the new political structure and, if anything, grew worse. Juan Bautista Alberdi, the brilliant nineteenth-century Argentine essayist, described the situation thus:

> America is misshapen. . . . We must redraw its economic, political, and geographical map. It is an old construction, built according to an outmoded design. It was formerly a Spanish factory, of which the various departments were devoted to special tasks distributed in accordance with the industrial plan required by the manufacturer. Today each of these departments is an independent nation, and each should work according to its own inspiration.
>
> As an example, I take the towns of Bolivia, which under the colonial régime were Spanish-owned foundries and mints. Today they cannot

[6] Simón Bolívar, 'Contestación de un Americano meridional a un caballero de esta isla', *Obras completas de Bolívar* (Caracas, 1947).

be the commercial and industrial centres they are called upon to be because they lack sea-ports and shipping with which to communicate with the outside world, with Europe.[7]

Trade in the new republics continued to be centrifugal. The Latin American countries persisted in looking towards the sea, across which their products were shipped to the European markets. They continued to turn their backs on one another. Regional interdependence was lacking, and even the few lines of communication that had existed under the colonial system were no longer in evidence. The new highways were built to lead to the new capitals where each of the young republics had established the centre of its political activity, or to serve the needs of trade with Europe. In effect, the new 'nations' were even more isolated from one another than in their colonial past.

Nor was there any evidence of integration in depth. The mixing of races grew, but the 'apparent' nation still overshadowed the 'real' nation. Economic activity was organized primarily around the export trade, which benefited the minorities holding the reins of power. If the benefits of this centrifugal trade no longer flowed to Spain and Portugal, as in colonial times, neither did they flow to the body politic, but remained in the periphery, in the new, still thin and impenetrable stratum of the ruling classes.

The economic and social structure inherited from the colonial system was largely characterized by the concentration of agricultural production and mining in a few hands. Latifundia and agriculture were synonymous. How the best lands came to be given over to export crops, and the economic and social consequences of this anomaly, have been the subject of repeated and exhaustive study by many leading authorities on Latin America.[8]

Industry was still in its infancy, and generally controlled by the landholders and mine owners who were the source of capital. Financial capital too was dependent on external sources. The ruling class in America and merchants and capitalists in Europe were closely bound by common interests.[9] Herein lay the

[7] 'Memoria sobre la conveniencia y objetos de un Congreso General Americano', thesis, Faculty of Law, Univ. of Chile, 1884, *Obras completas de J. B. Alberdi* (Buenos Aires, Imp. Lit y Enc. de *La Tribuna Nacional*, 1866).

[8] Mariátegui, *Siete ensayos.*

[9] Jorge Basadre, *Historia de la República del Perú*, 5th ed. (Lima, 1963).

beginnings of external indebtedness, through advances of capital made by foreign consignees of exports to individuals and governments in the new republics. The Peruvian export trade in guano, and later in nitrates, is a case in point. In general, then, we have a picture of a dependent economy lacking any drive towards national development, with its inevitable consequences of social frustration and political and cultural backwardness.

Alberdi expressed the frustrations of the young American nations in these words:

> It is the very vastness of America that explains her disorder and backwardness. . . . America contains her present enemies within her: her trackless deserts, her unexplored rivers, her coasts depopulated by petty restrictions, the anarchy of her customs and tariffs, the dearth of credit, that artificial speculative wealth that is the producer of real and positive wealth.

With a vision that transcended his own times and bore him into our own era of the common market, he counselled 'the unification of continental trade, which must include the abolition of provincial and national internal customs, and the retention only of customs duties on imports from abroad'.[10]

Naturally, the picture was not the same for all parts of Latin America. In Chile, for example, the 'apparent' and 'real' nations tended to blend more closely than was generally the case. The geographical isolation in which Chile's colonial life had developed, the type of colonist drawn to a relatively stern environment in which agriculture and shipbuilding were the principal economic activities, a greater homogeneity because of the absence of large Indian populations with their own patterns of culture, a rapid consolidation of independence that spared Chile prolonged wars of liberation, the firmness and keen practical sense of Portales, who put down all outbreaks of anarchy and encouraged the adoption of sound and efficient institutions appropriate to the country's social structure—these were factors that permitted Chile to define a personality of her own and progress towards greater national coherence than was possible in neighbouring countries.

Integration seemed more firmly rooted in Central America because differentiation factors originating in the apparently unifying colonial system were less marked. For all that, separatist interests prevailed against the idealism of Francisco Morazán.

[10] Alberdi, 'Memoria'.

In Mexico nationalism was deeply rooted in the population of mixed blood, and was accentuated by the French invasion and by proximity to an expansionist United States. Earlier than in any other Latin American country, this Mexican nationalism was to come to a climax in the Revolution, the vehicle for unification in depth. The process is now largely completed, and Mexico is one of the countries whose national development is most advanced.

It was in the River Plate countries that foreign trade played the major role in the accumulation of capital and in development. It was here that the European immigrants were to generate the beginnings of a Latin American middle class, which in Argentina was to come to power under Yrigoyen and his Radical Party during the second decade of this century. The same trend was reflected in Uruguay in the intellectual and political movement headed by Batlle.

The transfer of the seat of the Portuguese colonial empire to Brazil gave that country's independence a special flavour. Portuguese colonization was confined to the coastal areas, and even the hesitant thrust inland during the nineteenth century meant a great strengthening of Brazil's economic foundations.

In some countries more than others dependence on foreign markets and the close ties between local ruling classes and foreign economic interests led to foreign capital gaining control of public services and the main sources of export production. There were also countries in which the semblance of liberal democracy and its institutions was more fictitious than in others, while there were some where dictatorial power persisted. But in the nineteenth century at least, the common denominator of the Latin American republics was their economic dependence on foreign markets, their isolation from one another apart from contact between the intellectual minorities, the absence or precarious nature of national and social integration, the lack of sectors that might have encouraged interdependence because it was in their interest to do so, and the imitation of systems and institutions originally devised for alien conditions.

It was not until the twentieth century that echoes of the European industrial revolution and its new economic and social concepts belatedly reached Latin America. With it were felt the first stirrings of the 'real' nation, awakened by new internal economic relationships and the negative effect on Latin American development of the external factors on which the ruling élite had based its expectations of development. These two influences were to become important elements in transforming the isolated societies of the region and in orienting them towards integration in depth and interdependence.

The Awareness of Interdependence

Progressive nineteenth-century thinkers preached that the political and social structure of the Latin American countries did not reflect the conditions necessary to the advancement of their peoples, considering the latter as a whole and distinguishing between their interests and the exclusive interests of the ruling classes. But neither external circumstances nor internal conditions as yet permitted the support of this idea by the classes and sectors which were to champion it in the twentieth century.

As might have been expected, the dynamic pressure against the antiquated structure first manifested itself in the countries where a relatively greater accumulation of capital and the beginnings of an industrial system had created a middle class. This is worthy of note because insufficient attention has been paid to the revolutionary role of the new Latin American middle classes [11] which replaced the traditional middle classes, composed of small merchants and landowners, government servants, and the few professional men who were not of the ruling élite.

In Mexico it was the peasants who, rifle in hand, gave the Revolution its earthy, social quality, and not the middle-class intellectuals around Madero, who sought no more than to eliminate the political conditions of *Porfirismo*. But in Argentina, as in Uruguay and Chile, it was the middle classes that bore the brunt of the struggle for the rebirth of the nation. This struggle was slowest to develop in those countries where the economic and social structure inherited from the colonial system had been most rigid.

Many factors helped to produce this phenomenon, and some have already been mentioned. A few were external, and they included the upheaval of the First World War, a drive towards industrialization, the impact of new social and economic doctrines, the post-war crisis and the economic depression of the 1930s, and, finally, dissatisfaction with rigid dependence on foreign economic

[11] John J. Johnson, *Political Change in Latin America* (Palo Alto, Stanford Univ. Press, 1958).

interests. Other factors were regional in nature, such as the overt presence—aggressiveness in the case of Central America and the Caribbean—of what Latin America called 'Yankee imperialism', for in many countries south of the Rio Grande United States capital had replaced European capital, which had hitherto controlled public services and the sources of production. There was also the powerful influence of the Mexican Revolution, whose slogan of 'Land and Liberty'—used for the first time by a major national movement—struck a responsive chord in the Latin American masses.

Other factors were local in origin and included an increase in the educated sector of the population, incipient interests of the emerging industrial bourgeoisie that clashed with those of the old economic sectors tied to the export trade, university reforms induced by young middle-class students who now occupied a position that had been the exclusive preserve of the élite a century before, the slow but growing awareness of the existence of a genuine nation that was not reflected in formal institutions or protected by existing laws, and the simultaneous growth of a new national feeling that was deeper and broader than the primitive nationalism of the nineteenth century.

The middle classes had come to power in some countries, and were preparing to do so in others. Mass political parties with social programmes were coming into existence, led by the same young men who only yesterday had been defending in the universities the postulates that they were now to defend in political pamphlets and street-corner meetings. In this process, in which each country began its self-discovery, the new forces discovered their community of interest with those of other American countries which were making identical efforts to resolve identical problems and combating identical opponents. Thus the first important factor making for unification appeared on the Latin American scene: the first effective pressure groups for integration were the new political forces formed by the middle classes.

This had been foreseen by Venustiano Carranza, the Mexican Revolutionary leader, who predicted that once the armed conflict had ended, the 'formidable and majestic social struggle, the struggle of the classes' would begin.

Whether we wish it or not [he said], whatever the forces in opposition the new social ideas must impose themselves on our masses. It is not merely a question of distributing land and natural resources, of effective suffrage, of opening more schools, of equal sharing in the national wealth. It is something much greater and more sacred than that: it is the establishment of justice, the search for equality.[12]

Carranza spoke of the regional implications of the programme of integration in depth when he said: 'At present we are the makers of a revolution not only in Mexico but in all of Latin America. . . .'[13]

The political movement towards internal reforms and giving the people their rights through institutions and laws adapted to their progress coincides with the beginnings of regional solidarity. Yrigoyen, Sáenz Peña, and Ingenieros held similar views in Argentina. When Yrigoyen convened a meeting of non-belligerent American states in 1917, he said:

The essential point of this meeting is to affirm the emancipation of our governments with respect to foreign policy. . . . It is essential that we safeguard the personalities of our republics, for if we do not do so, when the destinies of the world are settled for half a century at the next peace conference, they will dispose of us as they did of their African markets.[14]

On the same grounds, Sáenz Peña called for a Latin American League.[15]

The same reasons were advanced by Ingenieros in advocating a Latin American Union, formed of the association of peoples rather than of governments, to defend Latin American independence. He contended that

the old plan, essentially political and aimed at a direct confederation of governments, cannot now be realized because most of the governments are controlled by the Yankees who are their moneylenders. . . . Action by the youth of Latin America, once public opinion is crystallized and the spiritual revolution is complete, may enable the peoples to exert pressure on their governments and compel them to successively create legal, economic, and intellectual organisms of continental scope that will form the basis for a subsequent confederation.[16]

---

[12] Venustiano Carranza, 'Discurso en el Ayuntamiento de Hemerillo', in *Hispanoamérica en lucha por su Independencia*.

[13] 'Discurso de San Luis Potosí', 26 Dec. 1915, ibid.

[14] Gabriel del Mazo, *El pensamiento escrito de Yrigoyen*, 2nd ed. (Buenos Aires, 1945).

[15] Ricardo Olivera, *Escritos y discursos de Sáenz Peña: La Doctrina de Monroe y revolución* (Buenos Aires, Peuser, 1935).

[16] Address delivered on 11 Oct. 1922 at banquet of the Society of Argentine Writers in honour of José Vasconcelos, in *Hispanoamérica en lucha por su Independencia*.

These ideas were shared and expressed by the Mexican Isidro Fabela in his plan for 'Ibero-American Action', and by Haya de la Torre, founder of the *Alianza Popular Revolucionaria Americana* (APRA), whose influence was manifest in the programmes of several of the major social-democratic parties organized in Latin America during the 1930s.

Just as the leaders of independence had a common enemy in the Spanish Crown, which was a factor in stimulating regional interdependence, so did the makers of the new political and social creeds find a common enemy in imperialism, but with one important difference. The new movement sought the social and economic vindication of large backward masses of the population, and found its justification in them. Hemispheric integration now became a necessary condition of national development, and regional integration and integration in depth coalesced because it was the people, the national bourgeoisie, the middle classes, and the working classes that were to benefit from both.

Consequently today emphasis on anti-imperialism is subordinated to the regrouping of inter-American and world economic and trade relations. That is the difference between the 'Big Stick Policy' and the Alliance for Progress. But the basic postulate of the interdependence of national development and regional solidarity has been strengthened. Hence the idea of regional integration has ceased to be utopian and has become part of the immediate agenda. Latin America today holds that to think of national development without regional interdependence is a form of retrogression inimical to the dynamic factors now transforming the region and hastening its transition from traditional economic and social patterns to a new industrial society.

Despite their obvious importance, historical and cultural factors alone have not brought Latin America to a critical point in its pursuit of integration, but a variety of external influences and imperative internal development needs are impelling the Latin American countries towards it, as a means of ensuring economic and social progress.

Integration is aided by the common ethnic, cultural, and psychological base that has produced a distinctive Latin American personality, moulded by geography and history.[17] But the driving

[17] Luis Alberto Sánchez, *Examen espectral de América Latina* (Buenos Aires, Edit. Losada, 1962).

force behind it comes from the conviction that economic inter-dependence makes development less difficult than if each country pursues this alone. Integration has become a need for the future rather than an imperative of the past.

The Progress Attained

Development and integration have been accelerated over the past five years within the Inter-American System and through new sub-regional economic and commercial associations, of which the most important are the Inter-American Development Bank, LAFTA, and the Central American Common Market. They have also been stimulated by a new inter-American economic policy expressed in the Charter of Punta del Este, and the growing strength of the multilateral concept clearly defined in the Alta Gracia agreements supported by Latin American delegates at the UNCTAD Conference in Geneva in 1964.

The Inter-American Development Bank was set up for the express purpose of enabling the Latin American countries to achieve integrated, and not merely individual, development. It also signified a reaction against the rigidity of a system of international finance, based on the erroneous idea that all countries were theoretically equal, when in practice variations in development placed the more underdeveloped countries at a disadvantage. Latin America was, moreover, the first underdeveloped region to stress the need for external financing sufficiently flexible to meet the special requirements of each region, and this goal was achieved despite the opposition of those who maintained that such region-alization of financial mechanisms would misfire.

The experience of the Inter-American Development Bank has persuaded other regions to establish similar agencies. Even the international financing organizations are considering more flexible policies, and traditional arrangements are being revised to modify the terms of loans and to permit greater flexibility in the activities for which loans are used. Precisely because the bank is an institution with a Latin American regional outlook, it has *de facto* become an integrating factor. When its Charter was approved five years ago integration was still in the stage of discussion and its practical application seemed remote, but the bank's regional outlook has brought it into the realm of fact.

The Charter states that one of the functions of the bank is to contribute to the individual and *collective* development of the member countries. It thus became possible to finance multi-national programmes and projects as well as national ventures, and to evaluate loan applications in terms of the 'integration factor'— the impact of a given project beyond the borders of any single country. It also became possible to create a system for financing the intra-regional export of capital goods and to stimulate many aspects of integration, including promotion, programming, regional infrastructure, intra-regional trade, multi-national projects, frontier development, and co-ordination with other financial and technical development agencies. Almost as a matter of routine, the bank has been projecting its policies from the national on to the regional plane, on the premise that no solutions to development problems can be definitive if they are restricted to the national scene. This consideration has led it to establish an Institute for Latin American Integration, which has opened in Buenos Aires. The institute will promote theoretical studies to speed up institutional, legal, social, political, and economic integration, and will provide courses, seminars, and publications to train officials and specialists from public and private sectors of member countries and keep them informed.

LAFTA and the Central American Common Market are tangible steps towards establishing a regional common market. Both are sub-regional associations, and each reflects a different approach. The Montevideo Treaty that created LAFTA seeks integration through the liberalization of intra-regional trade, to be re-negotiated at periodic intervals, and through reduced restrictions on reciprocal trade. It is thus an instrument for commercial integration.

The Central American countries, on the other hand, did not restrict themselves to intra-regional trade, but laid the foundations of a true common market. They have gone so far as to establish a common tariff for all imports into the area and have created means to co-ordinate their monetary policies. They are also co-ordinating their development plans on a regional scale, with a bank of their own to finance multi-national projects, and they are striving to co-ordinate their social policies and educational programmes as well. In short, they are moving towards an integrated geo-economic complex.

Both approaches have yielded positive results, but that of the Central American Common Market has enabled the Central

American countries to advance more rapidly. Trade among them is now seven times as large as it was ten years ago. New buildings and factories reflect increased local and foreign investment throughout the area. In contrast to this, LAFTA is not progressing fast enough, undoubtedly because of its narrow and hesitant terms of reference. If the purpose of Latin American integration is to create a favourable environment for self-sustaining regional development that will lead to a better economic and social life, it cannot be limited only to commerce and to something resembling the integration of stagnation. It must be an integration of development with all the necessary social and economic transformation which this implies.

If the approach to development is not on a regional basis, the less developed areas will become the 'periphery' of the more developed, while the more advanced areas will enjoy greater possibilities of further progress, and the process that now puts Latin America at a disadvantage in relation to more highly industrialized regions will be repeated within its own borders. Thus even though the Montevideo Treaty is flexible with respect to the relatively less developed countries, that is not enough. Effective Latin American integration must go beyond the underlying concept of LAFTA. The Montevideo Treaty should be revised and LAFTA and the Central American Common Market should be consolidated in a single economic system to include countries that have not yet joined either of these associations. In addition to a customs union and regional clearing house, the economic community to be established should consider the adoption of a regional investment policy within the framework of regional planning, or at least the co-ordination of national development plans. It should also consider a regional central bank—or at least the co-ordination of national monetary policies—and an agency for economic co-operation and development with the necessary authority and technical resources to guide and co-ordinate the decisions and applications of a regional policy at an executive level. Such an economic community would find its indispensable regional financing agency ready-made in the Inter-American Development Bank.

Despite the limitations of the Montevideo Treaty, LAFTA can point to some progress in increasing trade among its members. In the three years since the treaty came into effect, intra-zonal trade has risen from $300 to $450 million. It is estimated that it will reach $1,500 million by 1970, a figure equivalent to 20 per cent of the foreign commerce of the nine member countries of LAFTA up to 1963. (Venezuela has announced her intention of joining the association.) Moreover, despite the timidity of the Montevideo Treaty and the corresponding limitations on the benefits to be obtained from the Association, LAFTA is a distinct improvement on the former isolation or bilateralism of its members. If LAFTA is to be criticized, it should be criticized constructively, with an eye to enlarging its present potential.

The Charter of Punta del Este, which reaffirmed the new concepts of inter-American organization contained in the Act of Bogotá, is a milestone in the reaffirmation of Latin American regional integration: first, because the Alliance for Progress gave tangible proof of a changed United States attitude towards the problems of Latin American development, and secondly, because the Charter confirmed the decision of the Latin American countries to abandon the bilateralism that had in practice governed their relations with the United States, despite the inter-American legal and political system, and to adopt a policy of multilateralism. In emphasizing the importance of this Charter the writer has frequently said [18] that it represents approval of a series of Latin American ideas and aspirations that formerly had found no acceptance in the United States. Today it can be affirmed that probably the Charter's most important feature is the United States acknowledgement in it of the need and desirability of Latin American integration. Europe's experience did much to bring about this change in the United States. The Charter demonstrates that the United States has come to understand the limitations of bilateralism and the advantages of a strong, united, and prosperous Latin America in forging a continental system of economic and political relations. In this connexion, it may be stated that Latin America's need to defend its raw materials is as important a unifying factor as was the European Coal and Steel Community

[18] See *América Latina: integración económica y reintegración política*, address to Conference on Tensions of Development in the Western Hemisphere, San Salvador, Brazil; *Relaciones económicas interamericanos*, paper delivered to Georgetown Univ., 2 Apr. 1964; *Aspectos políticos y económicos de la integración de América Latina*, lecture to Colombian Society of Economists, Bogotá, June 1964 (all published in Washington by the Inter-American Development Bank).

before the Common Market. It is also very significant that the UNCTAD Conference gave Latin America an ideal opportunity to affirm its importance as a region to the other underdeveloped blocs, with which it entered into multilateral arrangements for the first time.

Looking back in the light of these recent experiences, it is not necessary to go farther than 1959 to see the remarkable progress that has been made. A mere five years ago there was no Inter-American Development Bank, no LAFTA, no Central American Common Market, no Charter of Punta del Este. Few then thought that a multilateral stance would be possible in so short a time in relation to the developed blocs and in agreement with the African and Asian regions which face the same need to defend external trade.

Impediments to Integration

To achieve the goal of integration, it is essential to modify agreements, institutions, and mechanisms that at present achieve only co-operation—a necessary but insufficient first step. Where necessary new ones must be created. If they are to solve the problems and remove the geographical, social, economic, cultural, and political obstacles delaying integration, the Latin American countries must quickly take a collective political decision that will permit a gradual transition from co-operation to integration. Among these obstacles, mountainous regions, dense forests, climatic extremes and immense distances impeding communication can be overcome by technological advances. The lack of basic communications is still a serious problem that is being attacked by various multi-national efforts, but if we are to think in terms of real integration, priority must be given to infra-structural investments facilitating inter-communication. The problem of the lack of social integration exists in each of the countries of the region, though it is less serious in the relatively well-developed ones. In most of the countries, however, there are large rural masses whose progress is stifled by their cultural and technological backwardness, by a subsistence economy, and by a land tenure system of unproductive large holdings or uneconomic smallholdings.

These social shortcomings reflect a deficient political and institutional structure controlled by minorities which are the chief beneficiaries of existing conditions and in which economic power is concentrated. These minorities oppose change, and therefore oppose integration, and in this are supported by traditionalist sectors with a stake in national underdevelopment and dependence. Since regional integration—the integration of national processes of change and development—requires radical modernization of the state, groups associated with traditional bureaucracies are reluctant to accept it. Moreover, Latin America's rate of population growth, which reached 2.7 per cent a year during the 1950-60 decade—the highest for any major region in the world—aggravates tensions created by the inability to provide employment for the active population.

Latin America's economic relations with the rest of the world continue to follow the traditional pattern of raw material exports and imports of manufactured goods of varying technical complexity. This has led to a progressive weakening of the region's foreign trade, its share of world commerce dropping from 12.3 per cent in 1950 to 7.9 per cent in 1963. This situation is one of the chief causes of development lag, but it also conditions other features of the economy, including the dominance of export activity and agricultural stagnation—except for export products—because of the social structure and insufficient modernization of production. It also leads to unbalanced industrialization, because of industry's dependence on imported capital goods and intermediate products, and the juxtaposition of highly developed and uninhabited or extremely backward areas. It is also mainly responsible for poor organization of domestic markets reflecting the failure to link urban and rural areas; competitive manufacturing, because national industrial efforts are aimed primarily at replacing imports; technological backwardness; the minor role of intraregional trade; and the meagre reciprocal flow of capital and manpower. Finally, it is a contributory factor in monetary and fiscal policies that are often chaotic and contradictory.

This economic structure and the lack of an infrastructure explains the centrifugal behaviour of Latin America's national economies and their marked dependence on the great foreign industrial centres.

Mobilizing and assigning investment resources to regional development is hindered at present by a shortage of multi-national projects and a lack of priorities relating to regional as opposed to national development. The mobilization of internal public resources for integration is complicated by insufficient sources of capital, defective tax structures, low levels of public savings, the crushing inflation suffered by some countries, and internal financial difficulties caused by enlarged expenditure for development without corresponding increases in revenues to finance them. Similarly, the mobilization of internal private resources is discouraged by factors that prevent the formation of private savings and their flow towards productive activities. The most important are political instability, inflation, and—for the purposes of integration—the lack of ties linking the financing and capital markets of the various countries. These factors also make it difficult to obtain private savings from abroad, apart from the added complication of the failure of the Latin American countries to adopt uniform conditions and guarantees.

As a consequence of the economic and social characteristics that have been outlined, a wide cultural gap exists between urban and rural areas, and the illiteracy rate in some Latin American countries is as high as 50 per cent. With such a tenuous cultural base, it obviously becomes difficult to mobilize the broad masses for integration. Moreover, Latin American education tends to be formalist, literary, and rhetorical, and in too many respects is out of touch with modern needs. There is also a shortage of the professional, scientific, and technological personnel and intermediate manpower required for development. Only 3.5 per cent of primary school students go on to college. The total estimated university enrolment in 1970 is 900,000 for the whole region—a meagre 4.2 per cent of the 19–24 age-group. Latin America had only 26,000 agronomists in 1962. It will need at least 60,000 in 1970 to meet the requirements of agrarian reform programmes to increase production, yet all the agricultural schools of the region together produce only 2,000 specialists a year. The same holds true of forestry—the region had only 600 forestry engineers in 1962 and will need 5,000 by 1970; of sanitation—500 sanitary engineers are needed each year and only 100 are produced; and of industry and all professions connected with development.

A further cultural obstacle to integration is a lack of uniformity in the various educational systems and curricula. There is no equivalence of studies and degrees at the university level, nor is there any co-ordination among universities to reduce duplication of effort and merge resources to permit specialized research and teaching that would be beyond the means of any single institution.

Finally, there is a restricted flow of news and information from one Latin American country to the other that is a distinct cultural handicap. There are no regional information services, and what little news each country publishes and reads about its neighbours is usually of a sensational type that makes for anything but better mutual understanding. One often learns more about Latin American countries in newspapers printed in the United States or Europe than in the leading dailies of the countries themselves.

Politically, the spread of nationalism and strident national feeling in the nineteenth century, especially in the more developed countries of the region, hinders the transition from co-operation to integration, which requires revision of the traditional concepts of purely national sovereignty. As we have seen, there are circumstances in each country that encourage a growing understanding of the need to give nationalism a regional projection. But a platform is still needed to give ideological support to integration and awaken public opinion to its advantages for the region as a whole and— because this will be of the greatest interest to the average Latin American—for each country in particular. The transition from co-operation to integration, and the intermediate process of co-ordinating mechanisms and policies for integration, calls for a system of institutions that either do not exist at present, or are inadequate for the task.

Successful integration demands technical and economic mechanisms to perform a number of special functions. These include at least the co-ordination of the general trade policies of the region, the liberalization of intra-regional trade, and the creation of a regional payments mechanism to stimulate Latin American domestic commerce.[19] It will also be necessary to co-ordinate national investment policies to make possible the direct integration of each country's economy with the regional framework. However, if attempts at integration are limited only to the freeing of trade, the positive effects of the expansion of the market will be greatly delayed. This would mean abandoning regional

---

[19] Miguel J. Wionczek, 'Condiciones de una integración viable', in *Integración de América Latina; experiencias y perspectivas* (Mexico City, Fondo de Cultural Economica, 1964).

investment to the free play of market forces and the parochial out-look of each country. A regional investment policy, however, offers a working solution that is compatible with national interests, since each country will be able to make a comparative evaluation of the benefits it can obtain from the regional solution. It also becomes the principal means of obtaining the balanced participation of the less developed countries in the process of regional economic integration.

A simple reduction of preferential tariffs would not suffice to overcome intra-regional imbalances because of the limited ability of the less developed countries to promote investments and increases in the production and export of items receiving a preferential trade treatment.

Integrated development in itself can be counted on to take care of geographical, social, economic, and cultural problems, but the speed with which Latin America can achieve this objective will depend on how long it takes to conquer political obstacles. Integration requires decisions at the highest political level, and until they are taken, technical planning will be hamstrung by an inability to put the technical and economic mechanisms to a use that will shape the economic community needed for regional development. Integration presupposes a political definition which must be expressed in appropriate organs, and this can only be done through the creation of an Inter-American Parliament, with sufficient authority to approve agreements for putting regional measures into effect. Such agreements today are subject to lengthy and tedious procedures of ratification by each national legislature. A Latin American Parliament would also serve as a forum for the many facets of Latin American public opinion to which political parties, labour, management, technicians, intellectuals, and many other groups contribute.

Yet another indispensable mechanism is a Latin American Court of Justice, to pronounce definitive judgement on disputes or conflicting interpretations of the commercial and contractual issues proceeding from the regional relations of many national agencies. It could also sit in judgement on other issues, including non-compliance by a country with regional agreements, and grievances based on the adverse effects of one country's economic policy on its neighbours, to cite only two.

Latin American economic integration also requires an institution to co-ordinate educational and cultural systems and investments for scientific and technological research at the university level. The action of the Inter-American Development Bank in organizing its Institute for Integration has filled a vacuum in the training of cadres of leaders and executives. Institutional mechanisms of this scope presuppose an ideological and political maturity which in some respects is still lacking. There is a strong tendency towards nationalism, which weakens with awareness of the extent to which integration makes reassessment of this concept necessary. But it cannot be over-emphasized that the lack of current ideological support of the highest calibre is a major obstacle.

The leaders of Latin America, absorbed as they are by complex and urgent national problems, are not devoting to integration all the attention it merits. If Latin America wishes to play a significant role in the future, it must unite; otherwise the growing inter-nationalization of world economic and political relations will inevitably lead to the destruction of the cultural identity of the countries of the region. Latin America must unite to preserve this cultural identity, and simultaneously ensure its historical survival as a community of nations, with a distinctive political and economic personality, in a new international system based on the relation-ships of super-nations or 'nation-continents'. Moreover, Latin America's existence as a distinctive region is not merely of interest to its members, who will safeguard their development through integration, but to the world at large, for it will be an important balancing factor in international relations.

[*Felipe Herrera, formerly Professor of Economics at the University of Chile and Minister of Finance in the Carlos Ibañez administra-tion, has been President of the Inter-American Development Bank since 1960. His principal publications include* Elementos de economia monetaria *(1955) and* Desarrollo económico o estabilidad monetaria? *(1958).*]

Index